DISCARD

MAN, MYTH, AND MAGIC

MAN, MYTH,
AND MAGIC

Beliefs, Rituals, and Symbols of Ancient Egypt, Mesopotamia and the Fertile Crescent

Cavendish
Square

New York

Published in 2014 by Cavendish Square Publishing, LLC
303 Park Avenue South, Suite 1247, New York, NY 10010

Website: cavendishsq.com

This publication represents the opinions and views of the author based on his or her personal experience, knowledge, and research. The information in this book serves as a general guide only. The author and publisher have used their best efforts in preparing this book and disclaim liability rising directly or indirectly from the use and application of this book.

CPSIA Compliance Information: Batch #WW14CSQ

All websites were available and accurate when this book was sent to press.

Library of Congress Cataloging-in-Publication Data

Brandon, S.G.F.
Beliefs, rituals, and symbols of ancient Egypt, Mesopotamia, and the Fertile Crescent / by S.G.F.Brandon.
p. cm. — (Man, myth, and magic)
Includes index.
ISBN 978-1-62712-569-7 (hardcover) ISBN 978-1-62712-570-3 (paperback) ISBN 978-1-62712-571-0 (ebook)
1. Egypt — Religion — Juvenile literature. 2. Mythology, Egyptian — Juvenile literature. 3. Mythology, Assyro-Babylonian — Juvenile literature. 4. Assyro-Babylonian religion. I. Title.
BL2441.3 B73 2014
299—d23

ISBN 978-1-62712-569-7 (hardcover)   ISBN 978-1-62712-570-3 (papeback)   ISBN 978-1-62712-571-0 (ebook)

Editorial Director: Dean Miller
Editor: Fran Hatton
Art Director: Jeffrey Talbot
Designers: Jennifer Ryder-Talbot and Amy Greenan
Photo Researcher: Laurie Platt Winfrey, Carousel Research, Inc
Production Manager: Jennifer Ryder-Talbot
Production Editor: Andrew Coddington

Cavendish Square would like to acknowledge the outstanding work, research, writing, and professionalism of Man, Myth, and Magic's original Editor-in-Chief Richard Cavendish, Executive Editor Brian Innes, Editorial Advisory Board Members and Consultants C.A. Burland, Glyn Daniel, E.R Dodds, Mircea Eliade, William Sargent, John Symonds, RJ. Zwi Werblowsky, and R.C. Zaechner, as well as the numerous authors, consultants, and contributors that shaped the original Man, Myth, and Magic that served as the basis and model for these new books.

Printed in the United States of America

Contents

A Reader's Guide to *Man, Myth, and Magic: Beliefs, Rituals, and Symbols of Ancient Egypt, Mesopotamia, and the Fertile Crescent*

Wherever cultures have grown up, there are common universal themes running through their religions and mythologies. The myths and legends of the ancient world, in what's been called the cradle of civilization, make a wonderful, colourful tapestry expressing the variety of local experiences and attitudes. The gods and goddesses of these ancient civilizations reflect man's desire to explain the nature of the universe and the human psyche, the mysteries of birth and death, the progression of the seasons, the riddle of creation, and so much more.

Man, Myth, and Magic: Beliefs, Rituals, and Symbols of Ancient Egypt, Mesopotamia, and the Fertile Crescent is both a new book and a revised work from a set of volumes with two decades of bestselling and award-winning history. It is a fully comprehensive guide to the people, customs, and faiths of some of the oldest civilizations on the planet.

Religions are concerned not only with the deities who personify and explain the various manifestations of power that men encounter in the world, but also with human nature and destiny.

Objectives of *Man, Myth, and Magic*

The guiding principle of the *Man, Myth, and Magic* series takes the stance of unbiased exploration. It shows the myriad ways in which different cultures have questioned and explained the mysterious nature of the world about them, and will lead teachers and students toward a broader understanding of their own and other people's beliefs and customs.

The Text

Within this book, expert international contributors have created articles arranged alphabetically, and the depth of coverage varies from major articles of up to 10,000 words to concise, glossary-type definitive entries in short paragraphs. The work is highly illustrated, and subjects of major interest are provided with individual bibliographies of further reading on the subject at the end of each article.

What made it possible to create this work was the fact that the last century has seen a powerful revival of interest in these subjects at both the scholarly and the popular levels. At the same time there has been a flourishing revival of popular interest in ancient civilizations, mythology, magic, and alternative paths to truth. This interest has shown no sign of diminishing in this century; on the contrary, it has grown stronger and has explored new pathways. Since the last edition of the series, scholarly investigation of our subjects has continued and has thrown much new light on some of our topics. The present revision of *Man, Myth, and Magic* takes account of both these developments. Articles have been updated to cover fresh discoveries and new theories.

Illustrations

Since much of what we know about myth, folklore, and religion has been passed down over the centuries by word of mouth, and recorded only comparatively recently, visual images are often the most powerful and vivid links we have with the past. The wealth of illustrations in *Man, Myth, and Magic* is invaluable, not only because of the diversity of sources, but also because of the superb quality of colour reproduction.

Index

The A-Z index provides immediate access to any specific item sought by the reader. The reference distinguishes the nature of the entry in terms of a main entry, supplementary subject entries, and illustrations.

Skill Development for Students

Man, Myth, and Magic can be consulted as the basic text for a subject or as a source of enrichment for students. It can act as a reference for a simple reading or writing assignment, or as the inspiration for a major research or term paper. The additional reading at the end of each entry is an invaluable resource for students looking to further their studies on a specific topic.

Ahriman

For more than fourteen centuries Iran has been a Moslem country, but before the Moslem conquest the state religion was Zoroastrianism. Ahriman is the Zoroastrian Devil (not the Moslem one, whose name is *Shaitan*, more familiar to us as Satan). We first hear of Ahriman in the 7th century BC when he plays a significant part in the *Gathas*, or 'Songs', of Zoroaster, the prophet of ancient Iran and the founder of Zoroastrianism.

Zoroastrianism is generally held to be a classical form of religious dualism; that is to say, it holds that the universe is not the creation of one god or principle but of two—a holy power and an evil one. Some religions identify evil with matter, with what Christians call 'the flesh'; but in Zoroastrianism matter, far from being evil, is the creation of the holy god and is therefore in itself entirely good. Evil is a *spiritual* power, negative and destructive: it is called the 'Lie' and is the principle of disruption and death, the adversary of Truth.

In the *Gathas* there is the basic dualism between Truth and the Lie: these are principles which exist in opposition to each other for all time. Of the origin of the Lie nothing is said. Truth, however, is seen as an aspect of the One True God, or Ahura Mazdah, 'the Wise Lord': twice it is called his 'Son'. If the 'Lie' is the principle of evil, Ahriman is its personification. He is not yet the eternal Adversary of the One God but he *is* the eternal Adversary of an entity called the 'Holy Spirit'. From the beginning the two Spirits face each other in implacable hostility. But evidently there was a beginning, for the Holy Spirit, like God the Son in Christian theology, was born of the Father and it appears that he was also the twin brother of the Evil Spirit:

In the beginning those two spirits who … were twins known as the one

An old tomb of the Zoroastrianism religion in the Sulaymanlyah province. The inside has been robbed and is empty.

good and the other evil, in thought, word, and deed. Between them the wise chose rightly, not so the fools. And when these Spirits met they established in the beginning life and death that in the end the followers of the Lie should meet with the worst existence, but the followers of Truth with the Best Mind. Of these two Spirits he who was of the Lie chose to do the worst things; but the Most Holy Spirit, clothed in rugged heaven, (chose) Truth as did (all) who sought with zeal to do the pleasure of the Wise Lord by (doing) good works. Between the two the demons did not choose rightly; for as they deliberated delusion overcame them so *that they chose the most Evil Mind. Then did they, with one accord, rush headlong unto Fury that they might thereby extinguish the existence of mortal men. From this passage two facts emerge. First, the two Spirits are twins and since Ahura Mazdah, the Wise Lord, is the father of the Holier, it follows that he must also be the father of the Evil One. Secondly the Evil Spirit, though he is 'of the Lie' must choose evil: he is not evil absolutely but becomes evil by choice. Once the choice is made, however, he is no more capable of change than is Satan in the Christian tradition: he is forever committed to the Lie.*

Declaration of War

Zoroastrianism is above all the religion of free will. Not only is Ahriman, the Evil Spirit, evil by choice and the Holy Spirit holy by choice, but the One Supreme God, Ahura Mazdah, has also to commit himself—has to choose between Truth and the Lie.

Ahura Mazdah chooses Truth. 'Holy and good Right-mindedness do we choose: let it be ours'. This is a declaration of war on the Lie and those who have chosen the Lie. On both sides this is an irrevocable decision and the battle must be fought to the finish.

In the *Gathas*, then, which are now generally admitted to be the work of the prophet Zoroaster himself, the supreme God aligns himself with the Holy Spirit against the power of the Lie. The Evil Spirit, on the other hand, chooses to lead the powers of the Lie against the Holy Spirit and therefore against the Supreme God. But though he is the sworn enemy of the Holy Spirit, he is also his twin and must therefore also be the son of his father, the 'Wise Lord'. Would it not, then, be more true to say that the Zoroastrianism of Zoroaster is not a dualism at all but a form of monotheism (belief in one god), at least in the sense that the Wise Lord is the First Cause of all things? In later times the Zoroastrians became divided on this issue.

A purely dualist solution was favoured by the fact that in the course of time the Holy Spirit was simply identified with the Wise Lord. The name Ahura Mazdah took on its later form Ohrmazd, and Ohrmazd and Ahriman then appear as independent principles eternally separate and distinct, eternally opposed. This is the form of Zoroastrianism that we meet with in the Sasanian period, from the 2nd to the 7th centuries AD, when the Persian Empire was revived under the house of

Sasan and Zoroastrianism became the official religion of the Empire.

By this time Ahriman had grown in stature: he had become an independent monarch who held undisputed sway in his own kingdom of darkness and death. But the myth of the two eternal twins lingered on because the problem of evil is at the very centre of Zoroastrianism.

Our experience of life seems to show that if God is all-powerful, he cannot be absolutely good—because he lets evil exist; and conversely, if he is absolutely good, he cannot be all-powerful—because he evidently cannot

Man must become mortal and accept bodily existence in order in the end to annihilate the force of destruction, death, and all evil.

prevent evil. A cut-and-dried dualism absolves God from any responsibility for evil, however indirect, but he necessarily pays for his goodness at the price of his omnipotence. But if the old legend of the primordial twins was retained, and since the Wise Lord and the Holy Spirit were now identified in the single person of Ohrmazd, could it not be that these twin poles of good and evil themselves derived their being from a neutral principle which was the original Unity?

Such a principle some of the Zoroastrian theologians thought they had found in Infinite Time, which was also Infinite Space, and which they called by its ancient name Zurvan. The myth was therefore modified to suit this new theology. It has totally disappeared from the Zoroastrian texts of the period but it is preserved in Christian and other sources and is certainly authentic. The myth which has come down to us is a popular presentation of a far more subtle theological

position, which seeks at all costs to preserve both the original Unity and the absolute goodness of God.

Zurvan and the Birth of Evil

The myth says that the great god Zurvan existed before there was anything else. He offered sacrifice so that he might have a son but after a long time he began to wonder whether his hopes were vain. As soon as this thought occurred to him, Ohrmazd and Ahriman were conceived—Ohrmazd because of Zurvan's sacrifice and Ahriman because of his doubt. Zurvan decided that whichever of them came to him first, he would make king.

When Ahriman heard this he ripped the womb open, emerged, and advanced toward his father. Zurvan, seeing him, asked 'who are you?'

And he replied: 'I am your son, Ohrmazd'. And Zurvan said: 'My son is light and fragrant, but you are dark and stinking'. And he wept most bitterly. And as they were talking together, Ohrmazd was born in his turn, light and fragrant; and Zurvan, seeing him, knew that it was his son Ohrmazd for whom he had offered sacrifice . . . And he said (to him): 'Up till now it is I who have offered sacrifice for you; from now you shall offer sacrifice for me'. But . . . Ahriman drew near and said to him; 'Did you not vow that whichever of your sons should come to you first, to him you would give the Kingdom?' And Zurvan said to him: 'O false and wicked one, the Kingdom shall be granted you for 9,000 years, but Ohrmazd I have made a King above you, and after 9,000 years he will reign and do everything according to his good pleasure'. And Ohrmazd created the heavens and the earth and all things that are beautiful and good; but Ahriman created the demons and all that is evil and perverse. Ohrmazd created riches, Ahriman poverty.

Ahriman is born of Zurvan's doubt and rules the world, but only for 9,000 years. This partial solution of the problem of evil which made the Evil One 'prince of this world', if only for a relatively short time, did not in the end satisfy the majority of Zoroastrians. The myth of the primordial twins was set aside and the universe was neatly divided into two separate halves, light and darkness, good and evil.

In the beginning, then, 'the Light was above and the darkness beneath; and between them was the void—Ohrmazd in the light and Ahriman in the darkness. Ohrmazd knew of the existence of Ahriman and of his coming to do battle: Ahriman did not know of the existence and light of Ohrmazd'. He soon found out. Roaming around in his dismal kingdom, he reached the upper confines of his realm and saw a ray of light. He longed to get hold of it and to destroy it. Ohrmazd in his goodness offered him peace, which the Evil One summarily rejected, and leapt forward to attack the light. Ohrmazd repelled him, 'laid him low by the pure power of the Law and hurled him back into the darkness'. There he lay unconscious for over 3,000 years.

Having foiled this first onslaught, Ohrmazd realized that he must create a bastion between himself and Ahriman, the eternal aggressor. For this purpose he first created a spiritual universe which is an 'ideal' model of the material universe, then the material world itself.

The ideal world was to remain forever free from the pestilential attacks of Ahriman, and at its summit were the souls of the human race. When Ahriman's attack on the material world took place, it was Ohrmazd's plan that these souls should acquire bodies and go to live in the world 'to do battle with Ahriman and the Lie'. But Ohrmazd demands the free cooperation of man, he does not and will not violate the freedom of man's will.

He took counsel with the consciousness and preexistent souls of men and infused omniscient wisdom into them saying: 'Which seems more profitable to you, whether that I should fashion you forth in material form and that you should strive incarnate with the Lie and destroy it, and that we should resurrect you at the end, whole and immortal, and recreate you in material form, and that you should eternally be immortal, unageing, and without enemies; or that you should eternally be preserved from the Aggressor?' And the preexistent souls of men saw by that omniscient wisdom that they would suffer evil from the Lie and Ahriman in the material world, but because at the end they would be resurrected free from the enmity of the Aggressor, whole and immortal for ever and ever, they agreed to go into the material world.

For the defeat and destruction of Ahriman, then, man's cooperation is essential. Man must become mortal and accept bodily existence in order in the end to annihilate the force of destruction, death, and all evil.

Gayomart and the Lone-Created Bull

Once the souls have consented to this, Ohrmazd creates the material world: he creates the sky, water, plants, the animals in the shape of the 'lone-created Bull', and finally the first man, Gayomart 'shining like the sun'. All is now in readiness and Ahriman prepares his attack. It is devastatingly successful. Each of Ohrmazd's creations he defiles and corrupts; he slays the Bull and mortally wounds Gayomart. His triumph seems to be complete and he cries out in savage exultation:

Perfect is my victory; for I have rent the sky, I have befouled it with murk and darkness, I have made it my stronghold. I have befouled the waters, pierced open the earth and befouled it with darkness. I have dried up the plants and brought death to the Bull, sickness to Gayomart . . . I have seized the Kingdom. On the side of Ohrmazd none remains to do battle except only man; and man isolated and alone, what can he do?

But Gayomart's seed had fallen into the earth as he died and from his seed sprang up a rhubarb plant which split in two to form the first human couple: the human race was therefore saved to continue the long arduous battle against evil which it had already freely accepted.

Moreover, the material universe was bounded by the sky which Ahriman had rent open, forgetting that it was made of 'shining metal that is the substance of steel'. He has entered into his Kingdom but the Kingdom is his prison.

This does not matter so long as he and the vices he has brought in his train can prey upon the creatures of Ohrmazd; but in the end evil which is of its nature destructive, finding that Ohrmazd's creation is slowly slipping from its grasp, will be forced to disrupt and destroy itself.

Ahriman and the demons in the world are like wild beasts that have broken into a garden, but once they have wreaked all the destruction they can, they find that they have been trapped. They make frantic efforts to get out and in doing so they use their own strength against themselves and ensure their own destruction.

The End of the Lie

Ahriman's end comes about when Ohrmazd's creation has become so spiritualized as to escape his power. Pandemonium breaks out; demon attacks demon, each destroying the other until only Ahriman and Az, the demon of death, greed, and lust, are left.

Az turns on Ahriman and threatens to swallow him, and Ahriman is forced to appeal to his eternal enemy to deliver him from his former ally. Ohrmazd will not relent. The Spirit of Obedience destroys the threatening demon Az and Ohrmazd himself lays Ahriman low.

Does this mean that Ahriman is finally annihilated? According to popular mythology, yes: 'he is dragged outside the sky and has his head cut off'. But according to more sophisticated accounts, he cannot be annihilated because he is the *substance* of evil and, according to the particular brand of philosophy the Zoroastrians had adopted, a substance by definition cannot be destroyed.

The technical term used means literally to 'put out of action': 'he is thrown out of the sky through the hole by which he rushed in; and at that hole he is laid low and knocked unconscious so that he will never arise again . . . He will be forever powerless and, as it were, slain and henceforth neither he nor his creation will exist'.

With his destruction a new heaven and a new earth are created, all men are resurrected, and those who were confined to hell are released from their torments, and all enjoy perpetual bliss for evermore in the company of Ohrmazd, the Wise Lord.

While he still exists as a conscious being, Ahriman is intensely active in this world. He is the Adversary of both God and man, the Destroyer, the author of death, a 'liar and a deceiver'. His aim is to deceive men as to the true nature of God, and so to bring them to hate Ohrmazd and to love himself. By these means he entices them into hell of which he is the overlord. In fact he is not the equal of Ohrmazd and never really stands a chance because he 'comes to know things too late'. So he is defeated as much by his own stupidity as by Ohrmazd's wisdom and power.

R. C. ZAEHNER

FURTHER READING: R. C. Zaehner. The Dawn and Twilight of Zoroastrianism. (Weidenfeld & Nicolson, 1961).

Ahura Mazdah

A name of Ohrmazd, the good god of Zoroastrian religion, twin brother and opponent of the evil god Ahriman, who will eventually be overthrown by Ohrmazd after ruling the world for 9,000 years.

Amun

The king of the Ancient Egyptian pantheon during the period of the New Kingdom (1609–1550 BC), Amun's name means 'invisible' or 'hidden', implying that his true nature cannot be known. Amun began as a deity local to Waset, modern-day Luxor that the Greeks called Thebes. During the reign of Ahmose I and the subsequent New Kingdom period, Amun was fused with the sun god Ra, making him Amun-Ra. His position as the patron god of the Egyptian capital placed him at the apex of Egyptian religious importance. His power was so great that he overshadowed all the other gods, approaching a kind of monotheism. For a brief period the pharaoh Akhenaten established a monotheistic cult of the god Aten, but after his death his religious reforms were reversed promptly by the well-established priesthood of Amun. Akhenaten's son, the new pharaoh Tutankhaten changed his name to Tutankhamun. Amun-Ra presided over Egypt's golden age, but his hegemony gradually declined in the 1st millennium BC.

The avenue of ram-headed sphinxes, a symbol of the god Amun. Each one holds a statue of the king, Rameses II, in its paws. Built by the Ethiopian kings in 656 BC, the avenue leads to the first pylon of Karnak Temple in Luxor, Egypt.

The pharaohs during Amun's prominence built massive temples in Karnak dedicated to him. Eventually his influence spread beyond the Egyptian sphere of influence to other Mediterranean cultures. For example, Amun was associated with Zeus from the Greek pantheon and became the central deity in Kush and Nubia.

Amun-Ra is often depicted wearing a crown with two tall ostrich feathers and a solar disc, or with ram horns. His wife was Mut and their son was Khonsu, the moon god. Together they made up what is known as the Theban Triad.

FURTHER READING: Pinch, Geraldine. Egyptian Mythology: A Guide to the Gods, Goddesses, and Traditions of Ancient Egypt. *(Oxford: Oxford UP, 2004); Brewer, Douglas J., and Emily Teeter.* Egypt and the Egyptians. *(Cambridge, UK: Cambridge UP, 2007); Shafer, Byron E., John Baines, Leonard H. Lesko, and David P. Silverman.* Religion in Ancient Egypt: Gods, Myths, and Personal Practice. *(Ithaca: Cornell UP, 1991); Warburton, David A.* Architecture, Power, and Religion: Hatshepsut, Amun & Karnak in Context. *(Münster, Lit Verlag, 2012).*

Ankh

Ancient Egyptian symbol meaning 'life', also called 'the key of life'. Denotes immortality and, because of its universal association with the gods and pharaohs, power and divinity. In wall carvings Egyptian gods and pharaohs are often depicted holding the ankh by the loop at the top. Its precise origin is unknown. The ankh symbol has been co-opted in a number of ways by different ancient and modern cultures, and its ubiquity has also made the ankh a generic symbol of ancient Egypt. Some theorists compare it to the other Egyptian symbols 'tyet', or the Knot of Isis, and 'was', an implement associated with protection of the dead. The ankh is also compared to certain Minoan and Mycenean symbols that depict a sacred knot with a dangling cord, forming an ankh-like shape. In modern times, the ankh is widely used by New Age proponents as a symbol of magic and power.

FURTHER READING: Teeter, Emily. Religion and Ritual in Ancient Egypt. *(Cambridge, UK: Cambridge UP, 2011); Wilson, John Albert.* The Culture of Ancient Egypt. *(Chicago: University of Chicago, 1956).*

Anubis

Egyptian god of the dead, 'lord of the mummy wrappings' and inventor of embalming, who led the dead to the place of judgment after death and supervised the weighing of the heart; shown as a black jackal or a dog, both of which roamed the cemeteries in the Egyptian desert.

Anubis, shown seated in a wall painting at the necropolis Deir el Medina

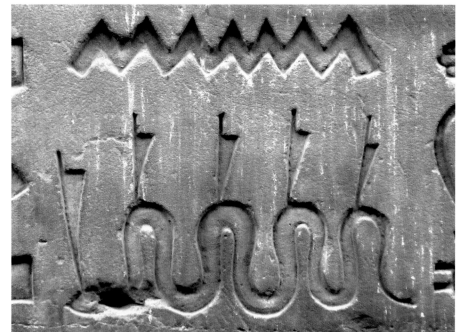

Wall relief of Apep, temple of Edfu, Egypt

Apep

Malevolent god of chaos and darkness in ancient Egyptian mythology, Apep is the nemesis of Ra, the sun god, and Ma'at, the goddess of truth. Especially during the Middle Kingdom of Egypt, Apep is described as the embodiment of all that is evil and what must be destroyed. Appearing in the form of a giant, earth-encircling snake or serpent, Apep battles Ra each day, either just before sunrise or just after sunset. The snake, therefore, resides just below the horizon, in the underworld. Egyptian priests had elaborate rituals for destroying Apep's influence over Egypt, including the creation of figurines which were then ritually decimated. Ra's solar boat, which he sailed in his orbit, was defended against Apep by the god Set, who would slay the monster. 'Apophis' is the Greek translation.

FURTHER READING: Wilkinson, Richard H. The Complete Gods and Goddesses of Ancient Egypt. (New York: Thames & Hudson, 2003); Wilkinson, Toby A. H. The Rise and Fall of Ancient Egypt. (New York: Random House, 2010); Pinch, Geraldine. Egyptian Mythology: A Guide to the Gods, Goddesses, and Traditions of Ancient Egypt. (Oxford: Oxford UP, 2004).

Aramaeans

Pastoralists and nomadic people who inhabited a region of what is now known as Syria. Well established as

The funeral stele of Si' Gabbor, priest of the Moon God. Dated early 7th century BC, found in Neirab (Syria), it bears an Aramaic inscription.

an ethnic and language group by 1100 BC, the Aramaeans spread east to the area around the Euphrates River in the 11th and 10th centuries BC. By the 9th century BC the relatively small but politically and militarily active Aramaean kingdoms were increasingly controlled by the Neo-Assyrians. Previous migrations east into Babylonia and Assyria led to the Aramaeans being absorbed into the larger Akkadian and Babylonian cultures, although Aramaic was widely adopted in the Neo-Assyrian Empire and Babylon as the language of trade and politics.

The lasting effect of Aramaean culture is linguistic; Aramaic remained the most sophisticated and powerful language in Mesopotamia for centuries, first appearing in 1100 BC, and only losing its universal appeal in around 200 AD. Aramaic was the default language of the Middle East until it was replaced by Arabic after the Islamic conquest of the region in 700 AD. Aramaic is closely related to Hebrew, and some Jewish ceremonies are still conducted in Aramaic. The Kabbalah and the Talmud, Jewish holy texts, are written in a combination of Aramaic and Hebrew. Aramaic was the choice of Jews in Babylon, and was the language that Jesus would have spoken.

FURTHER READING: Ascalone, Enrico, and Frongia Rosanna M. Giammanco. Mesopotamia. *(Berkeley: University of California, 2007); Van, De Mieroop, Marc.* A History of the Ancient Near East, Ca. 3000–323 BC. *(Malden, MA: Blackwell Pub., 2007).*

Assyria

Empire in northern Mesopotamia, which reached its peak of dominance in the Middle East in the 8th and 7th centuries BC; named from its chief town and god, Ashur.

Astarte

A great mother goddess was worshipped under various names throughout the Middle East, as Ishtar in Mesopotamia, as Ashtart or Asherah by the Phoenicians and Canaanites. The Greeks called her Astarte and equated her with their own love goddess Aphrodite, who was originally one of her many forms. Numerous clay plaques representing her have been found in Syria and Palestine, dating from 1700 to 1100 BC and probably worn as charms to promote fertility. She is mentioned frequently and with violent disapproval in the Old Testament and eventually, like many other deities who were rivals of the God of Jews and Christians, she turned into a demon and is one of

The fertility goddess Astarte, shown here on a fragment from a brooch

the fallen angels in Milton's *Paradise Lost*.

> Astoreth, whom the Phoenicians
>   called Astarte,
> Queen of Heaven, with crescent
>   horns;
> To whose bright image nightly by
>   the moon,
> Sidonian virgins paid their vows
>   and songs.

W. F. Albright has remarked that, 'Goddesses of fertility play a much greater role among the Canaanites than they do among any other ancient people': evidently because of their dread of drought and famine. Though these goddesses had different names and were independent personalities, they had similar functions and were essentially the same goddess. They ruled war as well as fertility, motherhood, and sex, and they were frequently represented naked and with the sexual organs emphasized.

The Bride of Heaven

Ashtart was the chief goddess of the Phoenicians at Tyre and Sidon, and wherever they established colonies they took her with them. She had a temple in their colony at Memphis in Egypt, for instance, and temples at Carthage. A Phoenician statuette of her in alabaster has been found at Galera, near Granada in Spain: she sits on a throne, flanked by sphinxes and with a bowl under her breasts. At some point in her ritual, milk was poured into the head of the statuette and flowed into the bowl through holes pierced in the goddess's breasts.

Asherah or Asherat, often called 'Asherat of the Sea', was the wife of the Canaanite supreme god El, whose name means simply 'the god', and by him was the mother of seventy deities. The same goddess was also worshipped in the south of Arabia and by the Amorites, the Semitic nomads who

by 2000 BC had spread northward from Arabia into Palestine, Syria, and Mesopotamia. There is an Amorite inscription to her of the 18th century BC, in which she is called 'the bride of heaven'.

In the Ugaritic texts, dating from c. 1400 BC, found at Ras Shamra in northern Syria since 1929, the goddess Anat plays a leading role. The chief god El stays in the background and the most active god is Baal, the storm god who sends the rains which bring fertility to the earth. Anat is his sister and wife, and she plays the vital part in killing the god of drought and sterility or, in other words, in reviving the life of Nature.

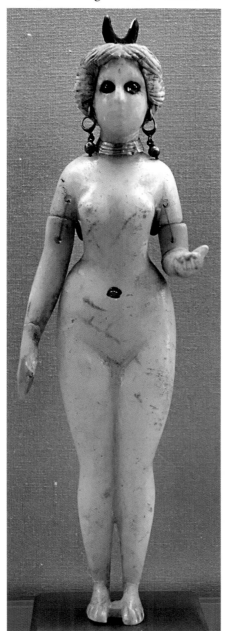

Asherah, the wife of the old supreme god El and the mother of Baal, seems to have been hostile to Baal at first but later joined forces with Anat to help him. Apparently, the followers of both goddesses tried to attach them to the fertility god as the cult of Baal developed.

All these goddesses were imported into Egypt and in the 13th century BC Pharaoh Rameses II called himself 'the companion of Anat'. Ashtart or Asherah appears in an Egyptian sculpture where she is called Qodshu or Qedeshat, 'the sacred prostitute'. She is naked, stands on a lion, and holds a lotus flower, a symbol of life, in her right hand. In her left hand the goddess holds a pair of serpents, which are symbols of life renewed because snakes slough their old skins each year.

In Canaan the symbol of Asherah was a wooden pole, called an 'asherah'. It might be a living tree but was more often a tree trunk with the branches lopped off, standing in a socket on a stone base. The upright pole is again a symbol of life, generation and fertilizing power, and may be the 'tree of life' which appears frequently in Canaanite art.

The Abomination of the Sidonians

When the Israelites invaded Palestine they found numerous local fertility gods and goddesses established, Baals and Ashtarts or Asherahs. The Old Testament writers called the goddess Ashtoreth, combining her name with the Hebrew word for 'shame', *bosheth*, as a comment on the licentiousness of her rites. But many Jews worshipped her. '. . . They forsook the Lord, the God of their fathers, who had brought them out of the land of Egypt; they

Statuette of a naked woman, possibly the Great Goddess of Babylon (or Ishtar). Alabaster, gold, terracotta, and rubies, 2nd century BC. From the necropolis of Hillah, near Babylon

went after other gods, from among the gods of the peoples who were round about them, and bowed down to them'. When Gideon pulled down his father's altar of Baal and cut down the asherah which stood beside it, 'he was too afraid of his family and the men of the town to do it by day, and he did it by night'. (Judges, chapters 2 and 6).

It was natural to feel that the gods already established in the country were powerful there, and the worship of a fertility goddess appealed to Jewish farmers who were just as concerned for the increase of their herds, crops, and families as the Canaanites were. In spite of the efforts of the prophets, many Jews continued to worship the mother. In the 10th century BC King Solomon built a 'high place' or sanctuary 'on the right hand of the mountain of corruption . . . for Ashtoreth, the abomination of the Sidonians' (2 Kings, chapter 23).

In the 9th century at Mizpeh, north of Jerusalem, temples of Yahweh and Asherah stood side by side. King Ahab and his wife, the notorious Jezebel, were devoted to the Canaanite gods and maintained 450 prophets of Baal and 400 prophets of Asherah. It was against these priests that Elijah fought his great ritual battle on Mount Carmel (1 Kings, chapter 18). He succeeded in calling down fire from heaven when they could not, but the reaction against him was so strong that he fled for his life.

In the late 7th century BC the prophet Jeremiah still bewailed that 'the children gather wood, the fathers kindle fire, and the women knead dough, to make cakes for the queen of heaven' but those he reproached answered that they would continue to burn incense to the queen of heaven and pour libations to her, as they and their fathers had done, because attempts to suppress her worship

had brought nothing but disaster (Jeremiah, chapters 7 and 44).

Priests and Prostitutes

As goddess of fertility, Astarte typified the reproductive powers of Nature and woman. She was associated with the moon, and often shown with the horns of the crescent moon, because the moon was believed to govern the growth, decay, and rebirth of all things as it waxed and waned in the sky. The dove, an amourous bird, belonged to her and at Ascalon in the 1st century AD a visitor saw 'an impossible number of doves' in the streets and houses, because they were sacred and no one ever killed

> *. . . their faces daubed with rouge and their eye sockets painted to bring out the brightness of their eyes.*

them. Fishes were sacred to her also, perhaps for their numerous offspring.

The Jewish prophets condemned the worship of Astarte, not only because they believed that Yahweh was the one true god but also because of the sexual rituals of the goddess, who was served by sacred prostitutes. Their activities had a practical use, for their earnings financed the goddess's cult, but the sexuality of Astarte's worship was basically imitative magic, intended to sustain the fertility of Nature.

Greek and Roman writers were also repelled by the worship of the Middle Eastern goddesses whose rituals spread westward, with their phallic symbols, sacred prostitutes and painted priests in women's clothes. In *The Golden Ass* Apuleius (born c. 123 AD) describes the priests, 'their faces daubed with rouge and their eye sockets painted to bring out the brightness of their eyes', who carried the image of 'the Syrian

goddess' about on an ass, dancing to the sound of castanets and cymbals, cutting themselves with knives and flagellating themselves for the edification of the spectators before going round with the collecting box. Earlier, in the biblical account of the contest between Elijah and the prophets of Baal, the Canaanite god's priests were said to 'cut themselves after their custom with swords and lances, until the blood gushed out upon them'.

The traveling lecturer and humorist Lucian, a contemporary of Apuleius, wrote an essay about the Astarte of Hierapolis, northwest of Aleppo in Syria. Tame bulls, bears, lions, and eagles were kept in the grounds of the temple and there was a lake full of holy fishes, some of which knew their names and came when called. In the early summer there was a great festival of the goddess, when trees were brought and erected outside the temple, with goats, sheep, and objects of gold and silver hung on them. The sacred idols were carried about among the trees and then burned.

The temple attendants were eunuchs who wore white robes with pointed caps. They cut their arms till the blood ran, and beat each other. Sometimes a young man, carried away in the ecstasy of the goddess's worship, would devote himself to her service by castrating himself. He would then run through the city and the occupants of the house into which he threw his severed members would supply him with women's clothes.

Princes of Amity

As a result of the denunciations of Ashtoreth in the Old Testament as an 'abomination' and an enemy of God, Jews and Christians decided that she was a demon but for unknown reasons the goddess turned into a male demon, with very bad breath. If he is summoned up by a magician, he appears in human form, half black and half white. He reveals all events of the past, present and future, and knows all secrets.

In the magical textbooks the demon Astaroth has lost all connection with sex but in the early seventeenth century Astaroth and Asmodeus were among the devils who possessed Madeleine de Demandolx. Under their influence, or so it was believed, she danced and sang lewd songs, writhed in indecent postures and told spine-chilling stories of orgies and cannibalism at witch revels she had attended. In 1673 Madame de Montespan sacrificed children to Astaroth and Asmodeus, 'princes of amity', in her attempt to secure her hold on Louis XIV's affections by black magic.

FURTHER READING: J. C. Gibson, Canaanite Myths & Legends. *(Attic Press, 1978); Donald Harden.* The Phoenicians. *(Praeger); E. O. James.* The Ancient Gods. *(Putnam, 1964); W. F. Albright.* From the Stone Age to Christianity. *(John Hopkins Press, 1957); Lucian's 'The Goddess of Syria' is in volume 4 of the Loeb edition of his works, though in an eccentric and tiresome translation.*

Aten

Or Aton, in Egyptian religion, the disc of the sun; in the 14th century BC Pharaoh Amenophis IV changed his name to Ikhnaton (or Akhenaten), 'pleasing to the Aten', denied the old gods and established a short-lived religion of the Aten as the only god.

Baal

The west semitic word *had* was applied to men and gods to mean ownership. It usually referred to the ownership of a place, so that there were many local gods who were Baals of their own areas, but it could also refer to ownership of a sphere of interest, as in the case of Baal Berith, 'the god of the covenant', who presided over agreements, or even to a god's ownership of those who worshipped him.

From c. 3000 BC probably, and certainly by about 2500 BC, the title was applied specifically to a god of the Amorites, a powerful group of Semitic nomads. He was the god of storm and the rain of winter, first found in Palestine and southern Syria, named *Adad* in Mesopotamian texts and *Hadad* in texts from Ras Shamra in northern Syria.

The texts found at Ras Shamra since 1929 contain versions, dating from about 1400 BC, of a large number of myths involving Baal, who was the most active deity in the fertility cult of the Canaanites, the early inhabitants of Syria and Palestine. This cult was particularly concerned with the winter rainfall, which was vital to the fruitfulness of flocks and fields. The texts make it possible to reconstruct the Canaanite cult of Baal. They sometimes confirm and sometimes correct the sporadic references in the Old Testament, which are generally criticisms of the abuses and grosser aspects of this Nature cult.

The Defeat of the Waters

The Baal myth of Ras Shamra describes in dramatic scenes how Baal (or Hadad) champions the gods and the order they sustain against the insults and threatened tyranny of the unruly waters, 'Prince Sea, even River the Ruler'. After a critical struggle Baal overcomes, slays, and disperses the waters, distributing them so that they are a good servant rather than a bad master. This conflict is described as a fight for kingship, and the victor Baal is acclaimed as 'king', his kingdom being 'an everlasting kingdom'. This was the Canaanite declaration of faith in the beneficence of Nature. It was an assurance to the worshippers and a relief to their fears and anxieties, which were expressed and purged by the drama vividly related in the texts. It was also an opportunity to influence the course of Nature by the speaking of words and possibly by an accompanying ritual in which Baal's victory was acted out and so magically recreated each year.

The main motifs of this Baal myth are reproduced in the Old Testament, notably in the psalms which assert or imply the kingship of God and in passages in the Prophets on the theme of the kingship of God and the maintenance of his order against the menace of Chaos in Nature and history. This was the theme of the Hebrew Feast of Tabernacles on the eve of the New Year, adapted from the chief seasonal festival in Canaan when the Israelites settled in Palestine, between c. 1225 and 1050 BC.

This same theme is the substance of hope for the future in apocalyptic literature. The imagery of the old Canaanite theme of the kingship of the god and his order in Nature, won in conflict with the unruly waters and certain sea monsters, such as Tin (the Biblical Leviathan), 'the Primeval Serpent, the Tortuous One with Seven Heads' is re-echoed from the Canaanite New Year ceremony.

The Warrior Storm

This is perhaps most familiar to general readers in the vision of the emergence of the reign of God and his saints after the succession of bestial powers, which significantly came up 'from the sea' in Daniel (chapter 7) and the culmination of the conflict against the bestial powers of evil in the establishment of the kingdom of God and his new creation, when 'sea shall be no more', in Revelation (chapter 21).

Opposite page:
Terracotta statue of Baal Hammon, the deity as worshipped in Carthage

Baal's character as the storm god is expressed in a sculptured stele (an upright slab or pillar) found near his temple on the acropolis of Ras Shamra and dating probably from c. 2100 BC. He is depicted as a helmeted warrior in a short kilt, striding into action, brandishing a mace (the weapon with which he overcomes Sea-and-River), and a spear, which is grounded, point downward. The butt of the shaft of the spear is depicted as branching, and this has been taken to simulate forked lightning, which is regularly noted as the weapon of Baal-Hadad (or Mesopotamian Adad) in texts and in sculpture. However, a seal design from Ras Shamra suggests that the branching spear may depict a cedar tree, expressing Baal's significance as a god of vegetation, particularly associated with the cedars which are the most splendid trees of the mountains of his Canaanite home.

The god's power of fertility is expressed by his association with the bull as his cult animal; he wears the bull's horns on his helmet. His stock epithet in the Baal myth is 'He who mounts the Clouds' (compare Yahweh, God of Israel, 'who makes the clouds his chariot'). The wavy lines shown beneath the feet of the god possibly represent the mountaintops and clouds (and again Yahweh 'treads the high places of the earth'). But they may also represent the waters below, over which he has triumphed.

The essential features of the warrior Baal are reproduced in the figurines of a young active god in bronze, sometimes inlaid in gold and silver, from various sites in Syria and Palestine. They indicate the widespread cult of the god, the Baal, the Master or Lord in the Nature worship of Canaan.

Baal, Zeus, and Hercules

Baal was one of the Semitic gods whose cult penetrated to Egypt, possibly carried there by the many Semites deported from Syria and Palestine in the various campaigns of the pharaohs between the 15th and 13th centuries BC. The pharaoh Rameses II (d. 1224 BC) himself affected Syrian cults.

The most notable cult centre of Baal in Egypt was Baal Saphon near Pelusium, east of the Nile Delta. The name reflects the proper home of the god, Mount Saphon, the modern Jebel al-Aqra, the Mount Kasios of the Greek geographers, a kind of Canaanite Olympus on the northern horizon of Ras Shamra.

Greek authors knew of a temple of Zeus Kasios near Pelusium and an inscription mentioning Zeus Kasios has been found there. The assimilation of Baal, the storm god who 'mounts the clouds', with the supreme sky god Zeus was natural, and equally natural was the worship, on this featureless but dangerous coast, of the god who established his kingship after winning victory over the unruly waters.

As the god of Tyre, whose worship Jezebel is depicted in the Old Testament as striving so hard to promote in Israel, Baal was assimilated in the Greek period (after the 4th century BC) to Hercules, the active young god who also sustained order against Chaos, which was depicted, like one of Baal's adversaries in the struggle, as a many-headed monster of the watery wastes, the Hydra.

The temple of Baal-Shamin in Palmyra, Syria

A similar theme was known between 2000 and 1000 BC in Asia Minor, as shown by mythological texts from the ancient Hittite capital of Hattusas (modern Boghazkoi) where the god who successfully overcomes the sea monster is Teshub, the weather god, who is represented in Hittite sculpture with the familiar features of the bronze figurines of Baal from Syria and Palestine.

The preoccupation with the fertility cult in Syria tended to give Baal-Hadad a predominance even beyond his proper sphere in Nature. It is significant that several of the kings of Damascus were called Ben-Hadad ('the son of Hadad'), which may have been a throne name of them all. It is a fair inference that the name reflects the conception of the king as the earthly guarantee of the kingship of Baal and the stability of order against the menace of Chaos. It was probably a trend to monotheism (the worship of one god) in the conception of Baal of the Heavens (Baal-Shamayim) in Syria between about 1000 and 500 BC which made Baal such a dangerous rival to Yahweh in Israel and prompted Elijah to his famous challenge to the prophets of Baal on Carmel (I Kings, chapter 18).

The Dying and Rising God

The bulk of the remainder of the Baal mythology in the Ras Shamra texts concerns Baal's conflict with Mot, the power of drought, sterility, and death, where Baal is a dying and rising god, the spirit of vegetation which wilts and dies in summer but revives again with the winter rain. These texts relate to the seasonal ritual of the Syrian peasants.

After Baal has succumbed to Mot, the latter suffers the vengeance of Baal's sister, 'the Virgin Anat', who cuts him with a blade, winnows him with a shovel, parches him with fire, grinds him with a millstone, and scatters him in a field. Here the rites of

desacralization (freeing from holiness) of the first or last sheaves of the grain harvest underlie the myth; such a rite, in fact, as is described in the Bible in Leviticus (chapter 2) which refers to the offering of the first sheaf, 'green ears of corn, dried by the fire, even corn beaten out of full ears'.

Baal eventually revives, and there is the glad prospect of the skies raining oil and the wadis running with honey (again an aspect of the establishment of the order of God in the Old Testament). Finally, 'after seven years' Baal engages Mot in a great struggle and overcomes him. This may be related to the Hebrew custom of allowing the land to lie fallow in the seventh year, thus simulating a famine, when the sinister power of sterility was allowed to exhaust itself, in the hope that the next six years would be normal.

Certain features of the myth suggest other rites mentioned in the Old Testament. On the death of Baal, 'the Virgin Anat' ranges the mountains searching for him with loud lamentation, suggesting the mourning for Hadad-Rimmon ('Hadad the Thunderer') in Zechariah (chapter 12) and the weeping for Tammuz by the women of Jerusalem (Ezekiel, chapter 8).

From the references in the Old Testament to repeated lapses to the cult of Baal and his female associates, we can infer that in settling in Palestine the Hebrews tended to assimilate the Baal cult without adapting it. Official authority was alarmed and the early calendar in Exodus (chapter 23) and the Ritual Code, also in Exodus (chapter 34), insisted that the festivals at the three great seasonal crises of the year be observed 'before Yahweh God of Israel', that is at the central sanctuary of the confederacy of Israel. Owing to this basic experience Israel was able to transform the theme of the Canaanite New Year festival, the kingship of God won and sustained against the menace of Chaos, and develop it as a fundamental

element of her own faith. The popular tendency, however, was to assimilate the grosser elements of Baal worship in the Canaanite fertility cult. To this the prophets are eloquent witnesses, especially Hosea, who inveighed against this materialistic Nature cult and the licentious rites of imitative magic with which it was associated.

JOHN GRAY

FURTHER READING: J. C. Gibson. Canaanite Myths and Legends. *(Attic Press, 1978); C. H. Gordon,* Ugaritic Literature (Argonaut)*; J. Gray.* The Legacy of Canaan. *(Humanities, 1967); J. Gray.* The Canaanites. *(Praeger, 1964).*

Babylonia

The area north of the head of the Persian Gulf, watered by the rivers Tigris and Euphrates, the centre of early civilization and religious development in the Middle East; in early times divided into two parts, the southern called Sumer and the northern Accad or Akkad.

Book of the Dead

It became the custom in ancient Egypt from about the eighteenth dynasty (1580–1320 BC) to place in the tombs of the dead papyrus scrolls inscribed with texts. These texts were designed to help the dead to rise to life again and obtain a happy lot in the next world. The name Book of the Dead is a modern one, given by Egyptologists. The ancient Egyptian title was Chapters for Coming Forth by Day. This title described what the texts would do for the dead, according to Egyptian belief. Briefly, it meant 'ability to leave the tomb' and it involved many strange and complex ideas about human nature and destiny. The Book of the Dead was the product of a long development of faith and ritual prac-

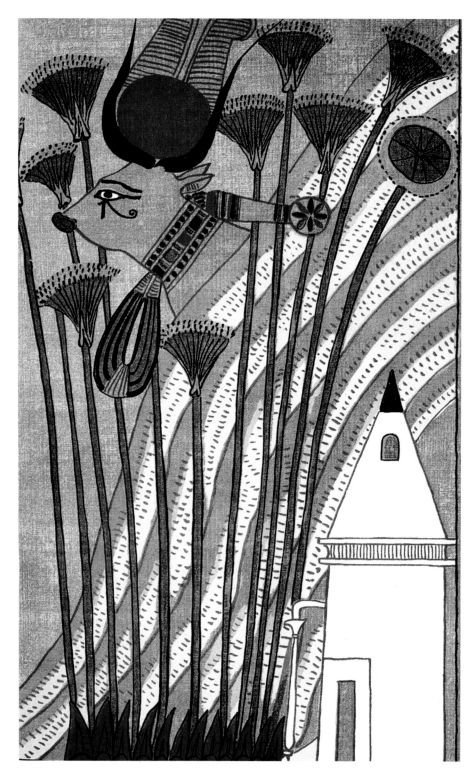

Facsimile of a vignette from the Book of the Dead of Ani. Hathor, as the Mistress of the West (a goddess of the afterlife) emerges from a hill representing the Theban necropolis. She is depicted as a cow, wearing her typical horns and sun disk, along with a menat necklace. Her eye is shaped like the sacred Eye of Horus. At bottom right is a stylized tomb.

The inscriptions were collected and arranged by the priests of Heliopolis, near Cairo, which was the ancient cult centre of Atum-Re, the sun god. In composing these texts, the Heliopolitan priests seem to have had a double purpose. The first was to provide the dead kings, buried in the pyramids concerned, with the magical means of securing resurrection from death and ascent to the sky, where they might join the sun god on his unending journey through the sky by day and the underworld by night. The sun god was imagined to make this journey by boat, and in the Egyptian mind eternal bliss was thus conceived as being forever in the company of Atum-Re as he made his unceasing circuit of the universe.

This linking of the kings' posthumous destiny with Atum-Re was evidently part of the policy of the Heliopolitan priests, intended to exalt the status of the god they served. The policy finds further expression in the texts by the presentation of Atum-Re as the creator of the universe, and Heliopolis as the place where he began his work of creation.

Guide to the Afterlife

The Heliopolitan priests were not skilful at literary composition, and the Pyramid Texts include rituals for use in embalming and funeral rites, hymns, incantations, magical spells, prayers, and myths in no apparent order. It appears that any material deemed to have a religious or magical efficacy was included. Some of it was evidently of a very primitive character. For example, the so-called Cannibal Hymn, which

tice concerning death and the dead in Egypt. Many of the texts can be traced back through two earlier collections of funerary texts: the Pyramid Texts and the Coffin Texts.

The Pyramid Texts have a unique place in human records for they are not only the earliest records we have of Egyptian thought, but they are also the earliest body of religious writings we

have of mankind as a whole. They are called 'Pyramid Texts' because they are inscribed, in hieroglyphic characters, on the interior walls of certain pyramids at Sakkara, the necropolis or burial place of the ancient city of Memphis. The Pyramid Texts date from about 2350 to 2175 BC, but it is clear that they contain traditional material which goes back to a much earlier period.

represents the dead king as eating the gods, doubtless reflects a practice of ritual cannibalism that had once, long before, existed in Egypt.

The priests of Heliopolis sought to associate the pharaoh's eternal future with their own god Atum-Re, but they could not ignore a more ancient mortuary god named Osiris. The Egyptians believed that Osiris, a good king of long ago, had risen from the dead after being foully murdered. They further believed that a dead person, who was ritually identified with Osiris, could also be raised to life again.

Originally, it would seem, this Osirian mortuary ritual was confined to royal use, and it was evidently so well established that the Heliopolitan priests felt obliged to incorporate it into their Pyramid Texts. Doubtless they could not safely ignore such ancient rites, which had long been practiced to secure resurrection for the kings of Egypt. But the Osirian idea of salvation from death logically contradicted the Heliopolitan view of a blessed afterlife with the sun god.

These two different views of the afterlife add to the confusion of ideas and imagery in the Pyramid Texts. Thus, while some texts are designed to enable the dead king to fly up to heaven as a falcon or climb up on a ladder, others deal with his embalming and resurrection according to the legend of Osiris. This discrepancy remained a permanent feature of Egyptian belief about the state of the dead as can be seen from the texts of the Book of the Dead.

The following translated extracts give some idea of the diction and imagery of the Pyramid Texts. First, an incantation designed to enable the dead king to join the sun god Re:

He flieth as a bird, and he settleth as a beetle on an empty seat that is in the ship of Re . . . He roweth in the sky in thy ship, O Re, and he cometh to land in thy ship, O Re.

The next illustrates the way in which the dead pharaoh Unas is ritually identified with Osiris, so that, invoking the principle of imitative magic, he is one with Osiris in his resurrected life:

Thy (Osiris's) body is the body of Unas. Thy bones are the bones of this Unas. (If) thou walkest, this Unas walks; (if) this Unas walks, thou walkest.

During the period from c. 2160 to 1580 BC, the nobility of Egypt adopted the custom of burying their dead in large wooden coffins, on the sides of which were painted texts designed to help the dead to pass safely to a blessed afterlife. The Coffin Texts are particularly characterized by the concern expressed by the deceased that he should have an adequate supply of food and drink, lest he should be forced to feed on his own excrement. He also asks that he should be assured of a supply of fresh air to breathe and that the integrity of his body should be preserved. Belief in the potency of magic is also abundantly attested.

The scales or balances, which were to be used in the dread judgment that faced the dead, are mentioned.

Facsimile of a vignette from the Book of the Dead of Ani. The scribe Ani and his wife, Tutu, the people for whom the papyrus was made, stand before a table piled with offerings.

The following passage, which takes the form of an invocation of the sun god, gives some idea of the terror this grim ordeal inspired. The balance is personified as an awful demonic being.

Thou canst protect me from this god of mysterious form, whose two eyebrows are the two arms of the balance, who casts his lasso over the wicked (to hale them to) his block, who annihilates the souls, in the day when evil is assessed, in the presence of the Master of all! Who is this god, whose two eyebrows are the two arms of the balance? It is Horus who presides at Letopolis. Others say: it is Thoth, it is Nefertem, the son of Sekhmet, this one who raises his arm.

This invocation is reproduced in Chapter 17 of the later Book of the Dead.

On some coffins, found in the necropolis of El-Bersheh and dating from the end of the eleventh dynasty (c. 2000 BC), a funerary text occurs which differs strikingly from the Coffin Texts. The text is also notable for the illustration that accompanies it, and which makes it a veritable guidebook to the next world. It shows a map of the journey which the dead had to make by either of two tortuous roads that were separated by a lake of fire. One was a land route, leading to the country of Ro-Setau, a mysterious place connected with the realm of Osiris. Its entrance was guarded by a gate of fire. The other route was by water to the lake of Ro-Setau, the entrance to which was watched over by a ram-headed crocodile, armed with a knife. Other dangers also beset the dead on the way—serpents, monsters, gates that could not be opened except by the right magical spells. This funerary text has, appropriately, been named the Book of the Two Ways.

The Pyramid Texts were compiled by the priests of Heliopolis for the

The Weighing of the Heart

One of the most famous scenes in the Papyrus of Ani shows the weighing of the heart after death in the Hall of the Two Truths. The heart of the royal scribe Ani is weighed in a balance against a feather, the symbol of truth. A dog-headed ape, associated with the god Thoth, sits on the beam of the balance, and Thoth himself stands at one side to record the result of the trial. The jackal-headed god Anubis tests the tongue of the balance. Behind Thoth stands the monster Amemet, 'the devourer of the dead'. The text reads:

Osiris, the scribe Ani, says: 'My heart my mother, my heart my mother, my heart my coming into being! May there be nothing to resist me at my judgment; may there be no opposition to me from the Tchatcha (the gods of the four cardinal points); may there be no parting of you from me in the presence of him who keeps the scales. You are my ghost (ka) within my body which knits and strengthens my limbs. May you come forth to the place of happiness to which I am advancing. May the Shenit (divine beings) not cause my name to stink, and may no lies be spoken against me in the presence of the god. Good is it for you to hear'.

Thoth, the righteous judge of the great company of the gods who are in the presence of Osiris, says: 'Hear this judgment. The heart of Osiris has in truth been weighed and his soul has stood as a witness for him; it has been found true by trial in the Great Balance. No wickedness has been found in him; he has not wasted the offerings in the temples; he has not done harm by his deeds; and he uttered no evil reports . . . on earth'.

The great company of the gods reply to Thoth dwelling in Khemennu: 'That which comes forth from your mouth has been ordained. Osiris, the scribe Ani, triumphant, is holy and righteous. He has not sinned, nor has he done evil against us. Let it not be given to the devourer Amemet to prevail over him. Meat-offerings and entrance into the presence of the god Osiris shall be granted to him, together with a dwelling forever in Sekhet-hetepu, as to the followers of Horus'.

Adapted from E. A. W. Budge, *The Egyptian Book of the Dead*

exclusive use of the dead pharaohs. No reference is made in them to the fate of other folk. The Coffin Texts reveal that later on nobles and other important persons had begun to take over this ancient royal ritual. In so doing, they did not change the royal references and terminology of the ancient texts, doubtless because they feared that any alteration in the traditional form might impair the magical efficacy of the spells and incantations. The resulting confusion, which also occurs in the later Book of the Dead, is very puzzling to the modern reader but it seems to have been no obstacle to Egyptian faith.

The process of democratization continued into the period from 1580 to 1090 BC, and it finds its complete expression in the Book of the Dead. By this time, any person who could afford the essential minimum of what was once the royal mortuary ritual could hope to enjoy the resurrection to a new life which had once been the privilege of the pharaoh. To enable the dead to achieve this resurrection, and to pass safely through all the grisly perils of the underworld to everlasting happiness, assistance had to be provided as it had been for the pharaohs in the Pyramid Texts and later for the nobles in the Coffin Texts.

Selections of appropriate texts were provided by scribes, written on sheets of papyrus, which were rolled up and deposited in the tomb. The selection and presentation of the texts, which thus formed the Book of the Dead, varied according to the means of the deceased or the generosity of his heirs. Cheap copies were available for the poorer members of society, which contained only what were regarded as the really indispensable texts. Spaces would be left in them for the insertion of the names of those by whom, or for whom, they were eventually purchased. The more elaborate versions contained varying numbers of chapters.

The Weighing of the Heart from the Book of the Dead of Ani. At left, Ani and his wife Tutu enter the assemblage of gods. At centre, Anubis weighs Ani's heart against the feather of Maat, observed by the goddesses Renenutet and Meshkenet, the god Shay, and Ani's own ba. At right, the monster Ammut, who will devour Ani's soul if he is unworthy, awaits the verdict, while the god Thoth prepares to record it. At top are gods acting as judges: Hu and Sia, Hathor, Horus, Isis and Nephthys, Nut, Geb, Tefnut, Shu, Atum, and Ra-Horakhty.

The larger and obviously more expensive versions of the Book of the Dead were generally illustrated by scenes of the funerary ritual and of the experiences of the deceased in the next world. What is probably the finest copy of the Book of the Dead is the Papyrus of Ani, now one of the great treasures of the British Museum. It was made for the royal scribe Ani, who held various important offices in Thebes around 1320 BC. The scroll measures 78 feet by 1 foot 3 inches, and is the longest known papyrus of its period. The text is written in hieroglyphic characters, and the illustrations are done in various colours and are well and clearly drawn.

The most impressive illustration in the Papyrus of Ani shows the judgment of the dead Ani in the Hall of the Two Truths. The scene depicts the heart of Ani being weighed against the feather-symbol of Maat (Truth). The next scene shows Ani, after the dread ordeal from which he has emerged justified or 'true of voice', being presented by the god Horus to Osiris.

This judgment scene usually illustrates Chapter 30 of the Book of the Dead which took the form of a prayer addressed by the dead person to his heart not to testify against him at the awful moment when it was balanced against the symbol of Truth.

Other scenes in the Papyrus of Ani show the funeral procession and the ceremony of 'Opening the Mouth', a magical rite designed to restore to the embalmed body certain of its faculties. The resurrection of Ani is also represented, and Ani and his wife are depicted in many scenes enjoying their new life in the paradise of Osiris. In one delightful scene Ani appears to be playing a game like chess, advised by his wife who sits behind him.

The production of copies of the Book of the Dead continued down the long centuries of Egyptian history into the 1st century BC. This lengthy tradition bears witness to the enduring strength of the Egyptian belief that the ancient Osirian mortuary ritual effectively provided the means of defeating the dreaded consequences of death and attaining a state of eternal bliss.

S. G. F. BRANDON

FURTHER READING: E. A. W. Budge. The Book of the Dead. (Routledge & Kegan Paul, 1950); S. A. B. Mercer. The Pyramid Texts. (Toronto, Longmans, 1952, 4 vols); T. C. Allen. The Egyptian Book of the Dead. (Chicago: Univ. of Chicago Press, 1960); S. G. F. Brandon. The Judgment of the Dead. (Weidenfeld and Nicolson, 1967).

Book of the Dead

Tibetan

The *Bardo Thodol*, as it is known in Tibetan, is a description of what happens after death. It represents only a small part of the Tibetan material on dying, and could better be called 'a' Tibetan book of the dead than 'the' one. The classic version in English was translated by a Tibetan lama, Kazi Dawa-Samdup, and edited by W. Y. Evans-Wentz, who was an enthusiastic Theosophist and admirer of Madame Blavatsky, and studied with Buddhist lamas in Tibet. The ideas and the complex symbolism involved are unfamiliar to most Westerners and, inevitably, neither of the two available modern versions is easy for the uninstructed to grasp.

The text treats death not as the end but as a recurrent stage in the cycle of lives, deaths, and rebirths which in Buddhist belief we all experience many times over, and from which only the enlightened can escape into Nirvana. Traditionally in Tibet the text was recited at a person's deathbed by a lama. It describes the extraordinary and frightening experiences which occur in the forty-nine days (the number is explained as symbolic rather than literal) in the interval between dying and being reborn. Its purpose is to teach the art of rightly dying and to banish fear of death and unwillingness to die, which produce 'unfavourable results'.

At the outset the dying person is told that the moment has come to leave the earthly plane and experience the Clear Light of the Void. Those who are exceptionally spiritually advanced will attain liberation; the great majority will be outside the body, but aware of the deathbed scene, hearing the weeping of friends and relatives, and wondering uneasily whether death has come or not. It will be some time before the truth dawns: now there follow awesome sounds and lights, but it is essential to understand that these are illusions, projections of the deceased's own consciousness.

Presently there are coloured lights and various deities appear. The blinding white light of wisdom will dazzle the dead person, who will shrink away, but must cleave to it rather than to the duller, smoky light which beckons the unwary to the hell-realms of misery. There are numerous visions of deities, terrifying sounds of thunder and voices crying 'Kill! Kill!', but these again are illusions.

The Wrathful Deities
Further testing comes with the appearance of Wrathful Deities—flame-wrapped beings with many heads, arms and legs, who brandish weapons in their numerous hands and drink blood from skulls: '. . . from the east, the Dark Brown Lion-Headed One, the hands crossed on the breast, and in the mouth holding a corpse, and shaking the mane; from the south, the Red Tiger-Headed One, the hands crossed downward, grinning and showing the fangs and looking on with protruding eyes; from the west, the Black Fox-Headed One, the right hand holding a shaving knife, the left holding an intestine, and she eating and licking the blood there from; from the north, the Dark Blue Wolf-Headed One, the two hands tearing open a corpse . . .'

These gruesome figures, too, can be vanquished by recognizing them for what they are and not giving way to panic. Lonely and afraid as the impulse toward rebirth gathers strength, the dead wander in a realm of illusions, confronted by thick darkness, beasts of prey, phantoms, snow and tempest, earthquakes, and hallucinations of being pursued by a raging mob and hiding in crevices in rocks. In a judgment before the Lord of the Dead, each person's good deeds and bad deeds are counted out in the form of white and black pebbles, and the deceased is agonizingly torn to pieces over and over again. But all this is still illusion.

C. G. Jung regarded the nightmare figures of the Tibetan text as images from the collective unconscious. The Buddhist tradition teaches that recognizing them for what they truly are is the path to enlightenment.

FURTHER READING: The Tibetan Book of the Dead, ed W. Y. Evans-Wentz (New York: Oxford University Press, 1960); The Tibetan Book of the Dead, trans F. Fremantle and Chogyam Trungpa (Boston: Shambhala, 1975).

Canaanites

Ancient inhabitants of Canaan, also known as the Levant, the area now occupied by Israel, Palestine, Western Syria, and Southern Lebanon, sometimes including areas further north or east. The term 'Canaanite' can refer to all inhabitants of the region, to speakers of any Canaanite language, or to the people known specifically as Canaanites. Aside from Canaanites, other cultures in the region that spoke languages very similar to one another were the Israelites, the Moabites, the

St. Simon the Canaanite temple in New Athos, Abkhazia, in present-day Georgia

The Battle of Jericho on Ghiberti doors, Grace Cathedral, San Francisco, California, USA

Phoenicians, the Amorites, and the Edomites.

Stone Age hunter-gathering tribes began to settle Canaan before 3500 BC, and by the 2nd millenium BC a series of city states had sprung up. Its location at the intersection of a number of large and powerful civilizations and empires meant that Canaan was at the heart of a series of invasions, conflicts, and other political and economic pressures. At times ruled by independent city states and confederacies, Canaan was variously ruled by the Egyptians, the Hittites, and the Assyrians. The geography of Canaan influenced its population in economic ways, as well. During periods of moderate climates, Canaan's mix of coast and hills was a prime agriculture opportunity. Because of its central location, economic prosperity for its neighbours also meant increased trade through Canaan's borders. Every advantage, though, made Canaan a more tempting target for conquest. The Egyptians in particular were very active in Canaan during the Middle Bronze Era (1550–1200 BC). During the Iron Age, Canaan was ruled by a succession of Empires, beginning with the Assyrians, followed by the Babylonians, the Persians, Alexander the Great from Greece, the Roman Empire in the 2nd century BC, the Byzantines, and finally Arab Muslims in the 7th century AD.

Canaan plays a central role in the Pentateuch of the Hebrew Bible: it is the Promised Land that God gives to the Israelites after their oppression in Egypt. Archaeological evidence suggests, however, that the Israelites were one of several groups already in Canaan for several thousand years. Jericho and Jerusalem are significant historical cities that appear in the Old Testament.

The Canaanite languages are part of the Semitic Language family. Canaanite languages had become extinct by the 1st century AD, but Hebrew was revived as a living language during the Zionist movement in the nineteenth century. Some versions of Aramaic are still spoken by pockets of people in Syria, Iraq, and Iran.

FURTHER READING: Van, De Mieroop, Marc. A History of the Ancient Near East, Ca. 3000–323 BC. *(Malden, MA: Blackwell Pub., 2007); Black, Jeremy A., Anthony Green, and Tessa Rickards.* Gods, Demons, and Symbols of Ancient Mesopotamia: An Illustrated Dictionary. *(Austin: University of Texas, 1992).*

Cheops

Ancient Egyptian pharaoh, 2nd king of the fourth dynasty of the Old Kingdom, Cheops ruled Egypt for several decades around 2580 BC. 'Cheops' is a Greek translation of his actual name, Khufu. Not much is known about Khufu's reign, nor his personal history. Everything that modern historians can surmise is drawn from documents that appeared long after his actual reign; some documents have his reign at sixty-three years, others less. Khufu's lasting achievement is the Great Pyramid at Giza, one of the Ancient Wonders of the World. Near the pyramid modern excavations uncovered a well-preserved wooden boat, buried near Khufu's resting place to take his soul to the afterlife. He is also possibly the builder of the Sphinx that guards the pyramid complex, although that attribution is debated. Khufu's reputation as a king is also a topic of controversy. While he was certainly powerful, given the scale of his funerary preparations, commentators from the 3rd century

The Meeting of Antony and Cleopatra, 41 BC, Sir Lawrence Alma-Tadema (1836–1912)

BC (more than 2,000 years after his reign) such as Herodotus criticized the ancient king for relying so heavily on oppressive mass slave labour to build his monuments.

FURTHER READING: Allen, James P., and Peter Der. Manuelian. The Ancient Egyptian Pyramid Texts. (Atlanta: Society of Biblical Literature, 2005); Wilkinson, Toby A. H. The Rise and Fall of Ancient Egypt. (New York: Random House, 2010); Wilson, John Albert. The Culture of Ancient Egypt. (Chicago: University of Chicago, 1956).

Cleopatra

Part of the Ptolemaic Dynasty in Ancient Egypt, Cleopatra VII Philopator (69 BC–August 12, 30 BC) was the last pharaoh of Egypt. In popular legend Cleopatra is portrayed as a famous beauty, and she cultivated the image of herself as an incarnation of the goddess Isis. Cleopatra courted Julius Ceasar while in exile during a dispute over the Egyptian throne with her brother Ptolemy XIII. Cleopatra and Ceasar began a love affair in 48 BC that resulted in a son, Ceasarion. Ceasar reinstalled Cleopatra to the Egyptian throne. After Ceasar's assassination, she supported Marc Antony over Octavion in the Roman civil war. Antony and Cleopatra became lovers and had three children. On August 1, 30 BC, Octavion defeated Antony's army near Alexandria, and Antony committed suicide. Cleopatra subsequently committed suicide as well, on August 12, supposedly by having an asp bite her chest. Her son Ceasarion was crowned pharaoh by his supporters, but Octavion had him killed soon after. Cleopatra's story is the subject of numerous theatrical adaptations, notably Shakespeare's *Antony and Cleopatra*.

FURTHER READING: Wilkinson, Toby A. H. The Rise and Fall of Ancient Egypt. (New York: Random House, 2010); Van, De Mieroop, Marc. A History of the Ancient Near East, Ca. 3000–323 BC. (Malden, MA: Blackwell Pub., 2007); Fletcher, Joann. Cleopatra the Great: The Woman Behind the Legend. (New York: Harper, 2011); Goldsworthy, Adrian Keith. Antony and Cleopatra. (New Haven: Yale UP, 2010); Schiff, Stacy. Cleopatra: A Life. (New York: Back Bay, 2011); Tyldesley, Joyce A. Cleopatra: Last Queen of Egypt. (New York, NY: Basic, 2008).

Code of Hammurabi

Code of laws recorded by Hammurabi, ruler of Babylonia from 1792–1750 BC. Hammruabi's Code is one of the oldest known legal documents in the world. The surviving copies, inscribed

Opposite page:
Bas relief showing Hammurabi, King of Babylon

in cuneiform on massive stone stele, can be dated to approximately 1772 BC. The Code is written in Akkadian and scholars suspect that the rules it sets out are much older, reflecting the Babylonian and Akkadian cultural heritage in the Sumerian culture. The oldest known legal code is the Code of Ur-Nammu, a Sumerian text dating three to four hundred years earlier than that of Hammurabi.

The Code of Hammurabi is most famous for its dictum 'an eye for an eye' which balances punishment with criminal behaviour. The Code, how-ever, also deals with numerous other aspects of society, including contract law, domestic issues such as marriage and sexual conduct, trade law, military conduct, and one instance of judicial conduct in which a judge may be removed from the bench for coming to the wrong legal conclusion. The punishments are graded according to the legal status of the individuals in conflict, whether they are slaves or free men.

The Louvre museum houses an original copy carved into a 7-foot-tall stone index finger. Other less complete versions have been found on smaller clay tablets that date from the same period.

FURTHER READING: Hammurabi, and Robert Francis Harper. The Code of Hammurabi King of Babylon, about 2250 BC. *(Honolulu, HI: University of the Pacific, 2002); Van, De Mieroop, Marc.* King Hammurabi of Babylon: A Biography. *(Malden, MA: Blackwell Pub., 2005).*

Dung-Beetle

The dung-beetle, or scarab, venerated in Egypt because it lays its eggs in a ball of dung which it rolls along the ground. A symbol of the sun, of the creation of life in matter, or resurrection. Amulets in the shape of a scarab were worn as good luck charms or placed in the tombs of the dead to ensure eternal life.

Egypt

Two factors have conspired to give ancient Egypt its unique appeal: its religion and the fact that its climate has so wonderfully preserved the relics of this religion for us. Religion permeated the whole life both of the individual Egyptian and of Egyptian society. It found expression in such a rich variety of forms that Egyptian religion provides the best introduction to the historical and comparative study of religion. Almost every aspect of religious faith and practice is found in this ancient religion: polytheism, henotheism (the worship of a single god), monotheism (belief that there is only one God), mythology, magic, ritual, divine kingship, mighty temples

Gold throne of King Tutankhamun depicts the ruler with his wife, Ankhsenamun

and mysterious tombs, a professional priesthood, illustrated religious texts, wisdom literature, and religious scepticism. It also embraced the most elaborate funerary cult, magical resurrection and a complex afterlife, and the earliest conception of a judgment after death. Although now extinct, Egyptian religion was the longest-lived religion yet recorded; it was already in being in 3000 BC and it survived until the forcible suppression of pagan cults by the Christian emperor Theodosius in 384 AD.

Egyptian religion is well documented. There is an abundance of texts inscribed on the walls of tombs, temples, obelisks, statues and stelae (stone memorial slabs), or painted on coffins or written on papyrus scrolls. They range in date from the Pyramid Texts of c. 2460 BC (see Book of the Dead) to texts of the 4th century AD. Monuments such as pyramids, temples and tombs have often been so well preserved that their ritual use can be easily traced. Temples and tombs were adorned with ritual scenes, and tombs with depictions of the underworld, all of which provide a vivid picture of Egyptian deities, worship, and belief about the next world.

The immense duration of Egyptian religion makes it necessary to know something of the course of Egyptian history, especially since Egyptologists use their own chronological scheme in making reference to various periods. This scheme is founded on a dynastic framework. The dynasties concerned are royal, but it is not certain why the various groups of monarchs are so related to each other. The dates given here are approximate, since only rarely can an Egyptian date be definitively established. The Thinite Period (3200–2780 BC), comprising

Dynasties 1–2, marks the beginning of the united kingdom of Upper and Lower Egypt under pharaonic rule. The Old Kingdom (2780–2280 BC), comprising Dynasties 3–6, was the pioneering period of Egyptian civilization, known as the Pyramid Age. The First Intermediate Period (2280–2052 BC), comprising Dynasties 7–10, was a time of social revolution when royal power was seriously weakened. At the time of the Middle Kingdom (2052–1778 BC), comprising Dynasties 11–12, the political centre had moved to Thebes in Upper Egypt. This was a period of great literary activity. The Second Intermediate Period (1778–1567 BC),

Dynasties 13–17, was a time of national eclipse, when Egypt was subjugated by Asiatic invaders. The New Kingdom (1567–1085 BC), Dynasties 18–20, was the period of Egypt's greatest imperial expansion; Tutankhamen was a minor king of the eighteenth dynasty. The Late Period (1085–330 BC), Dynasties 21–30, was a period of national decline, when Egypt suffered from Assyrian and Persian invasions. The last native Egyptian pharaoh was Nectanebo (359–341 BC). During the Ptolemaic or Hellenistic Period (330–30 BC), Egypt was ruled by Greek (Macedonian) monarchs, the last of whom was the famous Cleopatra. After her death, Egypt was incorporated into the Roman Empire; this was the Roman Period (30 BC–641 AD). The main pattern of its religion continued, with the Roman emperors taking the place of the pharaohs, until it was finally suppressed in favour of Christianity in 384 AD. Certain elements of the ancient faith passed into Coptic Christianity, which survived the Islamic conquest of Egypt in 641 AD and the subsequent conversion of the Egyptian people to Islam.

Two natural features have always dominated life in Egypt, namely, the River Nile and the sun. From them stemmed two of the basic themes of ancient Egyptian religion. Egypt has been aptly described as a land having length but no breadth. The description is not quite accurate, because the Delta area is certainly extensive. But south of Cairo, Egypt really consists of two strips of irrigable land on either bank of the Nile, with the desert stretching away on each side. The land consequently divides into two distinctive parts: Lower Egypt, comprising the Delta area, and Upper Egypt, formed of the long, narrow Nile valley. The fertility of the land depends absolutely upon the annual flooding of the Nile and the careful control and conserva-

tion of its life-giving waters. This entails the construction and maintenance of elaborate irrigation works. Consequently a strong centralized government, uniting Upper and Lower Egypt under one rule and able to direct the country's labour resources, has always been essential to the economic and social well-being of the people. Such a government was first established about 3000 BC in Upper Egypt, and the achievement was so important that the Egyptians looked back to this union of Upper and Lower Egypt as the starting point of their national life.

Because the sun so insistently dominates the daily scene in Egypt, it was venerated under the name of Re (Egyptian-Coptic for 'sun') as the supreme state deity, intimately associated with the monarchy. Known as the 'Great God', Re was conceived under various highly imaginative forms. As Re-Horakhti, an ancient falcon or falcon-headed sky god called 'Horus of the horizon' was associated with the sun god. Re-Horakhti was represented in art as a falcon-headed man, crowned with the solar disc. Sometimes this form of the deity was depicted as the solar disc, encircled by two serpents, between the outstretched wings of a falcon. As the sun at dawn, Re was represented as a beetle (Khepri) or a beetle-headed man. This strange concept had a subtle significance. 'Khepri' derived from the word kheper, meaning 'to become or exist', so that Re-Khepri indicated both the rising sun and the sun as the self-existent creator of the universe. The declining sun was Re-Atum, shown as an aged man of wise counsel. The word 'Atum' conveyed some idea of 'completion'. Atum was the god of Heliopolis, the old centre of sun worship.

Since Re, as the state god, was essentially connected with the kingship of the pharaohs, it was inevitable that his cult should be affected by political changes in Egypt. During the Old

Kingdom period, he was worshipped as Re-Atum in his ancient home at Heliopolis, where his temple was supposed to mark the primeval hill where he began the work of creation. When the political capital was moved to Thebes in Upper Egypt, during the Middle Kingdom, Re was associated with the local god of Thebes, Amun. Amun-Re was represented in art as a man wearing a cap, surmounted by two plumes and the solar disc. The great pharaohs of the New Kingdom were zealously devoted to Amun, building at Thebes for his worship huge temples, richly endowed, so that Amun became in effect the sole state god. This exaltation of Amun eventually produced one of the most interesting, though obscure, episodes in the whole of Egyptian history.

The Heretic King

It would seem that the priests of Heliopolis, the ancient cult centre of Re-Atum, attempted to combat the exaltation of Amun by promoting the worship of Re untrammelled by association with another god. Accordingly they proclaimed the Aten, the sun's disc, as the symbol of supreme deity. Meanwhile at Thebes the enormous power acquired by the priesthood of Amun had begun to challenge the royal power. When Amenhotep IV (1372–1354 BC) ascended the throne, he gradually set about supplanting Amun as the supreme deity by the Aten. This king, who soon changed his name to Akhenaten ('Pleasing to the Aten'), was a strange genius whose devotion to the Aten bordered on fanaticism.

Opposite page: Facsimile of a vignette from the Book of the Dead of Ani. The sun disk of the god Ra is raised into the sky by an ankh symbol (signifying life) and a djed pillar (signifying stability and the god Osiris) while adored by Isis, Nephthys, and baboons. The motif symbolizes rebirth and the sunrise.

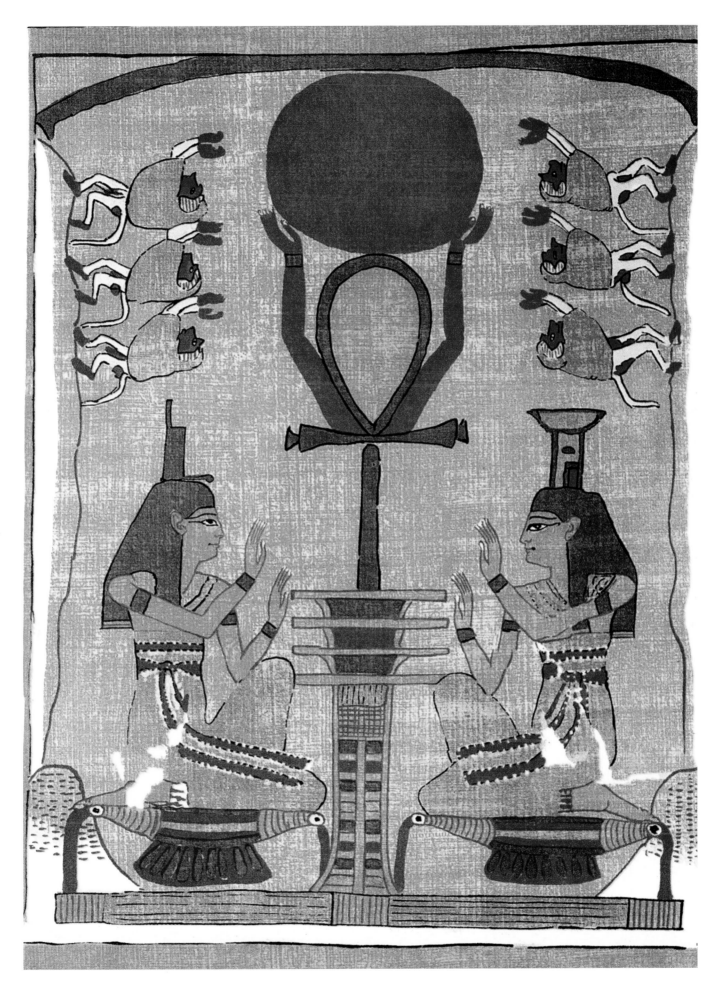

He moved his capital from Thebes, the stronghold of Amun, to a new city named Akhetaten ('Horizon of the Aten'), where he built a magnificent temple to his god, similar in plan to that at Heliopolis. He expressed his devotion in hymns to the Aten and he had himself frequently portrayed, together with his beautiful wife Nefertiti and their children, worshipping the Aten, whose descending rays, ending in hands, bless the pious family. He took measures to repress the cult of Amun, even to the point of causing the deity's name to be removed from monuments. However, the attempt to reform Egyptian religion did not survive the heretic king, and his successor Tutankhamen (1354–1345 BC) was obliged to submit to Amun's supremacy and bring the court back to Thebes. The memory of Akhenaten was execrated and his monuments destroyed. The ascendancy of the Amun priesthood reached its inevitable conclusion in about 1080 BC when Herihor, the 'First Prophet of Amun', took over the royal power at Thebes.

The third main theme of Egyptian religion was constituted by the funerary cult which centered on the god Osiris. This was essentially concerned with the spiritual needs of individuals, which were not served by the state religion. Osiris, the divine hero who died and rose again, had an intimate personal appeal and, since it was believed that resurrection to eternal life could be achieved through ritual assimilation to him, he came increasingly to dominate Egyptian religion. His cult was the longest lived of all those of the Egyptian deities.

The earliest texts record a multiplicity of gods and goddesses. The majority were local deities but some achieved a nationwide recognition. Amun is a case in point: the political supremacy of Thebes made him the supreme state god. Most local deities, like Bast, the cat goddess of Bubastis, and Sebek, the crocodile god of the Faiyum, had their chief sanctuary in their place of origin, with which they remained essentially associated. Sometimes their cult might be accorded a limited observance in one or two other places. The origin of these local deities is unknown. The fact that many of them had animal forms or animal heads has suggested the theory of their derivation from ancient totems, but there is no certain evidence that totemism existed as an institution in early Egypt, and many other local deities cannot be explained in this way.

Of the major deities after Re, Osiris, and Amun, whose worship was generally observed throughout the land, Horus and Isis enjoyed the widest recognition. Horus was a complicated deity who, under certain forms, achieved the status of a state god. His solar aspect as Re-Horakhti, under which he was associated with Re the sun god, was paralleled by another of equal importance but of confusing significance, especially since the two aspects became combined in one single deity. In the Osirian mythology Horus is the posthumous son of Osiris, who avenges his father's death and inherits his kingdom. Since the Egyptians identified a deceased king with Osiris, and his son and successor with Horus, the latter came to be regarded as the divine prototype of the reigning pharaoh.

In the Osirian mythology the god Seth figures as the murderer of Osiris and the opponent of Horus, who finally overthrows him. This god, who seems originally to have been associated with storms and the desert, and so regarded as a strong and fierce being, gradually became the Egyptian god of evil. Seth is generally depicted as an animal-headed man. The animal has never been certainly identified: it has a long curved muzzle, almond eyes, and sharp pointed ears. The Greeks later identified Seth with the monster Typhon.

The other chief deity of the Osirian mythology who can claim to have become, with Osiris, one of the two most popular deities of Egyptian religion and later of Graeco-Roman society, was the goddess Isis, the wife of Osiris and mother of Horus, the daughter of Geb and Nut.

Ptah, the god of Memphis, always enjoyed a position of dignity in the Egyptian pantheon, because Memphis had been the ancient capital of the land and continued an important city. He is represented in art invariably in human form, tightly wrapped in a robe like a mummy. He wears a skull cap and holds a curiously shaped staff or sceptre. The priests of Memphis attributed to him the creation of all things, including the other gods. Memphis was also the cult centre of the Apis bull, a primitive symbol of procreative vitality, which was associated with Ptah as the manifestation of 'his blessed soul'; later the Apis was also associated with Osiris.

The Divine Scribe

The Egyptians deified the earth as a male deity, Geb; but often he was represented as a goose. In the Heliopolitan story of the creation, Geb originally lay in close embrace with Nut, the sky goddess, until separated by Shu, the god of the atmosphere. The Pyramid Texts indicate that Geb was once venerated as the oldest of the gods, and the pharaohs were regarded as his successors, sitting on the 'throne of Geb'. A very different deity was Thoth, who was associated with the city of Hermopolis but acquired attributes that made him significant to all Egyptians. His appearance is one of the strangest among the many strange Egyptian deities, for on a human body he has the head of an ibis bird. Thoth was regarded as the god of wisdom and the divine scribe; he is generally represented holding the reed pen and colour palette of the Egyptian scribe. He assumed an important role in the judgment of the dead, where he recorded the verdict when the heart of the deceased was weighed. The Greeks identified Thoth with Hermes and, as Hermes Trismegistus ('Thrice-great Hermes'), he was the source of the mystic revelation incorporated into the so-called Hermetic literature of the Graeco-Roman period.

Hathor was a widely popular goddess, who manifested herself in various forms. As a beautiful woman, she was the divine patron of music and dancing, symbolizing the joy of life. In a bas relief at Karnak, recording the divine birth of the pharaoh Amenhotep III, Hathor is represented as animating the infant king and his ka, or other self, with the ankh, the symbol of life. The goddess was also thought of as a cow and was sometimes depicted suckling the king. She personified the sky and is often represented as a cow receiving the setting sun, an office which caused her also to be regarded as a guardian of the dead, whom she transported to the next world. But Hathor had another side to her nature: she was identified with the destructive 'Eye of Re', and as the 'Lady of Punt' she was a divine lioness. She was closely associated with Horus: her name Hathor (Het Hor) means 'House of Horus'. Hathor's ambivalence of character is similar to that of the Mesopotamian goddess Ishtar.

A god who deserves special mention, though he was not numbered among the greater gods of Egypt, is Bes. He was represented as a squat, dwarflike figure with a large grinning face. He may justly be called 'the poor man's god' because of his great popularity, despite his having no cult centre. Bes was the patron of fun and music, and helped women in childbirth. In many ways he could be regarded as the god of good luck; numerous amulets shaped in his image have been found.

The Egyptians were most obviously polytheists; but there is also evidence of a tendency to henotheism, if not monotheism, among them. Most notable is the use of the expression 'the Great God' in their wisdom literature and certain inscriptions. The use of this expression, without further qualification, is significant; it shows that the Egyptians recognized one supreme deity who needed

no distinguishing name. It seems certain that in the earlier period the title 'Great God' referred to Re, the sun god; later Osiris may sometimes have been so designated. Akhenaten's concept of the Aten certainly merits the description 'monotheistic'. But it seems likely that the worship of any specific Egyptian deity in its local sanctuary was a kind of henotheism; during the service, the deity concerned was conceived of as the 'one' god, there and at that moment.

Egyptian religion does not appear to have been so rich in mythology as was the religion of the contemporary civilization of Mesopotamia. It had indeed its creation myths and the fundamentally important Osirian myth. Three other myths are known which concerned Re and certain goddesses. One told how Re grew old and mankind rebelled against him. To punish them, Re sent forth his eye in the form of his daughter Hathor. So destructive was the goddess that the sun god had to make her drunk in order to stop her work of slaughter, for otherwise mankind would have been wholly exterminated. A variant version of this myth concerned the fierce goddess Tefnut, who lived as a lioness in the Nubian desert. Re, whose daughter she was, wanted her to return to him and he sent Shu and Thoth, in disguise, to persuade her to come back. On the return journey she transformed herself into a beautiful goddess at Philae, and revealed herself as Hathor at Dendera, which was her chief cult centre. The third myth told how the goddess Isis acquired her magical power. She made a serpent and caused it to bite Re. No god could cure Re in his agony. Then Isis appeared and offered to relieve him on condition that he revealed his secret name to her. The tormented sun god was forced to comply and the knowledge she gained gave Isis her great power. There are a number of

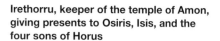

tales, such as that of the Two Brothers, which are full of supernatural details, but they are not true myths.

Ka, the Second Self

Religions are concerned not only with the deities who personify and explain the various manifestations of power that men encounter in the world, but also with human nature and destiny. The ancient Egyptians' concern with their personal destiny found expression in their elaborate mortuary cult. This cult presupposed a very complicated view of human nature. The individual person was conceived as a mixture of the physical and spiritual, made up of several constituents. The ka was a kind of alter ego or double,

created at conception together with the person whose ka it was. Egyptian texts give conflicting information about the nature of the ka and where it existed during the lifetime of the individual concerned. In art it was depicted as an exact replica of the individual, from whom it was distinguished by the ka symbol—shown as two arms extended upward—which was set on its head. Provision had to be made for the ka at death; in fact the tomb was called the het ka, the 'house of the ka', and it contained the ka statue in which the ka dwelt. 'To go to one's ka' was a euphemism for death. It is uncertain whether the Egyptians thought of the ka as a nonmaterial entity; it seems to denote

some vital force essential to the existence of the individual person.

The ka cannot properly be described as the soul. The ba, another constituent of human nature, had more claim to this description, though not in the sense of the 'soul' as the inner essential self according to the Greek idea of the psyche or the Hindu atman. In their concept of the ba, the Egyptians expressed their belief that at death a free-moving entity separated itself from the body but remained in close proximity to it. They represented the ba as a human-headed bird, giving it a male or female face according to the sex of the deceased. In the funerary papyri the ba is often depicted as perched on the portal of the tomb or flying down the tomb shaft to revisit the embalmed body lying in the sepulchral chamber below. Another important constituent of the person was the ib or heart. This was sometimes referred to as the 'god in man', since it was regarded as a kind of witness or censor of the conduct of the individual within whom it resided. The heart had a vital role in the judgment after death. The individual's shadow and name were also important to his being, though of lesser significance compared with the other entities. At death, the Egyptian trusted that the proper performance of the mortuary ritual would transform him into an akh or glorified soul.

Important as all these constituents were to the whole person, the body was always regarded as essential to life: this was why it was so carefully embalmed to preserve it from the disintegration caused by death. With their elaborate conception of human nature and the care given to ensuring eternal well-being after death, it is remarkable that the Egyptians never seem to have been curious about the purpose of human life in this world. In this lack of concern they contrast notably with the Mesopotamians, in whose mythology the origin and purpose of mankind was a primary topic.

Egyptian ideas of how and where the dead spent their afterlife are fundamentally confused. This confusion is already present in the Pyramid Texts (c. 2400 BC). It doubtless went back to predynastic times and stemmed from different local traditions. Three conceptions of the afterlife can be distinguished. What is probably the most primitive envisaged the dead as living on in their tombs, equipped with various everyday necessities and nourished on daily food offerings made by their relatives. In the Pyramid Texts the existence of a celestial realm of the dead is described. The idea takes two forms: that of ascending to heaven to join the sun god Re in his solar boat on his daily journey across the sky, or of ascending to join the 'Imperishable Ones', the circumpolar stars. The idea of accompanying the sun god became the more generally accepted view. The third conception was associated with Osiris and his realm, which was called the Duat or Ament (the West).

This realm was subterranean and was situated beneath the western horizon, which in Egypt was constituted by the western desert. The dead had to journey there, encountering many hideous monsters and fearsome obstacles on the way. This land of the dead was imagined as an idealized Egypt, where the blessed dead lived happily the same kind of life as in the Nile valley. Special guidebooks to the next world were provided for the dead. The Book of the Two Ways described alternative land and water routes, both equally perilous;

the Book of Gates divided the Duat by 12 gates; the Book of Duat told of the 12 time divisions taken by the sun god on his nightly journey through this underworld. What is particularly significant, in all this complex imagery and practice concerning the dead, is that the Egyptians continued, century after century, to embalm their dead and to furnish their tombs as though the dead really did live in them.

Magicians of the Nile

Magic played an important part in ancient Egyptian life and thought. It was mainly based upon the principle of symbolic imitation—that like will beget like. For instance a model of a wax crocodile, directed by an appropriate spell, might be transformed into a real crocodile to kill a rival; there is actual evidence of such a practice. Most things could be endowed with magical potency, from the pharaoh's crown to amulets such as the *udjat* eye (giving power to see everything, and promoting prosperity and fertility) and the ankh, a symbol of life and vitality, which was used by both the living and the dead. A statue of a god had to be animated by a magical ceremony similar to that of the 'Opening of the Mouth' which was performed on an embalmed corpse. The whole mortuary ritual was based on the magical assimilation of the dead to Osiris, so

that they would experience a similar resurrection from death. An indication of the Egyptians' belief in magic is provided by the custom of mutilating hieroglyphic signs representing dangerous animals or insects, or showing them as pierced with knives when they occurred in tomb inscriptions; it was a precaution against these potentially dangerous signs coming to life.

The service of the Egyptian gods was performed in temples by a professional priesthood, assisted by specially appointed laymen. This service had two main forms: a daily toilet and offering ceremony, and periodic festivals. The daily service was performed in the inner sanctuary of a temple by priests only, on the image of the god which was kept in a special shrine. The image was anointed and symbolically clothed and offerings of food and incense were made to it. The festivals commemorated various events in the annual calendar: New Year's Day, sowing and harvest, and the inundation of the Nile.

Some festivals were devoted to certain deities or their temples. A notable example was the annual visit of Hathor of Dendera (or rather her cult statue) to the sanctuary of her spouse, Horus at Edfu. The journey was made by boat, with halts at various towns on the banks of the Nile. The occasion was one of prolonged rejoicing and merrymaking among

Lady Meresimen, Singer of God Amon, giving presents to Osiris and the four sons of Horus

the people. It was only at festivals that ordinary folk saw the image of the god, which was carried out of the temple, mounted on a special boat, on the shoulders of priests; for inner courts of temples were forbidden to the public.

Egyptian temples were of three main types; some of them, like those of Amun at Thebes, were on a colossal scale. Sun temples, such as that of Atum-Re at Heliopolis and of the Aten at Akhetaten, were square in shape, enclosed by a wall and open to the sky. At Heliopolis the chief object of veneration was the ben-ben stone, a truncated obelisk which marked the place where Atum-Re had originally emerged from the primeval waters of Nun and commenced the work of creation. Other temples were of rectangular plan, comprising a series of courts. The inner sanctuary was reached through a pillared hall, and was in complete darkness. The third type of temple was the funerary temple, built for the proper performance of those rites, especially the food offerings, which were regarded as essential to the well-being of the dead man whose tomb they served. The great pharaohs of the New Kingdom erected vast funerary temples on the western bank of the Nile, opposite Thebes. These differed little in size and layout from the temples of the gods.

Since most of the extant evidence on Egyptian religion relates to the king and the upper classes of society, little is known of the religion of ordinary folk. Lesser deities, such as Bes, doubtless seemed to them more approachable than the great state deities, but Osiris had an intimate personal appeal to all classes. There is some evidence that Amun could be addressed as 'one who cometh at the voice of the poor'; however, it is significant that on the stele of Nebre, where these words occur, the Amun 'who hears the prayers' is depicted seated outside the portals of his temple, as a kind of vizier to the greater Amun who dwelt within the sanctuary.

The Dawn of Conscience

The 'dawn of conscience' has been located, with reason, in ancient Egypt. Already in the Old Kingdom the concept of maat, which denoted the qualities of truth and justice, was associated with the 'Great God' as the basic principle of an ordered universe. From this period, too, emerge the beginnings of the belief so important to the evolution of ethics and morality, that the dead would be judged on their conduct in this life.

The immense duration of Egyptian religion, and the impressive continuity of its traditional pattern of faith and practice, suggest that the Egyptians unthinkingly accepted an ancient priestly tradition, generation after generation. But there is evidence that this was not wholly so, and that there were those who could look critically at their ancestral faith, especially the funerary cult. There exist, inscribed on the walls of certain New Kingdom tombs, versions of what is known as the Song of the Harpist, which takes its name from the figure of a corpulent harpist who is depicted singing it. It was probably sung at memorial feasts held by relatives at the tombs of the deceased. In it the futility of the mortuary faith is frankly expressed: 'None cometh from thence that he may tell us how they (the dead) fare, that he may tell us what they need, that he may set our heart at rest, until we also go to the place whither they have gone'. The obvious conclusion is drawn from this scepticism: 'Be glad, that thou mayest cause thine heart to forget that men will (one day) beatify thee. Follow thy desire, so long as thou livest'.

A Mummy at the Feast

The expression of such sentiments is significant, for it shows that there did

exist at least a minority who could doubt the truth of their traditional religion and the effectiveness of its ritual technique for the achievement of a blessed immortality. Yet this faith was able to continue its serene tradition without the suppression of such heretical scepticism. That it did so attests the strength of two things: the spiritual satisfaction which the average Egyptian got from his faith in Osiris, and the practical nature of his philosophy of life. The Greek historian Herodotus, who visited Egypt in the

5th century BC, records an Egyptian custom at banquets of showing the guests a model of a mummy with the admonition: 'Gaze here, and drink and be merry; for when you die, such will you be'. This curious custom was prompted by no spirit of cynicism or levity; it reflected the practical evaluation of life that characterized the Egyptians. They feared death, but they believed that they had the means of reversing its threat of personal extinction and they accordingly made provision to secure this immunity. But such pre-

occupation with death and the afterlife did not induce pessimism or prompt a this-world-denying attitude. The Egyptians sought to extract the most joy possible from life, while preparing for death and mindful of the judgment that faced them thereafter.

The legacy of Egypt's ancient religion cannot be accurately assessed. The famous American Egyptologist J. H. Breasted believed that Akhenaten's monotheism influenced Moses and found its fruition in the Hebrew concept of one single God, who is the creator and sustainer of the universe. The connection cannot be proved and the assumption that it did exist has not been generally accepted by scholars. More certain is the influence of Egyptian wisdom literature on the Jewish Book of Proverbs. The elements of Egyptian religion which passed into Coptic Christianity were chiefly related to the world after death. Such elements included the idea of a judgment immediately after death and of the assessment as being made by weighing the soul on scales. And the Egyptian elements have yet to be fully evaluated in the Hermetic literature, where the god Thoth figures prominently under the name of Hermes.

S. G. F. BRANDON

FURTHER READING: J. H. Breasted. Development of Religion and Thought in Ancient Egypt. (Peter Smith, 1959); R. Brier. Ancient Egyptian Magic. (Morrow, 1981); J. Cerny. Ancient Egyptian Religion. (Westport, CT: Greenwood, 1979); M. Lurker. Gods and Symbols of Ancient Egypt.

A 'house altar' depicting Akhenaten, Nefertiti, and three of their daughters. New Kingdom, Amarna period

(*Thames & Hudson, 1984*); D. A. MacKenzie. Egyptian Myth and Legend. (*Longwood Press, 1976*).

El

The supreme deity of the Canaanites and Phoenicians, whose wife Asherah, called Astarte by the Greeks, was the great mother goddess: his name means literally 'the god' and his other titles, 'Father of Men', 'Creator of Created Things', and 'the Bull' indicate his benevolence to man and his strength and virility. He is depicted on a stele as a bearded man wearing a crown adorned with a pair of bull's horns.

Enuma Elish

Babylonian creation myth, recorded on seven clay tablets in Babylonian cuneiform, probably composed in or around the time of Hammurabi, from the 18th to 16th centuries BC. The tablets were unearthed and translated by British archaeologists in the nineteenth century and have since provided modern scholars with a deeper understanding of Babylonian religion and society. The story of the Enuma Elish, the title of which refers to the opening words that mean 'when on high', is of Marduk's battle against Tiamat, goddess of chaos, Marduk's creation of heaven, earth, and time, and then his establishment as the king of all gods. The poem is significant because it symbolizes the Babylonian gods assuming dominance over older Mesopotamian gods such as Ea and Enlil. Scholars have drawn illuminating parallels between the Enuma Elish and the myths told in the Hebrew Old Testament in the book of Genesis.

FURTHER READING: Dalley, Stephanie. Myths from Mesopotamia: Creation, the Flood, Gilgamesh, and Others. (*Oxford: Oxford UP, 2008*); Heidel, Alexander. The Babylonian Genesis: The Story of Creation. (*Chicago: University of Chicago, 1963*); L. W. King. Enuma Elish: The Seven Tablets of the History of Creation. (*Minneapolis, MN: Filiquarian Pub., 2007*); Sandars, N. K. The Epic of Gilgamesh. (*Harmondsworth: Penguin, 1977*).

Gathas

The name given to certain sections of the Zend-Avesta, the sacred writings of the Zoroastrian religion; generally believed to have been composed by the prophet Zoroaster himself, they contain hymns and poems mainly addressed to the supreme god Ahura Mazdah. These holy writings are still used by the Parsees, the surviving followers of Zoroastrianism.

Gilgamesh

The great hero of Sumerian and Babylonian mythology was Gilgamesh. His deeds are recorded in an epic poem no less adventurous than the *Odyssey*, put into its final written form not more than about a century after the Greek poem. The received text of the Gilgamesh epic was written down on a series of twelve clay tablets inscribed in the cuneiform script used by the Sumerians, the Babylonians, and the peoples of Assyria. The fullest version that has come down to us was originally held in the great palace library of the king of Assyria, Ashurbanipal, who made a vast collection of contemporary and ancient texts in the course of three decades between about 660–630 BC.

This famous epic became a set book in the scribal schools and has been reconstituted from fragments found not only on many Mesopotamian sites, but

This is perhaps the most famous of all cuneiform tablets. It is the eleventh tablet of the Gilgamesh Epic, and describes how the gods sent a flood to destroy the world.

also at places as far apart as Megiddo in Palestine and Ugarit in Syria. Evidence of the poem has been found at Sultantepe and Boghaz Koi, the great Hittite capital in Asia Minor. The Assyrian version ultimately derives from a much older Babylonian text which must have been composed before 1800 BC, for there is no mention of Marduk the god of Babylon, whose cult became the state religion in the reign of Hammurabi. But the earliest versions of all stem from Sumerian texts of the late 3rd millennium BC, at which time this epic was perhaps not a continuous story, but consisted of a disconnected series of episodes in which Gilgamesh took a prominent place.

The epic itself is enthralling for the insight which it gives into the psychology of the Babylonians and their Sumerian forebears. We also become aware of the historical background and of a heroic age which, though associated with stories about the gods, may be authenticated by historical, or semihistorical, literature such as the Sumerian king lists, and by archeology. The historical position of Gilgamesh is firmly established by an episode in the Sumerian version of the story, which tells of a battle between Gilgamesh and Agga, King of Kish, a name already known from the Sumerian king lists. Indeed the name of Agga's father has been identified on an alabaster bowl from the Diyala valley, dated about 2700 BC. Thus in the epic we can visualize a real king, Gilgamesh, as well as a world famous historical event, the Sumerian Deluge, the memory of which has been preserved in the book of Genesis.

From this poem we learn that Gilgamesh was a renowned and powerful king who had built the great walls of Erech, one of the most extensive cities of Sumer and Babylonia. Gilgamesh, however, was an arrogant, oppressive,

and philandering ruler who had exasperated his subjects. In consequence an appeal was made to the gods for a champion who would contend for their rights against the omniscient and headstrong oppressor within the city.

The Hairy Hunter

The champion elected to liberate Erech was a hairy hunter named Enkidu, a Sumerian wild man who lived with the animals and protected them. He was seduced by a courtesan, who tempted him with the delights of the city, and Enkidu who had never before partaken of bread developed a taste for strong drink also. On entering Erech he

In a mountain of cedars, perhaps the Amanus or the Lebanon, they sought out the demon Humbaba and slew him.

engaged in a wrestling match with Gilgamesh, but after honour was satisfied on both sides the two heroes became firm friends and decided to embark on an adventurous journey together.

In a mountain of cedars, perhaps the Amanus or the Lebanon, they sought out the demon Humbaba and slew him. In this episode we may see a relic of early dynastic Sumerian conquests in Syria recently attested by excavations at Mardikh and Chuera. The two friends returned in triumph to Erech, and the goddess Ishtar became enamoured of Gilgamesh. Unwisely he spurned her advances and accused her of having seduced men and beasts. The goddess, a woman scorned and enraged, induced the high god Anu to send down from heaven an avenging bull to trample on the city of Erech, but Enkidu killed it, thereby sealing his own doom and initiating a long drawn tragedy. After his death,

which was foretold in a dream, there follows a lament for Enkidu, for whom an expensive funeral is arranged.

Gilgamesh, bereft of his friend, began to fear for his own life, and resolved to embark on a journey in search of the secret of immortality, although as we are reminded in the ninth tablet of the epic, 'two thirds of him is god, one third is man'. Between twin mountain peaks he penetrated the gate of sunrise which was guarded by the scorpion-man and his wife, and after a long journey through an immense and impenetrable darkness arrived in a garden where the trees bore carnelian and lapis lazuli. He was on his way to find Utnapishtim, the Sumerian Noah who, as he hoped, would reveal the secret of his immortality to him. The sun god warned Gilgamesh that he was on a vain quest and advised him to seek what pleasure he could in life:

Day and night be thou merry; Make every day a day of rejoicing.

This part of the narration in Tablet X concludes with a passage worthy of the book of Proverbs in which Gilgamesh reflects on the impermanence of life and its mutability.

The ensuing Tablet XI is the famous Deluge tablet, which breaks the thread of the narrative. This is thought by many authorities to reflect an identifiable event or events which, according to another Sumerian tablet, may be related to the reign of king Ziusudra who is thought to have lived not more than a century or two after 3000 BC.

Robbed by a Serpent

The conclusion of the eleventh tablet is that with the advice of a ferryman named Urshanabi, Gilgamesh, his feet

This relief decorated the lower course of the exterior wall of the temple palace of King Kapara. Two heroes pin down a bearded foe, while grabbing at his pronged headdress. The context may be related to the Gilgamesh epic, and display Gilgamesh and Enkidu in their fight with Humbaba.

weighted by stones, dived deep into the sea and discovered a plantlike a thorn, the wondrous plant whose name was perpetual youth. His triumph was short lived, for on his way home, whilst refreshing himself in a pool, a serpent robbed him of his trophy and stole the secret of eternal life.

The last tablet of the series, Tablet XII, is an appendix to the whole, for in it Enkidu lives once more. It contains a Semitic version of a Sumerian story. Here we have a remarkable episode concerning a willow tree and its magical properties coveted by Inanna, queen of heaven. Enkidu, who has meddled dangerously on her behalf, goes to his death, and the story ends with an interview between Gilgamesh and Enkidu's ghost, who gives a woeful account of the underworld. Here we have an unrelieved picture of gloom which, with few exceptions, is typical of Sumerian and Babylonian thought.

M. E. L. MALLOWAN

FURTHER READING: The Epic of Gilgamesh, *trans. N. K. Sanders (Penguin, 1960); S. N. Kramer.* Sumerian Mythology. *(American Philosophical Society, Philadelphia, 1944); A. Heidel.* Gilgamesh Epic and Old Testament Parallels, *2nd ed. (Chicago: University of Chicago Press, 1963); J. Tigay,* The Evolution of the Gilgamesh Epic. *(Philadelphia: Univ. of Pennsylvania Press, 2003).*

Hadad

Semitic storm, thunder and lightning god, also known as Rimmon in the Old Testament, Teshub by the Hittites, Adad by the Akkadians, Zeus in Greece, and Jupiter in Rome. Depicted with bull horns and thunderbolt, Hadad's rain-giving powers also made him important for growth and fertility. It makes a dubious appearance in the Old Testament when Elijah calls on Yahweh to rain down fire when the prophets of Ba'al (generic deity term meaning 'lord', but in this case referring to Hadad) are unable to elicit a response (1 Kings, 18).

FURTHER READING: Black, Jeremy A., Anthony Green, and Tessa Rickards. Gods, Demons, and Symbols of Ancient Mesopotamia: An Illustrated Dictionary. *(Austin: University of Texas,* 1992); Suggs, M. Jack., Katharine Doob Sakenfeld, and James R. Mueller. *The Oxford Study Bible: Revised English Bible with the Apocrypha. (New York: Oxford UP, 1992).*

Harranian Religion

The city of Harran in northwest Mesopotamia became in ancient times the centre of a mysterious religion that included the worship of the planets. Information about this religion is sparse and difficult to interpret, especially since much of it comes from

Cylinder describing repairs on the temple of the moon-god Sin at Ur by King Nabonidus, with a prayer for his son Belshazzar. Terracotta, 555–539 BC

hostile sources.

As far back as the 2nd millenium BC, Harran was an important centre of the cult of Sin, the moon god. The original centre of the cult was the Sumerian city of Ur, known in the Bible as Ur of the Chaldeans. The Bible preserves an interesting connection between these two cult centres of moon worship, for according to the book of Genesis (11.31) Abraham, a native of Ur, journeyed with his father Terah and wife, Sarah, from Ur to settle in Harran.

In Mesopotamian mythology, Sin was an important deity connected with the regulation of time through the lunar month. He was regarded as the father of Shamash, the sun god, and of Ishtar, the goddess of fertility, who was identified with the planet Venus. The great temple of Sin at Harran was patronized by various Assyrian kings, but its greatest patron was Nabonidus (555–539 BC), the last king of Babylon. He claimed that he had been directed in a dream to rebuild the temple of Sin, where his mother was priestess. A stele (monumental stone) commemo-

rating this rebuilding in 552 BC shows Nabonidus worshipping the emblems of the moon, the sun, and the planet Venus. The temple of Sin attracted many visitors during the Roman period, including the emperors Caracalla and Julian.

Although the great temple of the moon god at Harran has vanished without trace, recent excavation at Sumatar Harabesi, in the Tektek mountains about 18 miles from Harran, has provided some valuable evidence about Harranian religion. A group of seven ruined stone buildings around a central mound were found to be of various shapes—round, square, and round on a square base. Inscriptions in Syriac discovered there mention Sin and a deity named Marilaha. The identity of the latter is a mystery. 'Mara' (lord) was a title of Baal-Shamin, 'master of the heavens'. There is evidence that Sin was sometimes called 'Sin Marilaha', thus equating him with the supreme deity. The cult signs of Marilaha were a sacred pillar and stool; Sin's emblem was a pillar, crowned by the upturned crescent of the moon and adorned with

two tassels.

In neighbouring Edessa curious evidence of the cult of Atargatis, with whom Ishtar was identified, still survives in the form of teeming pools of fish which are tabu and never eaten: fish were associated with the ancient cult of the goddess.

This archeological evidence, fragmentary and enigmatic as it unfortunately is, is supplemented by equally puzzling accounts by early Moslem writers. They identified the Harranian pagans with the Sabians, mentioned in the Koran as one of the religious communities permitted to exist. According to these writers, the Sabians of Harran recognized a supreme deity who was the primal cause of the universe. This deity had no contact with mankind but had placed the universe under the rule of the planets. Hence the Sabians worshipped the planets, or rather the demonic beings that governed them.

Rites of Human Sacrifice

Each planet was believed to have a special influence over some particular type of person. The Sabians were also reputed to celebrate 'mystery' rites, addressed principally to Shamal, lord of the jinn. In these secret rites they were suspected of using human sacrifice. There was a curious Harranian taboo on the eating of beans, because they were elliptical in shape whereas the celestial sphere is globular.

The Harranians and their planetary religion disappeared during the Mongol invasions in the twelfth or thirteenth century. Some scholars believe that the Sabians still survive in the Mandaeans, a religious community on the lower reaches of the Tigris and Euphrates. On the available evidence this identification seems unlikely.

FURTHER READING: J. B. Segal. 'The Sabian Mysteries: the planet cult of ancient Harran' in Vanished Civilizations, ed. E. Bacon. (Thames & Hudson, 1963).

Hittites

German excavations since 1907 within the walls of an ancient city on a hillside near the Turkish village of Boghaz Koi in Asia Minor (Anatolia) have revealed the existence of a kingdom which had that city as its capital

Hittite bas relief in Ankara's Museum of Anatolian Civilization

and which lasted from about 1700 to about 1200 BC. It was called 'the Land of Hatti', its capital was Hattusas, and its people are known as the Hittites, by reason of the undoubted, though remote, connection of the name Hatti with the Hittites, or sons of Heth, mentioned in the Bible. During those five centuries the rulers of Hattusas extended their dominion over peoples speaking languages different from their own. One of these was the Hurrians, whose centre was in upper Mesopotamia and whose name is also reflected in the Bible in the form 'Horites'. Our present knowledge of Hittite and Hurrian religion and mythology is due entirely to the German excavations at Boghaz Koi, which have brought to light thousands of broken clay tablets inscribed in the cuneiform script, once the royal archives of the Hittite kings. The archives of the Hurrians themselves have not been found.

Land of 600 Gods

The Hittite texts present us with a bewildering number of divine names. This is mainly because not only each linguistic area within the Hittite empire, but each individual cult centre, had its own names for its deities, though they might have similar attributes to those in other places. For example, the weather god was Tarhun in Luwian (and probably in Hittite), Taru in Hattic, Teshub in Hurrian; the sun god was Istanu in Hittite, Estan in Hattic, Tiwat in Luwian, Tiyat in Palaic, and Shimegi in Hurrian. Some 600 names have actually been counted. The basic type to which a deity belonged is often shown by the word sign with which his name is written, meaning sun god, weather god, moon god, and so on. Otherwise it may be deduced from a description of his cult stature or emblem, from his association with

other gods of the same type, or from allusions to his sphere of activity in prayers, myths or other texts. But in many cases the texts give no information about the deity's other attributes, so that he or she remains a mere name to us.

The Hittites themselves occasionally recognized an identity, as when we read in a prayer: 'Sun goddess of Arinna, my lady, queen of all countries! In the Land of Hatti thou givest thyself the name "sun goddess of Arinna". but in the country which thou makest a land of cedars (Syria) thou givest thyself the name Hebat'. But when listing divine witnesses to a treaty with a vassal king they would include not only the sun goddess of Arinna and of Hebat as distinct deities, but also the gods and goddesses of the individual cult centres, even though they might not have distinct names.

The State Cult

The great goddess of Arinna (which has not been located) was exalted as patroness of the state. Her name in Hattic was Wurusemu, but the Hittites appear to have addressed her under the epithet Arinnitti. She is always called a sun goddess, but there are indications that in origin she may have been a deity of the underworld, her solar attributes being secondary. The king and queen were her high priest and priestess, and in this state cult her husband was the weather god of Hatti, a great figure who bestowed kingship, brought victory in war and might represent the nation in its dealings with foreign powers: thus a treaty with Egypt is said to be for the purpose of 'making eternal the relations which the sun god of Egypt and the weather god of Hatti have established for the land of Egypt and the land of Hatti'.

This national weather god is probably the original sky god of the Indo-Europeans, akin to Zeus and Jupiter, brought in by the immigrants

The Hittite mythological texts are, on the whole, poorly preserved, and consequently any account of Hittite mythology must necessarily be incomplete. It seems, however, that in Anatolia itself mythology remained on a rather primitive level. The most elaborate myths preserved in the Hittite archives are either of Hurrian origin or are simply Babylonian myths transmitted to the Hittites by the Hurrians. In the latter class (though it is legend rather than myth) is the Babylonian Epic of Gilgamesh, of which there is even a fragment in the Hurrian language. Even where the gods or heroes in these myths are ostensibly Hurrian, they can often be recognized as ancient Babylonian or Sumerian deities under a garbled 'Humanized' name. These tales appear to be recorded simply as works of literature. They are of considerable interest on account of features in them which reappear in Greek mythology.

The myth 'Kingship in Heaven' tells how the kingship was held by a series of gods for periods of nine years. Alalu is defeated by Anu and sent down to the underworld; Anu in turn is mutilated and defeated by Kumarbi, who is apparently overthrown by the weather god Teshub. Anu is the Babylonian sky god; the conception of former generations of defeated gods who were banished to the underworld also derives from Babylonia. But Teshub and Kumarbi are Hurrian gods. The myth closely resembles the Theogony of Hesiod, where the sequence Uranus-Cronus-Zeus corresponds to Anu-Kumarbi-Teshub.

A Monster of Stone

The longest mythological poem is titled 'Song of Ullikummi'. It has a similar theme and tells of a plot by Kumarbi to replace Teshub as king

who introduced the Indo-European Hittite language into Anatolia in the 3rd millennium BC, and married to the indigenous mother goddess. The weather god of another city, Nerik, was made their son, and they had daughters named Mezzulla and Hulla and a granddaughter, Zintuhi. Among the deities of the state cult must also be numbered the spirits of past kings and queens, who received regular offerings. 'Became a god' is the normal euphemism for 'died' used by the Hittites when referring to kings.

During the later years of the Hittite kingdom the state cult came under strong Hurrian influence. It was at this time that the sun goddess of Arinna and the weather god of Nerik were identified with the Hurrian Hebat and her son Sharruma. Finally, at a holy place near the capital, now named Yazilikaya, a rocky outcrop forming a natural open chamber was adorned with a series of figures in relief representing a national pantheon. The central group is recognizable as the family of the sun goddess, but the names in Hittite 'hieroglyphs' attached to each deity, including the central group, are those of the Hurrian pantheon. It therefore appears that by the end of the Hittite period, in the late 13th century BC, the Hittites had achieved a measure of unity of worship.

of the gods by a stone monster named Ullikummi, whom he begets for the purpose.

> Kumarbi takes wisdom into
>   his mind
> and an evil spirit as enemy
>   he raises . . .
> At Cool Pond a great Rock is lying;
> her length is three leagues,
> but her width which she has below is
>   one and a half leagues.
> His mind sprang forward,
> he slept with the Rock
> and his manhood flowed into her.

After a considerable gap the Rock bore a child, Ullikummi, who was made of stone. The child was taken to earth and placed on the shoulder of Upelluri, a giant like the Greek Atlas, who supported heaven and earth. Here he grew up in the sea, which only came up to his waist. The sun god saw him and went to report the matter to Teshub, who with his brother Tashmishu gave battle. At first they were unsuccessful and the Stone even came to overshadow Teshub's town Kummiya. Tashmishu reported to Teshub's wife, Hebat, that her husband would have to give up his throne, a message which almost caused her to fall off the roof where

she was standing. But Tashmishu and Teshub decided to consult the wise god Ea, who in his turn went first to Enlil and then to the giant Upelluri. Upelluri's reply was as follows:

> When heaven and earth were built
>   on me
> I knew nothing (of it).
> And when they came and cut apart
>   heaven and earth with a 'cutter'
> That too I knew not
> Now something is hurting my right
>   shoulder but I know not who he
>   is, that god.

When Ea heard these words, he had only to turn Upelluri's right shoulder and there was the Stone standing on it. But Upelluri's words had given him an idea. He ordered the 'former gods' in the underworld to produce the ancient tool with which heaven and earth had once been cut apart. With this he severed the Stone from Upelluri and so destroyed its power. Teshub went out to battle again, and though the end of the story is lost, we may be sure he emerged victorious in the end.

This tale too has its parallel in the Greek story of Typhon. The reference to the building of heaven and earth in one piece on the shoulder of a giant

and their separation by cutting is the only surviving hint in the Hittite records of a creation myth.

The myths associated with Anatolian—mainly Hattic—deities are much simpler and more primitive. The 'Slaying of the Dragon' is said to have been recited at a great annual festival called purulli and is connected with the Hattian city Nerik. The weather god and the dragon god fought together and the weather god was defeated.

According to one version of this particular myth, he then appealed to the other gods for help and the goddess Inaras, moved by his plight, planned a ruse. She invited the dragon to a feast with barrels of every kind of drink. The dragon came with his children and they became so completely drunk that they could not go back to their hole. So the goddess' human assistant was able to tie them up and the weather god came and at last killed the dragon.

According to another version of this myth, when the dragon and the weather god fought, the dragon not only defeated the weather god but incapacitated him by gaining possession of his heart and eyes. The weather god then begot a son by the daughter of a poor man. When this son grew up, he took as bride the daughter of the dragon and his father told him to ask for the stolen organs on entering his bride's home. The demand was instantly met and the weather god, fully restored, went out to battle again. He succeeded in defeating the dragon but his son took the part of the dragon and was killed with him.

Myth of the Missing God

Several myths about Anatolian deities belong to a type which we may call for convenience 'the Myth of the Missing God'. They tell the story of a god who disappears and thereby causes a blight on earth, the search for the missing god, his eventual return, and the restoration of health and vigour to the world. In one such myth the weather god withdraws in anger and the search is conducted by the sun god (whose messenger is an eagle), the father of the weather god, his grandfather, and his grandmother Hannahanna. In another it is Tehpmu, son of the weather god, who is angry, and the gods who search are the sun god, the weather god, and Hannahanna, the grandfather being omitted. In both these versions the missing god is found by a bee sent out by Hannahanna. In another similar story the sun god and Telipunu are missing, not from anger, but because they have been seized by Torpor, a demon who has paralyzed all Nature.

All these myths are accompanied by a magical ritual, the purpose of which is to attract the god back into his temple and to remove some misfortune which his absence is thought to have caused. They are 'ritual myths', recited to enhance the effect of the ritual. In no case is the ritual connected with the actual seasons. Such magical rituals are, in fact, rather common in the Hittite archives.

Other fragments of mythology are found embedded in rituals. One text tells how the moon fell down from heaven and how the weather god sent storms and wind after him to frighten him. Another describes how an eagle found two goddesses of the underworld in a forest holding spindles and spinning long years for the king—forerunners of the Green Moirai, the Roman Parcae, and the Germanic Norn (Fates). The underworld contained, besides the dead, an older generation of defeated gods and some others, such as the Fates just mentioned. Its ruler was a figure called Lelwanis, whose gender is uncertain and who seems to be identical with the 'sun god of the earth' and the sun goddess Arinna in some passages.

The Evil Thing

Magic was a familiar part of ordinary life in Hittite society. Illness or misfortune were assumed to be caused either by a god or by hostile sorcery and specialists in sacred matters—known as 'bird operators'—and priestesses called 'old women' were brought in to try to put things right. Anything from sexual problems to family quarrels, from failure of crops to the infestation of a house by ghosts, could be ascribed to evil magic, which was classified legally as a crime on the level of violent assault.

A typical text describes the procedure used by an 'old woman', who was in effect the local white witch, to cure impotence in men or barrenness in women. The patient dressed in black clothes and stopped his or her ears with black wool. After performing various preliminary rites, the old woman would take the patient's black shirt and tear it from top to bottom, take off the patient's black leggings and remove the black wool from the patient's ears,

Hittite basalt relief depicting musicians, 8th century BC. Istanbul, Turkey

while saying aloud that, in doing this, she was removing the 'darkness' caused by the 'uncleanness' of the hostile magic, which was the root of the problem. Then the black clothes and wool, and anything else which has been in contact with the patient, were taken away and thrown into a river, so as to get rid of the sorcery for good.

The power of incantation was used similarly to banish evil spirits from a house. A spell for ridding a royal palace of malevolent spirits involves making a little image of a dog out of tallow and then formally telling it that it is a royal guard dog. 'Just as by day you do not allow other men into the courtyard', it is instructed, 'so do not let in the Evil Thing during the night'. Image magic was also used to harm an enemy. A doll was made out of wax or mutton-fat to resemble the enemy and was thrown on the fire to make him shrivel and perish likewise.

'Come Back Into Thy Temple'

The Hittites regarded their relationship with the gods as one of servant and master. 'If a servant has anything on his mind', prays King Mursilis, 'he appeals to his master and his master hears him and takes pity on him and puts right what is troubling him. And if a servant has committed an offence and confesses his guilt before his master, his master may do with him what he pleases; but because he has confessed his guilt before his master, his master's spirit is appeased, and his master will not call that servant to account'. But a well-intentioned master might still also be capricious at times. 'Now if, honoured Telipinu, thou art up in heaven among the gods, or if thou art gone to the sea or to roam in the mountains, or to battle against an enemy country, come back into thy temple'.

A god must be fed, tended, appeased, and flattered. His actions, even when attending to his duties, might not always be wise and might entail unforeseen consequences. It would then be the duty of his faithful servant to point this out to him, so that he might correct his mistake. But if misfortune was a punishment for sin, it would not be lifted until the sin had been confessed and expiated. Possible cases of divine anger would be brought to light by questioning the priests or by searching the records. It was then necessary to find out by divination which particular offence was the cause of the present misfortune. 'Now, O gods, whatever sin you see, let the old wives, the seers or the augurs determine it, or let men see it in a dream'. The 'old wives' practiced a form of divination by throwing dice; the seers were the experts in the ancient art of haruspicy (telling the future by studying the entrails of sacrificed creatures); the augurs took the omens from the movement of birds. The omens, being either favourable or unfavourable, would give an answer 'yes' or 'no'; in this way, by a lengthy process of elimination, it was possible to discover the offence which required expiation. The records of these questions and answers (the latter in barely intelligible language) are among the longest tablets in the archive.

O. R. GURNEY

FURTHER READING: C.W. Ceram. The Secret of the Hittites. (Schocken, 1973); O. R. Gurney. The Hittites. (Penguin, revised edn 1980); J. Hicks. The Empire Builders. (Time-Life, 1974); J. G. Macqueen. The Hittites. (Thames & Hudson, revised edition 1986).

Horus

As the royal and national god of ancient Egypt, Horus enjoyed a position of such importance that no great national rite or festival was celebrated without giving him a prominent place. The great temple at Edfu belonged to him. In form he was a falcon—the peregrine falcon, fiercest of all the birds of prey in the Egyptian sky. His name means 'he who is on high' or 'the distant one' and refers to his domain as a sky god.

Horus was identified with the living pharaoh and from the first dynasty onward the pharaoh called himself Horus (with other names). In the Cairo Museum there is a beautiful statue of King Chephren of the fifth dynasty which shows Horus stretching out his wings protectively behind the king's head, recalling the Old Testament phrase 'in the shadow of Thy wings'.

Horus was the leading god of the confederation of clans or tribes which secured sovereignty over the whole of Egypt when the kingdom was established. The Horus confederation was apparently opposed, in the final predynastic struggle for Egypt, by a league under the aegis of the god Seth, a canine deity whose home was in Upper Egypt. The political strife which resulted in the unity of Egypt was reflected in the mythological conflict of Horus and Seth, although other explanations have been offered. According to the myth, Horus and Seth were feuding brothers, who inflicted frightful wounds on each other. Seth tore out an eye of Horus and devoured it, while Horus castrated Seth. A trial ensued before a divine tribunal, in which Horus was vindicated and awarded the legitimate sovereignty of Egypt.

Horus and Seth Reconciled

There are suggestions that the god Thoth had tried to intervene in the quarrel in a reconciling role although he sometimes appears as a helper of Horus, especially as the god who restored to him his lost eye, and more rarely as one who sympathized with Seth. A tradition of reconciliation is reflected in the symbolism of Egypt's dynastic unity, for while Horus is the victorious deity who is incorporated

in the personality of the pharaoh, the two gods are shown cooperating for the king's benefit in the ceremony of the 'Baptism of Pharaoh'. The king's jubilee festival (called the Sed) concluded with a procession to the chapels of Horus and Seth, and in the purification of 'baptism' of the king the two gods are shown pouring water over the pharaoh's head.

Similarly, in the ceremony of 'Uniting the Two Lands', the symbolic plants of Upper and Lower Egypt, the reed and the papyrus, were joined by the two deities; Horus being associated here with Lower Egypt. Again, the stolen eye of Horus which was healed and restored was symbolic of the crown. In a royal context, therefore, the ceremony of presenting the eye suggested that the sovereign power of the king had been confirmed. Early on, the myth of Horus was merged with that of Osiris; the reason for the merger was the double identification of the king. When he died he became Osiris, but as a living pharaoh he had been Horus. From this divine doubling followed a transfer of the conflict to Osiris. If Seth had been the enemy of Horus, he was now the enemy of Osiris, and the myth maintained that Seth had murdered Osiris. In the early Horus myth the mother of Horus was Hathor, and his father was Geb. Now Isis becomes his mother, Osiris his father, Seth his nephew, and a new Horus emerges—Horus the child.

Horus the Child

Horus the child (called Harpocrates by the Greeks) gradually assumed an important place in mythology. Many stories were told about his childhood, when he was nursed by Isis or by a foster mother in the papyrus swamps of the Delta and defended by his mother's magic against the wicked onslaughts of Seth. It will be recalled that Moses too was a babe hidden in the bulrushes, and the legend of Horus may well have influenced the Biblical episode. Among the misfortunes inflicted on Horus the child was the homosexual attack made on him by Seth; the first version of this appears in a Middle Kingdom papyrus, and it tells of the unavailing efforts of Isis to prevent the assault. Seth also attacks Horus in various unpleasant insect and animal forms; Horus may be bitten and injured, but he is healed by the magic of Isis his mother. A curious feature of the childhood legends is that they also tell of a disagreement between Horus and Isis. One version described Horus and Seth fighting in the form of hippopotami in a river. Isis expresses feelings in favour of Seth, whereupon Horus cuts off his mother's head; one source adds that Thoth restored it as a cowhead. According to the Book of the Dead, the hands of Horus were cut off and thrown into the water through a magical curse uttered by his mother. In a few sources the episode takes a sexual form and Horus violates his mother. Mother-incest has been attributed to the Egyptian idea of kingship, with Isis being regarded as mother and wife of the Horus-Pharaoh.

Horus as the ancient sky god maintained his later status only by a process of assimilation to the cult of another heavenly god, the sun god Re. Egyptian religion teems with theological 'take-over-bids' of this kind. The composite name thus evolved was Re-Horakhty (Re-Horus-of-the-horizon), and the amalgam was expressed in art by a falcon with the sun-disc on his head.

J. GWYN GRIFFITHS

Hurrians

A group of people that played a central role in Mesopotamian culture and politics during the 2nd millennium BC.

Hurrians are mentioned in documents from the end of the 3rd millennium BC, and are an established presence in an area north and east of the Tigris River. They then began a migration westward. After 1700 BC, with invaders from the east driving them, the Hurrians engaged in a larger migration, subsequently taking over in Assyria and weilding influence in the entire Fertile Crescent. In the 15th century BC the Hurrians formed a unified kingdom named Mittani which had a close relationship with the Egyptian pharaohs, trading children as wives, and was antagonistic toward the Hittites to the west. While the Hurrian kingdoms were influential for almost 1,000 years, they had disappeared by the 13th century BC and the Hurrians were assimilated into neighbouring cultures.

Kingdom of Mittani

Although Hurrian people did not tend to form large cities like the Sumerians or the Egyptians, in the 15th century BC Hurrians united under the kingdom of Mittani, whose early kings are unknown. The kingdom gained a significant amount of influence over several centuries of expansion both west and east, their realm stretching from the Mediterranean to the western edges

of modern-day Iran. The kingdom was a sophisticated feudal hierarchy with a military and landed noble class.

Hurrian Language

The early Hurrians spoke a Hurro-Urartion language, although during the reign of the Mittani kingdom the Hurrian speaking people were subjugated by an Indo-European speaking ruling class. Hurrian language is unrelated to the Semitic or Indo-European languages that dominated Mesopotamia, and it had disappeared entirely by the end of the 2nd millenium BC, but not before exerting influence on the Hittites linguistically as well as culturally.

Hurrian Religion

Hurrian mythology and religion had a strong influence on Mesopotamian beliefs, including Assyrian and Hittite theology, and even may have helped shape later Greek mythology. Their pantheon included Teshub, the god of weather, and Hebat, mother goddess and sun deity. Shaushka was the goddess of fertility and war, not unlike Ishtar in Assyria, and Kushuh was the god of the moon. The Hurrian influence on Greek mythology is theorized in the parallels between the Hurrian 'The Songs of Ullikummi' and Hesiod's *Theogony*, both of which tell of a patriarchal god being castrated by his son, and then a son overthrowing his father and forcing him to regurgitate his swallowed children. The Hittites adopted the Hurrian religious system even after the Hurrian kingdoms disappeared.

Hurrian Economics

As far as archaeological evidence can provide, the Hurrians were master craftsmen who were well known as ceramic artists, metalworkers, sheep and wool traders, and horse trainers. Their distinctive pottery was coveted as

Hurrian cuneiform tablet, from the Louvre collection of the Levant

far away as Egypt. Also, because of the Hurrian's geography they were heavily involved in the trade and production of metals such as silver, copper, and tin.

FURTHER READING: Ascalone, Enrico, and Frongia Rosanna M. Giammanco. Mesopotamia. *(Berkeley: University of California, 2007; Van, De Mieroop, Marc.* A History of the Ancient Near East, Ca. 3000–323 BC *(Malden, MA: Blackwell Pub., 2007).*

Ikhnaten

Pharaoh Amenophis IV of the eighteenth dynasty of Egypt, who adopted the name of Ikhnaten (or Ikhnaton, or Akhenaten) is the most remarkable individual figure in the history of Egyptian religion. After a period of sometimes excessive admiration, later scholars have sought to reduce his stature. It has been claimed that the introduction of new art forms, as well as the monotheistic religious teaching for which he is famous, had already begun before he ascended the throne—indeed, his monotheism itself has been questioned. It has been said that the more permissive, peace-loving, and internationalist values with which he has been credited are altogether illusory.

Though the new interpretations are partly justified, the greatness of Ikhnaten remains. Whether the force that drove him is called fanaticism, megalomania, or will and imagination, there can be no question that this pharaoh, by his own genius, succeeded in changing the overwhelmingly conservative traditions of ancient Egypt. Looked at from the point of view of later human history, it can be seen that his changes were truly enlightened. The fact that his endeavour plainly contained the seeds of its own destruction turns drama into tragedy. No wonder that modern man has been stirred by his story—even to the point of intensifying and recolouring it.

Amenophis IV was the son of Amenophis III and Queen Tiye. His boyhood was probably divided between their great Malkata palace at Thebes and Memphis, the old capital, which kept its importance as a royal city. During his father's long reign of some thirty-eight years, the New Kingdom attained its zenith of cosmopolitan opulence.

Problems with Dating

It is known that Ikhnaten's reign lasted for seventeen years, but the problem

> *Heiress, great in the Palace, fair of face, adorned with the double plumes, endowed with favours, at whose voice the King rejoices . . .*

is whether he was co-ruler with his father, Amenophis III, for several years before the latter's death. Some Egyptologists have maintained that Ikhnaten was crowned in his father's twenty-eighth year on the throne and consequently ruled beside him for eleven years or so. Others have doubted this, but in his recent and authoritative biography of the pharaoh, Cyril Aldred examines the evidence and accepts the co-rulership theory. He dates the reign of Amenophis III from about 1384 to about 1346 BC and that of Amenophis IV, or Ikhnaten himself, as running from 1358 to 1340 BC, giving the latter a maximum of six years of independent rule before his demise. The parentage of Ikhnaten's principal queen—the celebrated Nefertiti—is uncertain. She is hailed in an inscription as the 'Heiress, great in the Palace, fair of face, adorned with the double plumes, endowed with favours, at whose voice the King rejoices, the Chief Wife of the King, his beloved, the Lady of the Two Lands . . .'

Nefertiti was closely associated with her husband in his religious reforms and adopted the extra name of Neferneferuaten, meaning 'Good like the beauty of the Aten'. Statues of her emphasized her physical attractions as a goddess of love. She bore Ikhnaten six daughters and seems to have enjoyed happiness with him until she died, perhaps in the twelfth year of his reign.

Ikhnaten had another much-loved wife, whose pet name was Kiya, and the pharaoh also had sexual relations with his elder daughters and children by them, incest being the accepted method of perpetuating the royal line in Ancient Egypt. His eldest daughter by Nefertiti was later married to Smenkhare, an obscure figure who was co-ruler with Ikhnaten for a short time but survived him by only three years. Smenkhare was succeeded in his turn by the equally short-lived Tutankhamen, whose queen was another daughter of Ikhnaten and Nefertiti, and who is famous today for the astonishing quantities of treasures found centuries afterward in his tomb. It seems that Smenkhare and Tutankhamen were the younger brothers of Ikhnaten and sons of Amenophis III—not Ikhnaten himself, as at one time thought.

Radiance of the Aten

The Thebes of Ikhnaten's youth was dominated by the city god, Amun. Linked with the royal sun god, Re, he stood for the unseen, creative solar force, and the wealth and power of his priesthood was very great. Probably under the leadership of the priests of Re at Heliopolis, there was a tendency to merge the divinities of Egypt's be-

wildering pantheon with the sun god. He was seen most often in the form of Re-Herakhty, compounded of Re and the falcon sky god Horus—who was pharaoh. In one early text Re is the 'sole god who has made himself for eternity', and other deities appear as his 'bodies'.

It has been supposed that the development of solar religion during the eighteenth dynasty may have been in part an attempt to return to the conditions of the Old Kingdom, when the solar cult of the northern city of Heliopolis gave the pharaoh unique power. This was part of a move by the crown and the northern priesthood to counter the near-hegemony of Amun. It is also suggested that the emergence of a new form of the solar cult, that of the visible sun disc or Aten (in which the spirit of Re was manifest) represented a compromise that could win new adherents.

There is no doubt that this growth took place. At their deaths several kings of the eighteenth dynasty were said to have been reunited with the Aten; under Tuthmosis IV the Disc appears as a distinct divinity associated with the power of the pharaoh. In his father's reign Ikhnaten would certainly have witnessed a mounting concern with the Aten. By now the god had a cult centre in Thebes, and the title 'Radiance of the Aten' was applied to the state barge, the Malkata palace and probably even to Amenophis III himself.

Although these developments may have anticipated Ikhnaten's teaching, they were still only a slender growth in the forest of Egyptian polytheism—and at Thebes they were quite overshadowed by the great cult of Amun. Amenophis III built several temples to Amun and to others of the old gods. The break which Ikhnaten had to make to achieve an uncompromising mono-

theism was therefore in truth more revolutionary than evolutionary.

Already in the second year of his reign he was planning a huge temple of the Aten at Thebes. At this time the deity was still shown as a falcon or falcon-headed man crowned with the sun disc. Now the first great innovation was made. The human and bird forms were swept away—presumably for the first time ever in Egyptian religion—and instead the divine power was expressed by a disc bearing the uraeus of kingship and long rays, each ending in a beneficent hand. These rays stretched out to all and sundry, giving a new unity to every scene, yet they offered the ankh, symbol of life, only to Ikhnaten and Nefertiti. At the same time the king seems to have demanded a deeper obeisance from those approaching him.

This intensified reverence, so contrary to other trends in the royal life, can be explained in both theological and personal terms. The living pharaoh had been one among the gods, the divine Horus. Now with one god alone, the pharaoh, too, became the sole divinity. The young king must also have felt complete identification with the godhead that had been revealed to him personally. On a boundary stone at Akhetaten he declares that it was his father the Aten, and he alone, who had shown him the site for this new city, and at the end of his famous sun hymn he says, 'there is none other who knows thee save thy son Ikhnaten. Thou hast made him wise in thy plans and power'. The same concentration on the divinity of the pharaoh is shown in the private tombs at Akhetaten. Where in the past the tomb owner himself would have appeared before Re-Herakhty, now there was only the divine Disc shining upon the royal family.

Temples Open to the Sun

After the adoption of the rayed disc, the next revolutionary step was the

move to Akhemtaten (now El Amarna) halfway between Thebes and Memphis. Thebes was heavy with the old gods and their powerful priesthoods. The new god Aten needed his own residence in his own city. The site was probably first established in the fourth year of Ikhnaten's reign, and was ready for occupation two years later. It was in this sixth year that Ikhnaten finally changed his name from Amenophis.

The temples of the new city imitated that of the sun god at Heliopolis. In place of the dark sanctuaries of most Egyptian temples their courts were wide open to the rays of the Aten. The royal family must often have worshipped in them. As for the litany, it must have followed the lines of the marvellous hymn to the sun.

The hymn hails the sun as a bringer of light and life to the world, which drives the night away and rouses all the inhabitants of the earth to joyful and productive activity. It is the sun which causes women to conceive, which quickens the child in the womb and the chick in the egg, which brings the Nile flood and gives life to the seeds in the ground. It is the god who made all the millions of forms that life takes and all manner and conditions of men and women, of all nations and languages and shades of skin colour—a novel inclusiveness.

The composition of the hymn is generally credited to the pharaoh himself. It celebrates the Aten's eternal return and nature is shown rejoicing in its creator: vegetation burgeons and grows green, beasts gambol, fish leap, and birds fly, raising their wings in the god's praise. The hymn uses accustomed phrases and brings together ideas often expressed in Egypt before, but significantly there is no mention of any other gods. The monotheism of the hymn is absolute.

Ikhnaten's teaching on the life after death is imperfectly understood. He had, of course, banished Osiris and his

the Nile. It would be foolish to judge these facts in the light of modern liberalism, but it is legitimate to see behind them a consistent mind and personality. Indisputably, they reveal a marked change from all earlier palace art, both in content and in style.

The inevitable negative side of the Atenist revolution is represented by the ruin of old temples and priesthoods, and the economic dislocation that resulted. Some authorities consider that it was only in his last years that Ikhnaten gave the command for all names of other gods, all words implying a plurality of gods, to be struck from the monuments. Possibly, opposition from the older priesthood had enraged Ikhtaten and led him to take such vandalistic action.

The closing events of Ikhnaten's reign have been much disputed, but his eventual successor, the youthful Tutankhaten, quit Akhetaten, then changed his name to Tutankhamen and busied himself with restoring the supremacy of Amun and the temples and statues of the old gods. With the coming of the nineteenth dynasty in 1299 BC, Ikhnaten's name was obliterated and removed from the king lists, to be almost completely forgotten for millennia.

JACQUETTA HAWKES
FURTHER READING: C. Aldred,
Akhenaten King of Egypt *(Thames & Hudson, 1988).*

Imhotep

The ancient Egyptian sage Imhotep has two claims to unique distinction. He provides the best documented instance of the deification of a man and he is the first individual of genius known to us. His reputation, moreover, was due to his wisdom and technological ability, not to success in war, too often the qualification for fame.

judgement of the dead. The sun hymn was inscribed in tombs, and its equation of night with death is suggestive. Pharaoh probably taught that through him all the dead could share in the solar resurrection.

The New Naturalism

Ikhnaten's ideas transformed not only religion but also art and the habits of court life. Until then, Egyptian art had for centuries always shown movement completely arrested; now it became an art of living movement. Where before

the pharaoh had been idealized to the verge of impersonality, Ikhnaten had his own distinctive peculiarities provocatively exaggerated.

The formal public scenes gave way to the liveliest portrayals of the royal pair embracing, eating, and driving out together, dandling their babies. Traditional scenes glorifying the pharaoh as hunter, warrior, trampler of subject races, were rare, and at Akhetaten, almost absent. The palaces at Akhetaten were bright with realistic paintings of the plants and creatures of

Imhotep was the vizier of the pharaoh Zoser of the third dynasty (c. 2778–2723 BC). Among his titles were 'overseer of the king's records', 'chief of all the works of the king', and 'supervisor of that which heaven brings, the earth creates and the Nile brings'. His personal name Imhotep meant 'he who comes in peace'. His father was Kanofer, 'chief of the works of the south and of the north land'; his mother's name was Khreduank. These facts are significant, for they show that Imhotep's human origins were well known and recorded.

One famous monument created by his genius still survives—the Step-Pyramid at Sakkara. This is the first-known stone building, and it was planned by Imhotep as a tomb for Zoser. Interesting evidence of the connection between king and architect has been provided by the finding, within the mortuary-temple complex of the Step-Pyramid, of a statue of Zoser bearing both his and Imhotep's names. The scientific and technological knowledge involved in the erection of the pyramid and its adjacent buildings at this early period impressively attests to the genius of Imhotep. But such an achievement does not explain how Imhotep came to be regarded as a god some 2,000 years later, in about 525 BC, according to the earliest available evidence of his deification.

From Egyptian sources, however, we learn that Imhotep had a reputation for other abilities than his skill as an architect. An inscription of the Ptolemaic period (330–30 BC), on the island of Sekel near Aswan, preserves an ancient legend about Imhotep. Egypt, during the reign of Zoser, was afflicted by a terrible famine owing to the failure of the Nile for seven successive years to reach the flood level necessary for the irrigation of the land. Zoser appealed to Imhotep to find the cause. After withdrawing to consult the sacred books, Imhotep revealed to the king 'the hidden wonders, the way to which had been shown to no king for unimaginable ages'. In the inscription Imhotep is described as 'the chief Kheri-heb priest . . . the son of Ptah'.

The description, in this context, is significant. The office of Kheri-heb involved the reading of magical texts during the performance of rituals believed to achieve supernatural results. Hence the holder of the office was associated with magical knowledge and ability. The legend indicates that Imhotep had a preeminent reputation in this connection. It also shows that he was regarded as the son of the great god of Memphis, Ptah, although the name of his earthly father was also known.

An interesting reference to Imhotep occurs in the curious sceptical poem known as the Song of the Harper, which dates from the Middle Kingdom (c. 2060–1788 BC), and was sometimes inscribed on the walls of tombs. It reads: 'I have heard the discourses of Imhotep and Hardedef, with whose words men speak everywhere—what are their habitations (now)?' The 'Harper' seems to imply that the wisdom of the great sages of old had not saved them from the ravages of time—Hardedef, incidentally,

The Step-Pyramid at Sakkara, tomb of the Pharaoh Zoser and first of the great Egyptian pyramids, bears witness to the technological genius of its architect, Imhotep, Zoser's vizier and 'chief of all the works of the king'.

was the son of the pharaoh Khufu (Cheops), builder of the Great Pyramid; but he never attained the posthumous fame enjoyed by Imhotep.

Healed in a Dream

In some way Imhotep also acquired great renown as a physician or healer of disease. A Greek papyrus found at Oxyrhynchus, an ancient city of the Nile valley, dating from the 2nd century AD but claiming to preserve an older Egyptian record, suggests that Imhotep's medical reputation was already well established by the reign of the pharaoh Menkaure (c. 2600 BC). The papyrus, which was written by a certain Nechautis, who sought appointment as priest in a temple of Imhotep, contains interesting evidence of the Egyptian practice of incubation—sleeping in a temple in the hope of divine healing. It relates how the mother of Nechautis, suffering from quartan ague, slept in the temple of Imhotep and was cured after dreaming that the god had visited and healed her by 'simple remedies'. After this miracle, Nechautis also became ill. He too slept in the temple, accompanied by his mother who remained awake. She suddenly saw 'someone whose height was more than human, clothed in shining raiment, and carrying in his left hand a book'. The presence intently regarded the sleeping Nechautis from head to foot and then vanished. Recovering herself, the mother found her son bathed in perspiration, but free of his fever. On awaking, he described a similar vision, and was conscious that Imhotep had cured him. When mother and son duly offered sacrifices of thanksgiving to Imhotep, they learned that the god wished Nechautis to fulfill a long-standing promise. This was to translate into Greek the ancient Egyptian book which the papyrus claims to embody, so that 'Every Greek tongue will tell thy story and every man will worship the son of Ptah, Imouthes (the Greek form of Imhotep)'.

The story graphically illustrates the manner in which the ancient architect of the Step-Pyramid had been transformed, some 2,000 years later, into a healing god. The Greeks identified Imhotep with their own divine physician, Asclepios.

The gradual deification of Imhotep seems to have been completed about 525 BC. It was paralleled by a change in his iconography. Previously he had been represented, in small bronze statuettes, as a man, generally seated, wearing a short waist cloth and skullcap, and without any symbol of deity; he held an opened papyrus scroll on his lap. Later, particularly in mural representations, he was shown with all the customary attributes of divinity: the Puntite beard, a long narrow artificial beard worn after the fashion of the men of Punt (Abyssinia), the was-sceptre and the ankh, symbol of life. His divinity is clearly attested in the following inscription, adjacent to his picture in the small Ptolemaic temple at Kasr el-Agouz, near Luxor: 'Son of Ptah, beneficent god, begotten by the god of the south wall (Ptah), giver of life, who bestows gifts on those he loves, who listens (to those who call upon him), who provides remedies for all diseases'.

Imhotep's deification led, in turn, to the deification of his mother and his wife Renpetnefert. His father did not share in this exaltation, for already Ptah had been credited with the siring of the divine physician. At Memphis Imhotep came to form a divine triad with Ptah and the goddess Sekhmet.

Three temples are known to have been dedicated to Imhotep in Egypt, the chief being at Memphis, which became a famous medical centre, and on the sacred island of Philae in Upper Egypt. Many temples contained special shrines for his worship; on the upper terrace of the temple of Hatshepsut at Deir el-Bahari there was a sanatorium

for those who sought his help. The centre of his cult was probably at his tomb at Sakkara, near the Step-Pyramid. Excavations are now in progress at Sakkara and there are hopes that the tomb of the man who became the Egyptian god of medicine will eventually be discovered.

S. G. F. BRANDON
FURTHER READING: J. B. Hurry. Imhotep. *(Humphrey Milford, 1926).*

Ishtar

Ishtar was the Semitic name for the old Sumerian goddess Inanna, the most powerful goddess in Mesopotamia. Representing the full potency of womanhood and maidenhood, and possessed of subtle powers in shaping the fortunes of man, she was worshipped for more than 2,000 years. Doubtless many facets of her character altered during this period; and different aspects of the goddess were venerated in different cities.

For the appraisal of Ishtar there is no more revealing source than the Sumerian hymn, 'The Exaltation of Inanna'. Composed in about 2350 BC by Enheduanna, the daughter of King Sargon of Agade in Akkad, in the north of Babylonia, this long poem describes the struggle for her supremacy over Nanna, the moon god in the southern city of Ur, and her final acceptance in the city of Uruk (Erech), also in the south, by the high god, An.

Reading between the lines, we can see how King Sargon, a usurper, set the divine seal to his empire over Sumer and Akkad by equating Sumerian Inanna with Akkadian Ishtar. Here is a glimpse of the kind of political and religious struggle so frequent in the long history of ancient Egypt, but more rarely revealed in Mesopotamia.

This poem, which begins with the description of Inanna as the lady who possessed all the attributes of divinity,

tells of her many accomplishments. Following the description of the dramatic struggle against the older divinities and against the wicked collusion of the older gods in Ur and Uruk, we end in a hymn of praise, through which the high priestess and her goddess emerge triumphant.

Inanna is the radiant lady rapt in beauty, terrifying and tempestuous, but she is also seen as a lady of resplendent light, beloved of heaven and earth. Inanna-Ishtar is also the dread goddess, who can, if she will, accurse vegetation and command fear in mankind. Not only is she possessed of sexual potency, able to control both fertility and sterility, but she is also a mighty goddess in battle, and this martial quality of Ishtar was as pervasive as any in the later development of her character.

Terrifying Seductress

In the hymn, she is described as 'the lady mounted on a beast' and as 'lent wings by the storm'; and in art she is frequently shown mounted on a lion or lioness, or leading both together. For example, on the high rock carvings of Maltai in Assyria, she occupied a prominent place in the procession of the gods; she was mounted on a lioness, and no doubt gave her blessing to the Assyrian armies as they marched through the defiles which separated Assyria from Iran, on their annual campaigns.

The description of her as having been 'lent wings by the storm' recalls the goddess's many sinister images, among which one of the most striking is the great terracotta, known as the Burney relief, in which the naked, winged goddess, usually called 'Lilith', with feathered legs and birds' talons, mounted on lions, appears in the guise of a seductive vamp of terrible aspect.

A vase with a carving of Ishtar wearing the horned tiara, surrounded by birds, fish, a bull, and a tortoise

Here she is seen to be of 'terrible countenance', in the words of the poem. In the early poems another side of Inanna-Ishtar's character is revealed, namely, of the goddess who presided over divination, incubation, and oneiromancy, the interpretation of dreams. She was invested with all the great powers of womankind, and while possessed of seductive beauty and charm, could, if so moved, turn rivers to blood.

Inanna-Ishtar presided over one of the most important ceremonies of the year—the ritual marriage of the god, in the course of which the king was wedded to the high priestess and in this way induced for his people the promise of agricultural prosperity. Indeed, on the famous stone vase from Uruk, c. 3300 BC, Inanna herself may perhaps be recognized, taking part in the spring festival. There is certainly evidence from later periods of the king's special relationship to Ishtar, the goddess who in the words of A. L. Oppenheim 'becomes the carrier, the fountainhead, of his power and prestige'.

For the people of Agade, Ishtar was an incarnation of the planet Venus, which was known as Dilbat. In military history, Ishtar of Nineveh and Ishtar of Arbela are prominent in battle and ensure victory for the Assyrian armies. A famous war poem of Tukulti-Ninurta I, referring to an event in the 13th century BC, tells how Ishtar intervened at a critical point in the battle as a result of which the Assyrians triumphed over Kashtiliash, King of Babylon.

Ishtar was also invoked as a healer; indeed she made a memorable journey in about 1375 BC from Nineveh to Thebes, in Egypt, in order to lay hands on the aged and ailing King Amenophis III. This was not the first occasion on which her powers had been so used.

Opposite page:
The reconstruction of the Ishtar Gate in the Pergamon Museum in Berlin

---

The Eyes of Death
In a Sumerian poem, the judges of the underworld pronounce death on Inanna:

The pure Ereshkigal seated herself upon her throne,
The Annunaki, the seven judges, pronounced judgment before her,
They fastened (their) eyes upon her, the eyes of death,
At their word, the word which tortures the spirit. . .
The sick woman was turned into a corpse,
The corpse was hung from a stake.
S. N. Kramer, *Sumerian Mythology*

But the most sinister episode in the mythology concerning this goddess is the account of her descent into Hades, a tale of early Sumerian origin, in which Inanna strives dangerously with her sister, the queen of the underworld, and only narrowly succeeds in escaping from it.

Lady of the Dawn

Ishtar, however, is often thought of as an erotic goddess concerned with sexual intercourse, and later in history her hierodules or prostitutes were to earn a licentious and evil reputation, especially in the city of Uruk, where there was an elaborately organized college of priestesses of Ishtar, the head of which was the high priestess herself. This cult enjoyed a considerable expansion elsewhere, and finally emanated in the lewd practices of the Phoenician Astarte, and Hebrew Ash-taroth, so much condemned by the Old Testament prophets.

There is evidence that organizations similar to the one in Uruk existed first in Ashur, and then in Babylon. In Ashur, the religious capital of Assyria, the remains of a temple which belonged to Ishtar dinitu, 'the lady of the dawn', or the 'lighting up' have been excavated. What happened within the

sacred precincts may be deduced from a series of lead discs and tokens found elsewhere in the same city. These plaques showed men, and women who were probably hierodules in the service of the goddess, enjoying sexual intercourse on the brick pillars of the temple. Other figures are also engaged in an erotic dance.

This practice has an interesting counterpart in Herodotus's account of a strange marriage practice in Babylonia, in the course of which eligible women sat in the temple and intending suitors cast a coin in their laps, invoking the name of the goddess in settlement and witness of the marriage contract.

M. E. L. MALLOWAN
FURTHER READING: W. W. Hallo and J. J. A. Van Dijk. The Exaltation of Inanna. *(AMS Press, 1979); S. N. Kramer.* Sumerian Mythology. *(University of Pennsylvania Press, 1972); A. L. Oppenheim.* Ancient Mesopotamia, Portrait of a Dead Civilization. *(Univ. of Chicago Press, 1964).*

Isis

The great goddess of the ancient Egyptians, Isis was the wife of Osiris, the god who died and was restored to life. He had been king of Egypt, but his evil brother Seth, whom the Greeks later identified with the monster Typhon, had killed and dismembered him and buried the pieces in various places. Isis searched for and found the pieces, put them together and revived him. Osiris became king of the underworld and their son Horus, called Harpocrates by the Greeks, became ruler over Egypt.

As Queen of Egypt, Isis' hieroglyphic symbol is the throne. She is also the exemplary mother who has taken infinite pains to nurse, protect and bring up her son Horus and she is frequently depicted suckling him. With care and

by Seth-Typhon, the hot wind of the desert. But Isis searches for the dead Osiris and finds him on the day of the Nile flood in the river's holy waters. The water, Osiris, flows over the withered earth, Isis, and fertilizes it.

The Nile flood coincides with the first appearance of Sirius, just before sunrise, and this was interpreted as a causal event; Sirius (Egyptian Sothis) was seen as the star of the Nile flood and the star of Isis. The day of the rising of Sirius and of the river's flooding became the sacred New Year's Day of the Egyptians.

After the conquest of Egypt by Alexander the Great in 331 BC the country was ruled by Greeks for 300 years, and during this period the cult of Isis became completely Hellenized. When the Romans took over the government in 30 BC they relied on the support of the Greek middle class in Egypt and the language of administration remained Greek; during this era, the goddess's cult spread over the entire Mediterranean basin. It was only when Constantine the Great, after his victory at the Milvian bridge in 312 AD raised Christianity to the level of the national religion, that the Isis cult lost its importance and was subsequently prohibited.

Seeking the Dead Osiris

The Greeks identified the Egyptian Isis with their Greek goddesses: Isis, the provider of corn, was the Greek Demeter; Isis, the goddess of love, was Aphrodite; Isis, wife of the king of the gods, was Hera; Isis, the goddess of magic arts, was Hecate, and so on. By depicting Isis as the prototype of the human woman, she was put

incantations she protected him from all diseases, and after the death of Osiris she saved him from Seth who wanted to murder him. When Seth brought a lawsuit against Horus before the court of the gods, intending to become king of Egypt himself, Isis intervened and enabled her son to win the case. Isis therefore did everything that a good woman can do for her husband and child, and became the model for all Egyptian women.

Her sacred animal is the cow,

the mother of calves and provider of milk, 'the fruitful image of the all-producing goddess'. For Isis gives life, fertility and prosperity to people, animals, and fields.

As man fertilizes woman, and Osiris Isis, so did the annual flooding of the Nile fertilize the soil of Egypt; coming in the middle of the hot summer, this inundation was looked upon as a miracle and attributed to Isis. When the river dried up in the summer, it meant that Osiris was dead, killed on a par with the Greek heroine, Io, who was loved by Zeus and had been changed into a cow, the Isis animal. A gadfly sent by Hera chased poor Io over land and sea until, after a long and frantic flight, she came to Egypt. There, on the banks of the Nile, Zeus changed her back into a woman. This myth was a consolation for everybody who was hunted throughout life as Io was; at the same time it demonstrated the close connection between Greece and Egypt.

Isis was also compared with other goddesses such as Artemis, Persephone, and Nemesis, and especially with Tyche, the goddess of fortune (the Roman Fortuna), and with Providence. These various identifications are the expression of living religious feeling. The great goddess appears in many different forms and always reveals new aspects. She is called Myrionymos, 'the one with 10,000 names', and a Latin inscription is translated as: 'Thou, the one who is all, goddess Isis'. Her whole being is impenetrable, but behind her many faces and names there is one and the same divine Unknown.

Next to Isis are always her husband, Osiris, and her son Horus, and she can never be viewed individually, without her family. However, during the Greek period of Egypt a change set in as other sides of the nature of Osiris were given prominence, and he was given the name of Osiris-Apis, abbreviated to Serapis. Apis was the sacred bull of Memphis, the old capital of Egypt, and Serapis was the god of this city. However, he also became the god of the new capital Alexandria and of the new Greek Dynasty, the Ptolemies.

Isis' ancient role as throne goddess, the Queen of Egypt was perpetuated among the Greek kings; Cleopatra appeared on official occasions in the costume, one might even say in the guise, of Isis. The Isis religion therefore had a political element. It was the national religion of the Egyptian state:

Isis greeting Nectanebo II, fragment of the door of a small temple built at the entry of the alley to the Serapaeum. Painted limestone, c. 359–341 BC (thirtieth dynasty). From the Serapaeum at Saqqarah

those who worshipped Isis and Serapis acknowledged their loyalty to the reigning royal house.

This fact encouraged the spread of the Isis and Serapis cult in the Greek ruling circles of the Ptolemies, in Cyrene, Cyprus, Crete, the coastal towns of Asia Minor, and the Greek islands whose religious centre was Delos. On the other hand, for political reasons, an expansion beyond the sphere of influence of the Ptolemies was not regarded favourably anywhere. There were only branches of the Isis cult in seaports, such as Athens, Salonika and on Euboea. But even in Egypt itself, linking the royal cult with the Isis-Serapis religion was in many respects a disadvantage as pure religious feelings cannot arise when the practice of a religion is welcomed and rewarded so distinctly by those in high places.

The political decline of the Ptolemies, which started in 200 BC,

followed by the complete loss of autonomy that resulted from Egypt's incorporation into the Roman Empire, provided a real opportunity for the Isis religion to expand. Having lost its political aspect, it became possible for the religious and ethical aspect to be strengthened. On Delos, for instance, the Isis cult became purely religious, and as Delos was an important centre for trade with Italy, the Delian cult even reached that country.

The transformation of the cult of Isis into a religion of Mysteries first occurred in the Roman Empire. Because there was no longer a political aspect to worshipping the goddess, the cult now appealed to people as individuals: each one was personally offered salvation, and promised regeneration after death. If a man entered into the service of Isis it was his own personal decision.

The consecration ceremonies of the Isis Mysteries during the Imperial

period are described in detail in The Golden Ass of Apuleius. There was a wealth of rites: the morning opening of the temple, the vigils, the abstention from wine, meat, and love; the rites of cleanliness which included wearing white linen clothes, shaving the head, and ablutions. Novices lived for a time within the precincts of the temple; the statue of Isis was contemplated, there was ecstatic prayer and obligatory tears were shed. The worthiness of the candidates was tested at a kind of hearing, and anyone who had sinned gravely was rejected. Sins were confessed and forgiven through immersion in water, and worshippers pledged themselves under oath to the service of the deity and to secrecy. With every new variation the sacred myth of Isis was restated, the seeking and the finding; in each procession Isis sought the dead Osiris, and found him every time the holy water was drawn.

The initiation into the Mysteries was in three stages and consisted of a voluntary ritual death and revival. The initiate stepped on to the 'threshold of Proserpina' (the Greek Persephone) and went on a journey 'through all the elements' for which mechanical appliances were probably used. As in the case of Freemasons, there also seems to have been a coffin ritual, and perhaps a baptism of fire. In all probability, a 'sacred wedding', a sexual union, was an integral part of the initiation. Finally, the initiate received a new name and the mystics then partook of a communal meal, with music and dancing.

Garden of Religion

There was an entire vocabulary of religious symbols: the life of man was a pilgrimage or a sea journey, the sinful world was the sea, the religion of Isis was the ship and the haven,

Isis seated with Sethos I; the goddess is the throne itself, the seat of power

and Isis herself the mast and the sail. Her priests were the fishermen who rescued the souls from the sea, the evil world, or bird-catchers who caught the souls (birds or butterflies) with their lime-twigs; the mystics were soldiers on holy military service for Isis, or gardeners who labouriously cultivated the garden of religion. The Isis priests were the true philosophers, who attained the perception of God, and the functionaries in the religious organization of the community were the legitimate 'consuls'; the community itself was called Ecclesia, like the Greek general assembly and later the Christian Church.

The wheel was the symbol of Isis, the sponge indicated the purification of the mystics, and the ladder their spiritual advancement. The anchor symbolized the religion that granted security, the bosom the all-providing goddess, the amphora, a two-handled vessel, the holy water; the lamp stood for the night-feast of the goddess, and the yardstick, justice. The winnow, in which the grain is separated from the chaff, represented the cleansing of the soul in the initiation, the palm the 'victory' of the mystic and his rebirth.

Great pilgrimages were undertaken in the service of Isis, from Rome to Egypt, and indeed as far as Syene, now Aswan, where the source of the Nile was said to be, and where the holy water was drawn when the Nile was in spate. Above all, outstanding festival cycles took place in the service of Isis. One of these was the festival of the goddess as mistress of navigation on 5 March. This was a spring festival, when the beginning of the navigation period was ceremonially inaugurated by the 'voyage of Isis'. The goddess's worshippers walked through the town in a long procession, wearing masks, and accompanied by music and choirs, and the first ship was then put to sea. The festival was also called *ploiaphesia*, which can be roughly translated as a

'launching'. Isis herself inaugurated the navigation for the year, as according to the myth she had been the first to set sail on a ship. There were two other important festivals, one on 24–25 December and the other on 5–6 January, dates which were also important holy days in the competing Christian religion.

The abolition of all frontiers in the Mediterranean area under the Pax Romana, with trade and communication among countries restricted less than at any time in history, encouraged the spread of the Isis Mysteries. Like the Jews and the Christians, the Greeks from Egypt formed small communities in all the towns of Asia Minor in order to practice their native cult, and also helped one another in other ways. Anyone who came into an Isis community did not suffer materially; he would have friends and helpers.

It is clear that the 'church' of Isis had a 'mission' during the Imperial period, and that Memphis and Rome were the holy cities. At four places in Greece and Asia Minor, when Isis sanctuaries were being excavated, identical sacred texts were discovered, depicting Isis proclaiming her power. There is therefore no doubt that propaganda was being spread. It may be assumed that there were Isis sanctuaries or shrines in all the Mediterranean ports, and also in many inland cities and towns.

The cult's growth was partly because of its rather exotic nature: the strange and mysterious rites were an attraction, and at the same time it was Hellenized to such an extent that people quickly became accustomed to it. On the other hand, many Egyptian concepts still clung like tiresome and disregarded eggshells to the Isis religion. This was particularly the case with regulations concerning priests. They had to be born into the caste, as they could not be elected, they had to cut their hair, wear only linen garments, refrain from eating various kinds of food and on the whole observe many taboos. Only a native Egyptian could be considered for high office in the priesthood; a large-scale mission was impossible and in view of the tolerant nature of the religion was probably never envisaged. In any case, a type of lay clergy had evolved in Greece and Rome, the 'bearers of the shrine', who held leading positions in the religious community. In Egypt itself they were a group of laymen who were

The goddess Isis on the foot of the outer coffin of the mummy of Ankh-Wennefer, Washington State History Museum

called in to act in a subordinate capacity without being accepted into the priest-caste.

Mistress of the Elements

In the Roman Empire the Isis and Serapis shrines had characteristic features in common. The temples were built in the Greek style; but instead of the old roof construction they often had vaulted roofs. Most of the statues were in the Greek style but there were also those in the style of Egypt, or simply stiff-limbed statues imported from Egypt. There were also representations of Apis, the son Horus with a hawk's head, the servant Anubis with a dog's head, and the sacred animals.

Several hymns were written in honour of Isis, but *aretalogies*, reports of the miraculous deeds of Isis and Serapis which were recorded in the temple, are the most characteristic feature of the literature that developed through the worship of the goddess. For fishermen who were dying with thirst on the high seas Serapis changed the saltwater into freshwater; he helped one of his priests on Delos in a critical legal dispute; and he also lengthened the life of a servant by causing a stranger to become drunk and die in his place, for this god was able to 'change the clothes of destiny'. According to a recent theory, the literary form of the love story developed from these accounts of miracles. Several classical novels, such as the story of Psyche and Cupid by Apuleius, would therefore be coded texts of the Isis religion.

During the period of the Roman Empire the Mysteries of Isis were strongly influenced by Greek philosophical theories. Isis is 'provider of all things in Nature, mistress of all the elements'. She embodies all contrasts: light and dark, day and night, fire and water, life and death, beginning and end. Whoever enters her service as a slave will achieve true freedom. Apuleius describes Osiris as Creator of the world.

The psychology of the Mysteries was apparently quite Platonic: the soul is not bound firmly to the body but comes from the Beyond; it plunged into the sinful body and must try to free itself and return to God. The whole life of man is governed by the goddess. The many external vicissitudes of life, all mishaps and trials, appear to be afflictions of wayward chance, of the goddess Fortuna. But if a man becomes

From the day that I became your husband until this day have I done anything that I should conceal?

converted and enters the service of Isis, it will be seen that all the vicissitudes were caused by Providence only in order to lead mankind to salvation. Fortuna and Providence therefore come together in Isis. The influence of the stars, blind Fate, so much feared by the people of late antiquity, was broken by Isis; her servants were confident that the goddess was standing above the stars and, as Providence, was guiding both them and Fate.

R. MERKELBACH

Letters to the Dead

The belief of the ancient Egyptians in a life after death is attested by a rich abundance of material, ranging from the great pyramids of Gizeh to the treasures of the tomb of Tutankhamen. But nothing more vividly illustrates the intense reality of that belief, and also its pathos, than what Egyptolo-gists call 'Letters to the Dead'.

The known examples range in date from the Old Kingdom (2780–2280 BC) to the nineteenth dynasty (1320–1200 BC), which indicates that these 'Letters' represent a long-established practice in Egypt. They generally take the form of messages written on pottery vessels, used for making food offerings to the dead. The logic behind the selection of such means for communicating with the dead is obvious. The dead would surely see the messages when they partook of the food in the vessels concerned.

The contents of the 'Letters' reveal that the dead were regarded as still having a lively interest in the affairs of their families, and able to work for their well-being. Thus a widow asks her dead husband to watch over the interests of his heirs, whom false friends were endeavouring to rob of their inheritance.

These messages to the dead were not all appeals for help to promote the interests of relatives in this world. The dead were also feared as being capable of tormenting the living, as the following 'Letter' shows. It was written about 1200 BC by a husband to his dead wife, Ankhiry. He asks: 'What harm have I done you that you so distress me?' He reminds her of their past life together: 'From the day that I became your husband until this day have I done anything that I should conceal? . . . I married you when I was young . . . I did not desert you. I refrained from any action that might grieve your heart'. To reinforce his appeal, he threatens that he will complain about his wife to the gods who sit in judgment as assessors of the dead in the next world.

In ancient Egypt attempts to communicate between the world of the living and the dead were not made only by the former. In some inscriptions the dead speak to the living from

imaginative effort that went to the composition of this inscription—did it record a message that the husband believed he had received from his dead wife?

Maat

Egyptian goddess of truth, justice and order, whose symbol was a feather; according to ancient Egyptian belief, in the judgment of the dead the heart of the deceased was weighed against the feather-symbol of Maat and if declared *maa kheru* (true of voice) the deceased was granted entrance into the kingdom of Osiris.

Magi

Or *magians*, 'wise men', plural of magus, a great adept of the occult arts; from a Persian word from which our 'magic' is derived: learned Persian priests, revered as sages, magicians and diviners: three magi, or wise men or kings, brought the infant Jesus gifts of gold, frankincense, and myrrh, an event commemorated in the festival of the Epiphany; according to tradition, their names were Kas-par, Melchior, and Balthazar, and their bones were buried in Cologne Cathedral.

Magical Papyri

Magic and religion always walked hand-in-hand in ancient Egypt, and are often hard to separate: even in the early hymns and prayers there is evidence of a strong magical element

their tombs. For example, warnings to would-be violators of their tombs were sometimes given, such as that by Harkhuf, an Aswan noble who lived about 2500 BC: 'As for any man who shall enter into this tomb as his mortuary possession, I will seize him like a wild fowl'. Even stranger, perhaps, in view of the situation implied of the dead as opposed to the living is a tomb inscription, now in the British Museum, dating about 71 BC. A lady, That-I-em-hetep, addresses her husband, who is still alive: 'O my brother, my husband, my friend . . . cease not to drink, to eat, to be drunken, and to marry wives, and to enjoy thyself, and follow the desire of thy heart by day and night'. After this generous exhortation, the dead lady tells of her own grim condition: 'I no longer know where I am, now that I have arrived in this valley of the dead. Would that I had water to drink from a running stream . . . O that my face were turned toward the north wind . . . that the coolness thereof might quiet the anguish of my heart'. We can only wonder at the

chapters of his Natural History to a description of the manufacture of papyrus in the Roman period; but, apart from a few references in the works of medieval scholars and humanists to surviving fragments, these were the first discoveries of actual papyri written in Greek.

It was Napoleon's campaigns in Egypt that laid the foundations for more systematic investigations in the nineteenth century, as a result of which so many Greek papyri were found that the work of deciphering and editing them became sufficiently important to justify the formation of a special branch of classical scholarship known as papyrology (a term first mentioned in 1898). Naturally scholars have paid most attention to the literary discoveries, but a large number of the texts are nonliterary, amongst them many magical papyri which cannot fail to be of interest to students of magic, ancient and modern.

In 1928 the first volume of Karl Preisendanz's work *Papyri graecae magicae* appeared, followed by the second volume in 1931 and the third, of which the stock was destroyed by an air raid over Berlin, in 1941. Other special collections of magical papyri are those of T. Hopfner and S. Eitrem, but many isolated texts have also appeared in the last seventy years or so, which add interesting details to the general picture without invalidating the conclusions that may be drawn from a study of the more comprehensive collections.

The range covered by these texts is a very wide one, extending from the long hymns in verse contained in Preisendanz's first volume (the 'Great Paris Magical Papyrus' has 3274 lines), to brief recipes and imprecations, many of them accompanied by elaborate, if sometimes crude, illustrations. The substantial magical books date from the

with the underlying purpose of gaining power over the deity for the furtherance of personal ends. Love potions, wax images, talismans, and curses were all extremely popular, and it was natural that the Greeks who settled in Egypt in large numbers from the 4th century BC onward should come under the spell of the ancient traditions of Egypt, and under Egyptian influence in their own approach to religion and magic. The magical papyri are a rich source of material for illustrating the ways in which the Greeks (and later the Romans) in Egypt attempted to combine existing magical practices with elements of their own religion and that of other cultures.

A merchant traveling in Egypt in 1778 was offered a jar containing forty or fifty papyri, which was said to have been discovered near ancient Memphis. He bought one of the rolls for a small sum and subsequently took it back to Italy where he presented it to Cardinal Stefano Borgia as a curio. The Danish archeologist Schow has told how he found the papyrus in the Cardinal's museum at Velitri ten years later. Details of the story, including the postscript that the rest of the jar's contents were burned for their pleasant aroma, have been questioned, but the fact remains that the surviving fragment, which became known as the Charta Borgiana, whetted the appetite of scholars, though it contained only a list of workers at Ptolemais Harbour in 192–193 AD.

It was well known that for centuries papyrus had been the staple writing material in Egypt. There were examples in the hieratic script (the simplified cursive form of hieroglyphic) which had survived from earliest times, and the elder Pliny had devoted several late 3rd and 5th centuries AD, but some of the smaller texts have been placed as early as the second century.

A. D. Nock, in his article on 'Greek Magical Papyri' in *Journal of Egyptian Archaeology* Vol. 15 (1929), expressed the opinion that the longer papyri were actual working-copies used by practicing magicians 'like the books burned by St. Paul's Ephesian converts . . . or the magical books handed down in Germany from generation to generation'. It is even probable that many of them belonged to the same library. The shorter texts appear to have been extracts from such magical books, supplied on demand to meet specific needs and occasions.

This view is supported by the existence of alternative versions of the same recipes containing variations of method and names, and often described as 'another copy'. For example, in the same text, the 'Great Paris Papyrus', there are two versions of the correct procedure for slandering one's rival to the moon, within 150 lines of each other. The general impression is of professional magicians compiling their handbooks from existing models without worrying too much about coherence or consistency, and selling the required extracts to their customers.

In language and style, as in content, the texts vary greatly, from the poetic to the semiilliterate. For example, an invocation of Helios, the sun, in the *Louvre Papyrus* (in Preisendanz's first volume) reads:

> Hither to me, greatest in heaven, for whom the heaven became a dancing-place (magical words followed by a Coptic word), do such and such (magical words), you who are the friend of oracles, golden of countenance, golden-gleaming, shining with fire in the night, mighty mighty lord of the universe, shining forth early in

the day, setting in the west of heaven, rising from the east, in form like a circle, running toward midday and passing the time in Arabia (magical words), harbinger of the holy light, circle in fiery form (magical words), brilliant Sun, sending light over the whole world, covering the Ocean (magical words), I pray you by the egg. I am Adam the first born, my name is Adam . . .

Contrast the lucidity and rhythmical symmetry of this calm invocation with the staccato incoherence of the following extract from a fragment published by A. S. Hunt as 'A Greek

> *I will not pour out the cedar-oil but will let it be, I will preserve Ammon and will not slay him, I will not scatter the limbs of Osiris, and I will hide you from the giants.*

Cryptogram' in the Proceedings of the British Academy for 1929:

> Adonai (magical word or words), accomplish for (name) what I have written hereon for you, and I will leave the east and west as it was formerly established and will save the flesh of Osiris forever and will not break through the bonds wherewith you made Typhon fast, and I will not call those who have died violent deaths but let them be, I will not pour out the cedar-oil but will let it be, I will preserve Ammon and will not slay him, I will not scatter the limbs of Osiris, and I will hide you from the giants . . . Eieieieieieiei choin (followed by several magical words of which only Aoth and Jacob are intelligible). Declare the secrets of Isis . . .

But even this cryptogram retains certain elements of formal style, how-

ever crude, when compared with many other texts like, for example, this agoge or spell for a lover from Eitrem's Papyri Osloenses.

> Write with a bronze stilus on an unbaked potsherd: 'Hecate, you, Hecate, of three shapes, all the magical signs of every one having been completed, I adjure you by the great name of Ablathana and the power of Agramari, for I adjure you, you, who control the fire of the Hawk and those in it, that (feminine name) be consumed, and to pursue (her) to me (masculine name), because I hold in my right hand the two serpents and the victory of Iao Sabaoth, and by the great name Bilkatri-mopheche, shaking the fire, Stoutou-katoutou, for her enflamed to love me, in fire for me, yes, tortured. Sunkout-ouel am I'. Write 8 magical signs, so; give me the favour of all things, Adonai.

Even this translation conceals the grammatical errors and peculiarities of spelling which, together with the accumulation of epithets and the use of what are to us meaningless combinations of words and vowels, are the main features of the language and style of popular magical texts on papyrus.

Two further examples from the same papyrus are also worth quoting. A 'remedy to break spells' runs as follows:

> You take (a piece of) lead, and you engrave upon it the figure Mononthoun (?), holding in his right hand a torch, in his left a dagger, and on his head three hawks, and under his feet a scarab, under the scarab a serpent biting its tail. That which is written round the figure is this. (Magical letters and sign follow.)

A curse combines in a most unusual manner all the features that have been mentioned as being typical of these papyri, with universal elements and an invocation of angels:

You take a plate of lead and write on it with a bronze stilus the following names and the figure. You anoint the plate with the blood of a bat and roll it up in the usual way; you open a frog (toad), and put it (the plate) into its stomach, sew up the frog with Anubis-thread and a bronze needle and suspend it on a reed taken from the spot with hairs from the tail of a black ox with its hind-legs (tied to the reed) in the eastern part of the place near to the rising sun.

Ousirisesengenbarpharanges. (This complex is written in the shape of a heart by cutting off the letters successively from each end.) Erikisepheararacharaephthisikera. Rikiseph-theararacharaephthisiker. Ikisephthearara-charaephthisike. Base. Lord angels, as this frog vanishes away and dries up, so may also the body of (masculine name), born of (feminine name), because I adjure you who are placed to command the fire, Maskelli, Maskello, and the rest . . .

Above all else, the magical papyri, the numerous amulets collected in one volume by C. Bonner, and the charms on lead tablets testify that the syncretism or fusion of different elements characteristic of popular religion from the Hellenistic period onward, has a prominent place in magical practice. Apart from the traditional Greek deities, of whom Hermes, Hecate-Selen, Apollo-Helios, Aphrodite, and Eros are predictably to be found most often (though the last two are not as important for the love charms as one might have expected) there are Egyptian deities like Isis, Osiris, Horus, Anubis, and Seth-Typhon, side by side with very strong Semitic, especially Jewish, and other oriental ingredients as well.

Threatening the Gods

One papyrus, the large Berlin text which opens Preisendanz's work, illustrates the typical mixture with its association within a relatively narrow compass of the names Apollo, Paieon, Iao, Michael, Gabriel, Abrasax, Adonai, Pakenbeth (for Seth-Typhon), Aion, Physis, Adonaios, Eloaios (for Elohim). As H. I. Bell wrote in his *Cults and Creeds*: 'All was fish that came to the magician's net; the more deities he could include in his spells the more likely these were to be effective'.

It is not surprising, therefore, to find Christian references too, as in this early fourth century Coptic exorcism quoted by Preisendanz: 'Hail, God of Abraham, hail, God of Isaac, hail, God of Jacob, Jesus Christ, Holy Ghost, Son of the Father, who is among the Seven and in the Seven'. Angels, saints, the Virgin Mary, the Holy Ghost, Moses, all appear cheek by jowl, reinforced by citations from psalms, the Lord's Prayer, St. Matthew's gospel, and the book of Proverbs, to quote a few examples.

But M. P. Nilsson has rightly stressed that the Christian elements were relatively few if one considers that Christianity was the predominant religion of the period. He has explained this paradox as being the result of the natural hostility of Christians to magicians: to the latter Christ was merely one among many powers, to the former he was the most powerful of all mediators, the son of the only true God.

The attitude revealed by the magical papyri is essentially utilitarian. As Nock has picturesquely put it: 'the Gnostics were passionately eager to know how the wheels went round' but 'the authors and readers of the magic papyri desired simply to be able to make them turn'.

Their objects were to acquire power and through it to achieve success in love, beauty, popularity, health, wealth, and victory over, or revenge on, an enemy. The means to gain these objects were at hand, if men could but discover the secret of the right approach; and it is a characteristic of these magical papyri, as of Egyptian magic in general, that they threaten deities almost as often as they implore them, confronting them with others who may be even more powerful.

Underlying all else, however, there was a deeper concern, also typical of the period, to break the power of destiny, fate, or necessity, and this preoccupation led the magicians to use astrology as a means to achieve their ends. There are often signs too of an approach which is closer to that of contemporary mysticism: as the 'Berlin Papyrus' puts it, 'If you have the god for a friend, you will be reverenced as a god yourself'. This mystical piety is best seen in the process called 'introduction to the sun god', which involved winning over the deity as a familiar spirit, a guide, and companion to a new spiritual state and the acquisition of new and greater powers of magic.

The magical papyri are full of evidence, if evidence is needed, that religion is a house of many storeys and that, even if magic is the 'disreputable basement', it is not difficult to pass on to higher levels, and back again. Scholars have rightly emphasized the fundamental opposition of magic to true religion in its attitude to the gods but, by their adaptation of current religious ideas and forms, the magical papyri claim a place of honour among our sources of knowledge of the religion of Graeco-Roman antiquity.

B. R. REES

FURTHER READING: H. I. Bell. Cults and Creeds in Graeco-Roman Egypt. (Ares, 1975); C. Bonner. Studies in Magical Amulets. (University of Michigan Press, 1950); E. R. Dodds. The Greeks and the Irrational (University of California Press, 1951) and Pagan and Christian in an Age of Anxiety. (Norton, 1970); M. P. Nilsson. Greek Popular Religion. (Columbia University Press, 1940); A. D. Nock. Conversion. (Oxford University Press, reprint 1961); B. R. Rees. The Use of Greek. (University of Wales Press, Cardiff, 1960).

Manicheans

Manicheism was a gnostic, dualistic religion, founded by a Babylonian prince of Persian origin named Mani, who was born in 216 AD. According to the Fihrist of the Arabic author An Nadim, when Mani was twelve years old God sent an angel called at-Taum (twin) to him, ordering him to leave the ascetic sect to which his father belonged. When Mani was twenty-four, this same angel appeared to him and told him that now the time had come to appear in public and proclaim his own doctrine. From Manichean sources, partly written by Mani himself, we hear more about this twin or familiar. He is said to accompany Mani and protect him. Even at the hour of death, Mani was gazing at this familiar, the one who waited for him always and opened before him the gate unto the height.

So Manicheism is based upon a special revelation, a personal experience of the founder. The 'higher Self of Mani revealed himself to him, inspired him with the doctrine he had to proclaim to the world, protected him during his missionary journeys and awaited him at his death to bring him to the eternal realm of Light. Sometimes this Self is described in Christian terms: then it is designated Christ or the Holy Spirit. This is the case in Western sources, especially in the Coptic Psalms discovered at Medinet-Madi in Egypt, in 1931. The problem is whether we should interpret the experience of Mani in a Christian or in an Iranian perspective (as is supposed by G. Wid-

Manichaean Electae, Kocho, tenth century

engren and L. J. R. Ort).

The concept that man has a spiritual double or twin appears in the Greek author Lucian's *Dialogues of the Dead* (2nd century AD); according to him the 'shadow' (*eidolon*) of Heracles was his exact image and counterpart, his twin. In other sources it is stated that the 'daimon' or attendant spirit of a man is his image. This influenced the Jewish religion of the time, according to which the guardian angel was the *iqonin*, the image of the man to whom he belonged.

Through Judaism the concept was integrated into Christianity, where we find it at a very early date, allegedly already in the community of Jerusa-lem (Acts 12.15). From there it seems to have spread in many directions, especially to the Syriac Christianity of Edessa in Mesopotamia. In the *Gospel of Thomas*, written there about 140 AD, the guardian angel is called *ikon*, image, the eternal counterpart of man. In the 'Song of the Pearl', contained in the *Acts of Thomas*, also originating from Edessa (c. 225 AD), the encounter with the Self is described as the encounter with the eternal Garment, which is the mirror of its owner: 'for we were two in distinction, and yet again one in one likeness'. In the same *Acts of Thomas* the apostle Thomas is called the twin of Christ.

Mani seems to have known Christianity mainly in its Syriac form. He knew the Gospel of Thomas and he may very well have known the Acts of Thomas. From Syriac Christianity, which was strongly encratitic (prohibiting marriage, wine, and meat) he may have taken his severe asceticism, according to which the fall of Adam was his intercourse with Eve, and marriage as such is sinful. So Mani's religious experience, the revelation of the twin, which is the Holy Spirit, can be understood in a Christian perspective.

Christianity in Edessa, however, was not exclusively encratitic. Before the sect of Encratites, Jewish Christianity had come to the city, possibly from Jerusalem. These Jewish Christians called themselves Nazorees or Nazarenes, as the Syrian Christians did later on. The Manichean Kephalaia preserves a debate of Mani with a Nazoree about the problem of whether God, as judge, is not necessarily bound to use evil when he punishes. The implication seems to be that, according to this Nazoree, God was the origin of both good and evil.

Mani's abhorrence of the doctrine that God creates evil was one of the sources, and possibly the main source, of his absolute dualism. According to Mani, evil was Satan or Matter, not a god, as in Persian religion. This did not prevent Mani from taking over certain views of the Jewish Christians. During his trial, which ended with his death, he proclaimed solemnly that he had received his doctrine from God through the intermediary of an angel. So according to him, his twin and familiar, the Paraclete ('Counselor') or Holy Spirit, was an angel. This of course is in disagreement with orthodox Christianity, but can be found in the very archaic Ascension of Isaiah. Similarly, in the Manual of Discipline, one of the Dead Sea Scrolls, the Angel of Light (possibly Michael)

is called Holy Spirit and Spirit of Truth. On the other hand, Mani called Christ 'the right hand': this he must have taken from Jewish Christians, who used the same terminology. Of course, Mani took the designation Paraclete from St. John's gospel (14.16) but the fact that he considers this Paraclete to be an angel seems to hint at familiarity with Jewish Christians in Mesopotamia.

Mani in India

Mani considered Buddha, Zoroaster, and Jesus as his predecessors. He visited northwestern India and during his missionary trips in the Persian Empire, favoured by King Shapur I, he must have become thoroughly familiar with the Iranian religion. If he died in prison (possibly in 274 AD) owing

> *The father of greatness evoked the mother of life and the mother of life evoked the primal man.*

to the hostility of the official magians (fire-priests) who influenced King Bahram I, this does not mean that he did not integrate Iranian religious concepts into his system.

It is not quite clear which elements in Mani's religion are Iranian or Buddhist, mainly because it is not clear what these religions taught at that period. Later Buddhism of northwestern India, mother of Tibetan and Zen Buddhism, had very little in common with original Buddhism and may have been influenced by western Gnosticism. But Mani was probably inspired by Buddhism to respect the suffering life of the particles of light mixed up with matter, and perhaps drew the idea of reincarnation from this source. From Iranian religion he may have

taken his absolute dualism, the opposition of light and darkness; this he combined with the gnostic dualism of spirit and matter, and equated with the opposition of God and Satan.

Yet all these influences do not explain the unmistakably gnostic character of Manicheism. It has been established that Mani was familiar with the views of the Mandeans, a baptist sect still existing in Iraq, most probably originating from Palestine and possibly already then living in southern Babylonia. It seems plausible that the sect of the Mughtasila (Baptists), to which Mani's father belonged, was a sort of Mandean or Proto-Mandean sect.

The difficulty is that the Mughtasila are said to have been strongly encratitic, whereas the Mandeans are not, and never seem to have been. Moreover it is not certain that the Mandeans, now a gnostic sect, were already then gnostic to the same extent as they are now. And Manicheism has certain gnostic elements which seem to be absent from Mandeism. The god of this world, the demiurge, is called in Manichean sources Saklon or Saklas. This goes back to Saklas (Aramaic for 'fool'), which is the name for the Jewish god and creator in the gnostic *Apocryphon of John* (early second century), but has no parallel in Mandean sources.

Man the Work of Darkness

This Saklas, the ruler of darkness, together with his subjects, creates Adam after the image of the primal man, created by God. In the same way, in the *Apocryphon of John*, Saklas and his powers fashion Adam after the idea of God, his image, also called first man, who revealed his reflected image in the water of chaos. It is even said, in Manichean sources and in the *Apocryphon of John*, that Saklas made Adam after the image of God and after the image of himself and his fellows, so that man is a microcosm of everything: 'Come! Let us make a man according to the image of God and according to our likeness'. This, of course, ultimately goes back to the Timaeus of Plato, where God contributes only the divine part of man, the soul, and leaves it to lower gods to fashion the mortal part of man. But the concept must have reached Mani through gnostic channels.

There must be some relationship between Mani and the various gnostic schools and currents of the second century, quite apart from Mandeism. But at the moment we cannot be more specific, because the history of these sects in eastern Syria and Mesopotamia is almost completely obscure. This problem may come nearer to a solution when all the gnostic manuscripts found at Nag Hammadi in Upper Egypt have been published.

There is no doubt that Manicheism is a gnostic religion. It has a gnostic conception of man (as a divine spark), of the world (as a product of failure) and of God (as the suffering God), which is expressed in a systematic and consistent myth. Because this myth is so extremely complicated, even in the abridged form which we offer here, it is perhaps right to remember that according to Franz Cumont and Henri-Charles Puech the myth reflects and expresses the 'Self-experience' of Mani himself.

The Suffering God

From the very beginning, so the myth says, before heaven and earth and everything contained therein came into being, there were two principles, a good one and an evil one, the realm of light and the realm of darkness. In the realm of light dwells God, 'the father of greatness'. In Eastern sources he is called the 'four-faced God', because with his light, his power, and his wisdom he forms a sort of quaternity.

In the realm of the dark dwells the king of the dark. He arose from his domain to invade the realm of light.

Then God decided to go out and fight the battle against the invading forces. Thereupon 'the father of greatness evoked the mother of life and the mother of life evoked the primal man'. When God sends out the primal man, he is really going himself. The primal man and all the other light-figures of Manicheism are qualifications and manifestations of God himself. When the lost part of primal man, called *Jesus patibilis* (suffering Jesus), is said to hang on every tree, we should understand that it is God himself who is crucified in the world of darkness.

We have here a conception of God akin to, but not identical with, that of Christian theology. It is essentially gnostic. In the recently discovered *Gospel of Philip* it is said that the heavenly Christ saved his own soul, which he had lost since the beginning of the world. The idea of this Valentinian author is that the fall of divine, wisdom (Sophia), through which this world came into being, is essentially a split within the godhead itself. The divine element is dispersed in matter and God, when saving man, is saving himself. This astonishing conception of the suffering God is not to be found in India, Iran, or Israel. It seems to have its prototype in the Greek myth of Zagreus-Dionysus, who was torn in pieces by the Titans.

It is this gnostic and ultimately Hellenistic concept of God suffering in the world and in man which the Manichean myth tries to expound, in the following way. The primal man, in his glorious armour of the 'five bright elements', went forth to repel the forces of darkness. But this fight ended in defeat and the primal man was left in the darkness in a state of unconsciousness. On the other hand, it was a sort of divine sacrifice, for in this way the primal man could also serve as bait to catch the forces of darkness, so as to assuage them and to prevent their attack upon the realm of light. When the primal man recovered from

his swoon, he entreated the father of greatness to come to his support. From above he received 'the call', conceived as a spiritual being. To this he gave 'the answer', also a spiritual being. Thereupon the primal man returned to the realm of light but had to leave his armour behind.

The adventures of the primal man are described in great detail in the Coptic Manichean psalms, which show us how this myth reflected the situation of every Manichean. They too were living in the darkness of unconsciousness and matter, until the saving message of the doctrine appealed to them, revealed to them their real identity and so enabled them to return to the realm of light. A similar conception of salvation, and a similar myth, is found in second century Gnosticism, especially in the documents from the school of Valentinus.

Here, the perfect man is Jesus. He leaves his 'members' behind in the world, to be formed by their life in history and to discover their own identity. The end of the world-process is achieved when all spiritual elements have returned to their origin above. In the same way, the Manichean primal man returns to the realm of light, but leaves behind his armour, also called his members or his soul.

This shows that scholars (including G. Widengren and R. Bultmann) who interpreted Manicheism as a myth of 'the saved saviour' were right. They were wrong when they supposed that Mani took this idea directly from Iranian religion. Before him the Valentinian Gnostic had a similar conception, which seems inspired by St Paul's view that the Church is the body of Christ, and by a Jewish myth that Adam regained Paradise.

Seal of the Prophets

The elements of light which had been absorbed by darkness had still to be delivered. To this end, the world was created as a mixture of spirit and matter. The myth here becomes very obscure and obscene. By a strange mixture of generation and cannibalism Adam and Eve were brought forth by Saklon (the Jewish god). 'Jesus Splendor' aroused Adam from his sleep, so that Adam became conscious of himself.

This process was continued during the whole history of mankind. Ever and again, messengers were sent to remind men of the divine spark in them. Such apostles were Sethel (Seth, the son of Adam), Enosh, Enoch, Shem (the son of Noah); Buddha in the East, Zoroaster in Persia, Jesus in the West. But their doctrines were not complete and soon after their death were corrupted by their pupils.

Mani admitted that Jesus revealed himself in Palestine at the beginning of our era to reveal the gnosis to man, though the body of Jesus was not held to be material. He admired St. Paul, but he held the Church to have disappeared completely ('a tree without fruits') in his own lifetime. Therefore the Paraclete, the Spirit of Truth promised by Jesus, had been sent to Mani, who was called to reveal the definite and consummate gnosis. For that reason Mani styled himself 'the apostle of Jesus Christ' and 'the seal of the prophets'. He must have thought that he lived in the last generation of mankind, before the final separation of light and darkness. Then the 'earth of light', the abode of God and all the saved, would be healed of the wound inflicted upon it by the attack of darkness. The earth would be destroyed by fire, the powers of evil would be confined within their original domain, and unrepentant sinners would be compacted together in a great round clod, the globus. At last the realm of light would enjoy an eternal peace, no longer endangered by any attack of darkness. Dualism in the end will be permanent.

In order to realize the duality of man and his higher Self, Mani had to postulate a highly dualistic philosophy.

And this is understandable, because the unity of the innermost man with his heavenly Self, according to Mani, is only possible when man is ready to reject everything material.

Manicheism spread in the West, where the young St. Augustine was attracted to the sect, until it was completely suppressed by the combined forces of Church and State in c. 600 AD. In the East, especially outside the Roman Empire, it flourished in spite of persecutions and remained for 1,000 years one of the main religions of Asia. The medieval sects of the Bogomils and Cathars had much in common with Manicheism. The Cathars owed much to the Bogomils of Bulgaria, who in turn originated from the Armenian Paulicians and perhaps the Syrian Messalians. Neither Paulicians nor Messalians were Manichees and we have no evidence that Manichees were active in the Byzantine Empire at the time the Bogomils entered history. But the 'medieval Manichees' were so similar to the 'classic Manichees', that perhaps in the future some missing link will be discovered.

(Since this article was originally written a Greek papyrus has been discovered, which tells us explicitly that to the age of twenty-five Mani was a member of the Jewish Christian sect of the Elchesaites in the south of Babylonia.)

G. QUISPEL

FURTHER READING: F. C. Burkitt. The Religion of the Manichees. *(Cambridge University Press, 1925); H. C. Puech.* Le Manichéisme. *(Paris, 1969, 2nd edition); G. Widengren.* Mani and Manichaeism. *(Weidenfeld, 1965).*

Kudurru of the Babylonian king Marduk-balassu-iqbi, Vorderasiatisches Museum (Near East Museum)

Marduk

Marduk became the high god and patron saint of the city of Babylon, and eventually secured for himself an international prestige which went far beyond the natural confines of the Babylonian Empire.

The name first appears in about 2000 BC, at which time it was of little importance, but it seems possible that originally Marduk was a solar god, for later he was remembered under a Sumerian title, meaning 'the bull calf of the sun', and indeed throughout his career Marduk was one of the gods of light.

His ascent to fame, however, was first achieved under the Amorite Dynasty of Babylon, which reached its peak in the reign of King Hammurabi, c. 1792–1750 BC. On the famous diorite monument discovered at Susa, and inscribed with the text of the Babylonian 'code' of laws, Marduk is twice mentioned in the introduction. He had been allotted 'the divine worship of the multitude of the people', and thus before the end of Hammurabi's reign had become the Babylonian national god and patron, though perhaps not yet supreme. As administrator of justice Marduk was represented on the

contemporary cylinder seals with the toothed saw that cuts decisions.

From that time onward until the Seleucid era, beginning in 312 BC, the fortunes of Babylon were inextricably bound with those of Marduk, who, however, attained his greatest authority during the renaissance of the Babylonian Empire between the end of the 7th and 6th centuries BC. It is indeed apparent that when Marduk was down, Babylon's fortunes were at their lowest ebb and three historic events illustrate the point.

First, an inscription of the Kassite king, Agum II, recalls that he brought back to Babylon the statues of Marduk and his wife, Sarpanitum, after they had been in exile in Khana for thirty years. This banishment had followed the sack of Babylon by the Hittite king, Murshilish I, in 1595 BC. Only with the triumphant restoration of these divinities did Babylon begin to rise again, but it took many centuries for Marduk to recover his prestige.

The renaissance appears to have occurred shortly before 1100 BC when the god's statue was once again recovered, this time from Elam, to the east of Babylon. The reign of Nebuchadnezzar I, who was responsible for the victory over Elam, thus marked a turning point in Mesopotamian religion. This was indeed a signal triumph, for Elam which had been a deadly menace to Babylonia, was thereafter quiescent for nearly three centuries and, doubtless, the credit went to Marduk.

A third historic event which marks once again a low ebb in the god's fortunes was the devastation of Babylon in the time of Sargon, King of Assyria, and the neglect of the god's sanctuary by Sargon's son, Sennacherib, in the years 705–703 BC. The New Year ceremonies were at that period several times suspended. But Babylon, which had suffered so much devastation under the early Sargonids, was restored to favour again by the superstitious Assyrian King

Esarhaddon. Even after the conquest of Babylon in the 6th century BC by the Persian monarch Cyrus, the fortunes of Marduk waxed strong, though heresies in the form of worship were alleged to have been perpetrated by his predecessor, Nabonidus. Thus, Marduk's fortunes may be followed from historical records and are also attested by his fluctuating popularity as a component of personal names.

Victory Over Chaos

Information about the character of the god comes to us from religious and magical texts. First comes the famous epic of Creation, a long poem recited in the god's honour on the fourth night of the New Year's festival. It was known in antiquity as the *Enuma elish* from the first line which runs, 'when on high the heavens were not named'. There were seven tablets in all which varied in length between about 115 and 140 lines. They tell us about the creation of the universe,

Commemorative stone stela (kudurru) set up in honour of Adad-etir, an official of the Marduk Temple, by his son Marduk-balassu-iqbi. From the Temple of Marduk in Babylon

and proclaim the Babylonian belief that in the beginning the first gods were generated out of the mingling of waters which had preceded the formation of the earliest Mesopotamian slime.

As the gods multiplied there was a schism in the course of which the respectable High Gods such as Anu, Ansar, and Ea became divided against the detestable aboriginal dragon Tiamat, representing chaos and supported by her evil myrmidons. The good gods, threatened with destruction, were saved from annihilation by the birth of Marduk, son of the magical god Ea, and destined to restore order to the universe. In agreeing to fight Tiamat, Marduk struck a bargain with his superiors and was promised the power to declare fates and work miracles. The magical 'appearing and disappearing' act of Marduk's garment is a notable forerunner of the conjurors Maskelyne and Devant. The saviour's destruction of Tiamat with the aid of the Seven Winds is a theme frequently illustrated on Babylonian seals, but we cannot recognize in iconography his creation of man out of the blood of Kingu.

Marduk's victory was celebrated by his reorganization of the heavens, by a drunken thanks-offering banquet of the gods and by the decision to build Babylon, the shrines of Esagila and the ziggurat, the great temple tower.

Banquet of the Gods

At the end of the festival, Marduk led the great procession of gods which passed along the sacred way, flanked by enameled brick reliefs of lions, and his personal symbol, the Musrussu dragon, to emerge at the Akitu temple where he entertained the divine assembly to a banquet.

The belief that in the course of this festival Marduk was entombed and resurrected is based on a misinterpretation of an Assyrian text and has no foundation. It has been shown that in two late texts the resurrected god was Nergal, king of the underworld, and that this emergence probably represented the victory of the sun after the winter solstice.

The cult of Marduk flourished in Assyria from the 14th century BC onward, but in the seventh century he was displaced by the national god Assur: a late Assyrian text describing the capture of Marduk and his committal to the ordeal by water is a political tract designed to discredit the god. However, Marduk's popularity was due to his reputation as assistant magician to his father, Ea, in the rituals for alleviating sickness and misfortune, and as an exorcist. In a literary work named the *Ludlul Bel Nimeqi* Marduk appeared as the saviour of the righteous sufferer, who was a kind of Babylonian Job.

The power of the priesthood of Babylon over a dynasty of successful soldiers and notables, not of royal blood, ensured the glorification of Babylon and the rich endowment of the temples. However, the god's fame throughout the ancient world and for posterity derives from the imperial victories of Nabopolassar and Nebuchadnezzar II who rebuilt the city on a magnificent scale.

M. E. L. MALLOWAN

FURTHER READING: G. R. Driver & J. C. Miles. The Babylonian Laws. (Clarendon Press, Oxford, 1952–55, 2 vols.); S. Langdon. The Babylonian Epic of Creation. (Clarendon Press, Oxford, 1923); A. L. Oppenheim. Ancient Mesopotamia, Portrait of a Dead Civilization. (Chicago Univ. Press, 1964); H. W. F. Saggs. The Greatness that was Babylon. (Sidgwick & Jackson, 1962).

Mesopotamia

In the ancient world religion was not a distinct or optional activity but the attitude to life which gave it cohesion, meaning, and pattern. Mesopotamian religion, like Hinduism, had its roots in prehistory and was not attributed to a specific founder. Despite the 3,000 years over which the evidence extends, and the several distinct groups of peoples concerned, there is a sufficient continuum to justify treatment of the whole of the evidence as belonging to one cultural stream, and to speak of Mesopotamian 'religion' rather than 'religions'. Some distinction can be seen between the systematized theology of the scribes, which provides the bulk of the evidence and the popular religion, but since evidence of the popular religion appears only incidentally and allusively, little specific can be said of it.

Mesopotamia here means the pre-Christian cultural area approximating geographically to the modern state of Iraq. In the context of ancient times the southern part of this region is known as Babylonia, the northern as Assyria.

The earliest evidence of the occupation of southernmost Mesopotamia comes from c. 5000 BC. By 3500 BC this region was settled by the Sumerians. This ethnic group, of unknown origin, initiated a cultural revolution which gave the world writing, cities, and a corpus of religious practices and concepts. From their original area of settlement in southern Babylonia, where their city-states flourished during the third millennium, Sumerian cultural influence permeated as far north as the area later known as Assyria, but was less marked there than in the south.

The period 2750 to 2500 BC saw considerable immigration into Babylonia of peoples from the Arabian desert, speaking the Semitic language Akkadian, who in the course of their assimilation to the higher Sumerian culture profoundly modified it, not least in religion. Further Semitic immigration brought about, by c. 2000 BC, the disappearance of the Sumerians as an ethnic or cultural entity, and in the north overlaid the aboriginal inhabitants of Assyria with a mainly Semitic culture.

The beginning of the second millennium was marked by the rise of a number of Akkadian-speaking city-states, of which Babylon under Hammurabi ultimately achieved supremacy. Before 1000 BC political supremacy had passed to Assyria, which with brief intermissions remained predominant until shortly before the fall of Nineveh in 612 BC.

The Sumerians and their successors employed as their principal writing material tablets of clay, inscribed by impression with a stylus. Such tablets, virtually indestructible, have been found in hundreds of thousands. Many of them contain texts directly or indirectly related to religion, myth, or magic, one of the principal sources being libraries collected by Assyrian kings, particularly Ashurbanipal (668–629 BC) at Nineveh.

Opposite page:
Stele of Naram-Sin, the Akkadian king

Ancient man saw the universe in the form of conscious forces, which were conceived of in some specific shape. Such personification was originally not necessarily in human shape, since some of the most primitive concepts of divine powers invested them with animal aspects. Some aspects of the forces active in the world, certainly those thought of as universal gods, must have been personified by the Sumerians before their settlement in Mesopotamia. In addition, each early Sumerian settlement had its own local deity (sometimes identified with a universal deity), with attributed characteristics depending on the dominant features of the locality and community. As society developed, the deities of different settlements were brought into relationship, whilst additionally specific aspects of agriculture and technology (for example, corn or brick making) became personified in a deity. Thus arose a considerable pantheon, the names of its members being compiled in god lists before the middle of the third millennium. Genealogies of the gods, or *theogonies*, were developed to explain the relationship between deities.

The Great Gods

In one group of theogonies, Enlil is the first god, deriving from several generations of vaguely defined primeval beings. In other theogonies, this role falls to An (Akkadian Anum), with Enki (Akkadian Ea) as his son. These two concepts were theologically combined, so that heading the pantheon in its developed form there stood a triad of universal gods: Anum, the sky god and king of the gods; Enlil, 'Lord Wind', originally a wind and mountain god; and Enki (Ea), god of wisdom, originally 'Lord Earth'. Though Anum was nominally king of the gods, executive power was in the hands of Enlil, who often in practice usurped the supremacy. In the mythology of historical times the sphere of Ea's activity was the cosmic sweet waters (Apsu) beneath the earth, probably as a result of the Sumerian Enki absorbing the attributes of a divinity of an earlier stage of religion.

A second group of deities comprised the moon god Nannar (Sin); the sun god Utu (Shamash); Venus, known in Sumerian as Innin or Inanna, 'Lady of Heaven', and in Akkadian as Ishtar; and the weather god, who was of less importance in a purely Sumerian context than to the Semites, amongst whom he was called Adad. These four gods, manifestly related to the diurnal period, are specifically described as sleeping during part of the day. Since in the latitude of Babylonia the crescent of the new moon is seen on a level axis like a boat, Sin was said to ride across the sky in a holy ship. Though, like the other great gods, thought of also anthropomorphically, he bore the epithet 'Brilliant Young Bull', and in a myth took that form to impregnate a cow.

The sun god rode across the heavens in a chariot drawn by mules. It was to him that prayers were addressed by those who lived by the ancient pre-agricultural pursuits of hunting and fishing, although all civilized men bowed to him at his rising. Seeing all that happened on earth, he became god of justice and the divine lawgiver, and also controlled omens. He was sometimes thought to pass through the underworld at night.

The importance of Adad, the weather god, increased as one left Babylonia, a region watered almost wholly by irrigation, and moved northwestward into areas dependent upon rain. Because of the sound of his voice in thunder, Adad was associated with the bull: he was also represented by the lightning symbol.

Inanna-Ishtar, a very complex figure, Queen of Heaven and Earth, the only prominent goddess of historical times, seems to have personified the vital forces of the crises of life. She

'Winged deity by the sacred tree', a relief from the palace of Ashurnasirpal II at Kalhu, Nimrud. Alabaster, 9th century BC. Hermitage Museum, St. Petersburg, Russia

could be felt as the loving mother who had suckled the king, or as the goddess controlling sexual powers, or as goddess of battle. She was also associated in myth and popular religion with a consort Dumuzi (Tammuz), a fertility deity who was annually lamented when absent in the underworld.

Other deities of major significance included Marduk, originally an aspect of the sun god. As god of Babylon, he ultimately achieved supremacy in the Babylonian pantheon, assimilating the characteristics of Enlil; he was also equated with a god Asallukhi, in which context, he was god of magic. Nabu, god of Borsippa, the nearest city to Babylon, was (probably for this geographical reason) regarded as Marduk's son; he was also patron of the scribal profession. The latter function had earlier been attributed to a Sumerian goddess Nisaba, and the conflict between the two concepts was resolved by Nisaba being (by the first millennium) regarded as Nabu's wife. In Assyria it was Ashur, originally the Assyrian tribal god, who ultimately usurped leadership in the pantheon, bearing the title 'the Assyrian Enlil'. Another god who became of particular significance in Assyria was the warrior god Ninurta, son of Enlil.

Though there are indications in mythology that a number of female deities originally held a significant place in Sumerian religion, from the beginning of the second millennium the only goddess of independent significance other than Inanna (Ishtar) was Ereshkigal, Queen of the Underworld, and even in her case a myth describes how she gained a dominant spouse, Nergal. Each of the male deities had a nominal consort, sometimes a pale reflection bearing the feminine

form of his own name, sometimes an old Sumerian goddess who originally served an independent function in the pantheon or even existed before the developed pantheon.

The great gods, whilst regarded as being concerned with the life of Babylonia and Assyria as a whole, might at the same time be thought of as having their abode particularly in a certain city or cities. Anum lived in Erech or Der, for instance, and Shamash in Sippar or Larsa. The deities were in no sense tied to these places but if the proper rites were performed, an aspect of the deity might take up residence in an image, which then represented the god's presence and became a focus of the cult, although the god was not theologically thought of as bounded by the visible statue. A considerable wardrobe of clothing, insignia, and jewelry would be available to dress and adorn the god's image. Daily food

offerings were made, and privileged persons, including the king, might be permitted to eat the food remaining from the god's meal table. The deities, in the form of the statues, might upon appropriate occasions make journeys from one shrine to another, either by ship or upon the shoulders of bearers. Their accidental movements on such occasions were of great significance as omens to bystanders.

There is some ambiguity about the relationship felt to exist between Mesopotamian man and the great gods. On the one hand, the great gods were concerned not with the individual but with the maintenance of cosmic and political order and the course of Nature. On the other hand, there are indications that the relationship between a worshipper and a god might be felt as a very intimate one. In the third millennium, Gudea, a city ruler, says to his god: 'You are my father, you are my mother'.

In general, the gulf between the worshipper and the great gods was bridged by the concept of the 'personal god', a minor deity rather like a guardian angel, who could bring the supplication of the ordinary man before the major deities. It seems probable that only a king would have a major deity as his personal god.

Defeated Gods

Behind the deities prominent in historical times there are traces of an earlier stage of religion, hinted at in the genealogies of the gods, and represented in myths and incantations which mention divine beings thought of as slain, defeated, or suppressed. Whilst the deities of historical times are primarily anthropomorphic, some of the divine powers of the earlier stage were conceived in animal form. Anzu (or Zu), a divine being who once challenged the great gods, had the form of a bird, whilst Tiamat, the primeval being from whom in one myth the gods originated, was some-

times represented as a dragon, and another proto-deity whose attributes were absorbed by Ea may have been thought of as an ibex. The supersession of the earlier stage of religion is reflected not only in the various combat myths, but also in the fact that the victor gods bear the characteristics, and sometimes the names or titles, of those they overcome. Thus Ea not only overcame Apsu, the primeval waters, but bore the title 'the Ibex of the Apsu' and is even identified with Apsu. Ninurta not only defeated Anzu, but had applied to him the name Imdugud, elsewhere used of Anzu. Marduk not only subdued Tiamat's marshal Kingu, but could actually be called Kingu.

The number of deities in the pantheon was ultimately much reduced by identifying one deity with another or with aspects of another. For example, one hymn specifically states that a number of great deities are incorporated in the god Ninurta. Such a process would logically have concluded in

monotheism. The claim has been made that this was actually achieved in Babylonia, but this remains questionable.

Like a Thrusting Bull

Myths, either as long literary productions or embedded in fragmentary form in incantations, ritual texts or hymns, are known in both Sumerian and Akkadian. The value of myths for the understanding of Mesopotamian religion has been variously estimated, one extreme view being that they primarily reflect primitive stories from the remote past rather than anything in the religious experience of Mesopotamian man of the second or first millennium. Against this, whilst their origin was certainly (in most instances) very ancient, their use until a late period in incantations indicates that they were still felt to have some relevance to the supernatural forces affecting mankind.

The main themes of myths concern (with variations between Sumerian and Akkadian examples) the creation and organization of the physical universe, the creation of the gods and their functions, the creation of man, the origin and prehistory of the existing order, the origin of disease and healing, and stories of the Flood and the underworld.

A Sumerian myth of creation offers an insight into the concept of the relationship between the gods and mankind. The composition begins with an account of the difficulties confronting the gods in obtaining their food. Their complaint is brought before Enki, god of wisdom, who describes to his mother how to make servants by moulding clay in the image of the gods. Theologically, this reflects the view that mankind exists primarily to serve the gods. When the creation of man has been successfully achieved, Enki and his mother, having become intoxicated in celebration, proceed to make seven abnormal beings, this part of the story being an attempt to explain the occurrence of malformed humans.

The myth of 'Enki and the World Order' described how Enki produced the features of the world as known to the Sumerians. He it was who had given cattle to the nomad 'who builds no city, who builds no house', and he it was who had decreed for the various lands their characteristic products, and who had instituted the various aspects of agriculture. A typical passage described how in the manner of a bull he impregnated the Tigris, giving it fertility, and making its water available for irrigation.

> *Like a thrusting bull he*
> *stood proudly,*
> *He produced an erection,*
> *he ejaculated,*
> *He filled the Tigris with*
> *clear water . . .*
> *The water he produced is*
> *clear water . . .*
> *The grain he produced . . .*
> *the people eat it.*

Some Sumerian myths reflect very early cultural advances or changes. The earliest Sumerian settlements were in the extreme south around Eridu, but the cultural centre subsequently moved north to Erech; this situation is reflected in the following myth. Inanna, goddess of Erech, visited Eridu, whose patron Enki, god of wisdom, had in his charge a collection of objects basic to civilization, called in Sumerian 'me', and representing features of civilization which in modern terms would mainly be thought of as abstract concepts, but which the Sumerians, conceiving

them as embodied in their symbols, could regard as physical entities. They included such aspects of Sumerian life as kingship and royal insignia, various priestly offices, sexual relations and prostitution, musical instruments, truth and falsehood, various crafts, peace and victory. A feast ensued at which Enki, generous in his wine, gave these functions over to Inanna. Subsequently repenting of his generosity,

The other gods proving powerless to challenge her, Ea's virile son Marduk appeared as champion on condition that he should receive supreme power . . .

Enki dispatched monsters to intercept Inanna on her voyage home, but failed in his attempt.

One of the most striking myths, centreed on Inanna (Ishtar) and extant, with variations, in both Sumerian and Akkadian versions, describes the visit of the goddess to the underworld, for reasons which are not made explicit but which some scholars have suggested (on little evidence) was to gain possession from her older sister Ereshkigal. Inanna's descent took her through seven gates, at each of which the gatekeeper removed part of her garments and insignia. Emerging through the final gate naked, she encountered the deathly glance of Eresh-kigal and the judges of the underworld, and became a corpse.

Anticipating disaster, Inanna had left her vizier, Ninshubur, with instructions to seek help from various other deities, if she did not return within three days. After unsuccessfully visiting Enlil in Nippur, and the moon god in Ur, Ninshubur went to Enki in Eridu. Enki created two sexless creatures (possibly a reflection of the occurrence of eunuchs in the cult of Inanna) and sent them to Ereshkigal, from whom after they had

ingratiated themselves, they were to beg the corpse of Inanna as a gift. The creatures then restored Inanna to life, but the rules of the underworld permitted her to leave only if she provided a substitute. Her return to the earth was therefore in the company of ghouls, serving as wardens. At the first two cities Inanna visited, she found the city god in mourning for her, and in gratification exempted them from being taken as substitute. At the third town, a suburb of her own city Erech, she found the god Dumuzi, her own spouse, rejoicing instead of lamenting. In chagrin she handed him over to the representatives of the underworld who, despite desperate attempts by Dumuzi to escape, finally took him prisoner, to Inanna's ultimate grief.

Amongst myths preserved only or primarily in Akkadian the best known is the relatively sophisticated Creation myth 'Enuma elish' ('When above'). Recited at Babylon during the New Year festival, this began with a description of the origin of the universal deities Anum and Ea from a chain of beings descended from the primeval Tiamat and Apsu, the cosmic ocean and sweet waters. Eventually the bustling activities of the younger gods disturbed the primeval beings, and conflict ensued. After Ea had overcome Apsu, Tiamat herself entered into hostilities.

The other gods proving powerless to challenge her, Ea's virile son Marduk appeared as champion on condition that he should receive supreme power in the pantheon. With this granted, he fought and defeated Tiamat, splitting her body like a shellfish, and spreading it out as heaven and earth. From the blood of Kingu, leader of the host of Tiamat, Marduk created man, and imposed on him the service of the gods. In gratitude to Marduk the other gods built him a shrine in Babylon.

This myth reflects theological ideas concerning the origin of man (created to serve the gods but yet containing a divine element), and also concerning the reason for the political supremacy of Babylon.

The myth of 'Adapa', the ending of which is missing, concerns the limitations of human beings in the face of the gods. A fisherman, Adapa, was summoned to heaven for breaking the wing of the south wind. After Anum had forgiven him, he had immortality within his grasp when the supreme god offered him the bread and water of life but—falsely advised by Ea— Adapa rejected these gifts.

In the relatively late myth of the pestilence god Erra, datable in origin to the end of the second millennium, Erra is represented as offended by mankind's neglect of his cult. He therefore came to Marduk, god of Babylon, to pick a quarrel. By this period Marduk had acquired attributes originally belonging to Anum, and was called 'king of the gods'. For reasons which are not clear, Marduk had to leave his city to go to the underworld, and conciliated Erra by allowing him to take charge during his absence. Breaking trust, Erra proceeded to devastate Babylonia, including the capital itself. Finally Erra's anger was calmed by his vizier, and he confessed himself at fault. This may represent a mythological explanation of an outbreak of plague in Babylon, possibly during the New Year festival, when on the human level the city was dangerously crowded and on the mythic level Marduk was, for part of the period, absent. The epilogue states that the presence of this myth in a house will give protection against plague, and it is known that extracts from this myth served as amulets.

The Prowling Dogs

The great gods were probably of less immediate concern to the ordinary man than the demonic powers with which his imagination peopled the world. Spirits were of many kinds, including both ghosts of humans who had come to a violent or tragic end— 'a man lying dead in the open country, uncovered with earth', 'a weeping nursing mother'—and nonhuman devils, amongst others the 'Croucher', the 'Seizer', the 'Ghoul', Lilith and Lamashtu, a female spirit which preyed upon women in childbirth and upon infants. Such spirits lurked in corners, in graveyards and in the desert. They were likened to prowling dogs, and their motion could be so rapid that they were said to flit past like shooting stars. They could get into houses by many means:

A door cannot exclude them,
A bolt cannot turn them back;
They slither through the door like
*   a snake,*
They blow in by the hinge like
*   the wind;*
They bear off the wife from a
*   man's embrace,*
They snatch the son from a
*   man's knee.*

A vast corpus of magical incantations and rituals grew up to deal with them, some collected into series which developed a standard form. Amongst these the principal are Utukku limnutu, 'Evil Spirits', and Asakku limnutu, 'Evil Disease-demons'. Typically these contain incantations and ritual instructions represented as derived from Enki (Ea) and his son Marduk, god of magic. These were used by the exorcist, who spoke in the name of Enki:

I am the man of Enki! . . .
The great Lord Enki (Ea) has
*   sent me;*
He has put his pure spell to my spell;
He has put his pure mouth to
*   my mouth;*
He has put his pure spittle to
*   my spittle;*
He has put his pure prayer to my
*   prayer . . .*
By the magic of the word of
*   Enki (Ea),*
Those evil ones will be taken away.

Some of the incantations in these series contain fragments of ancient myths. Others were strictly limited to a ritual and an incantation. For example: 'If dead men keep appearing, it is 'Hand of Ishtar'. To drive the dead men away, you shall mix vinegar with river water, well water, mundu water (uncertain meaning) and ditch water. You shall fill an ox horn, and you shall raise the horn in your right hand and a torch in your left hand and say thus: 'My (personal) god, turn to me! My (personal) goddess, look on me! Let your angry hearts be calm; let your ire be appeased; set forth well-being for me'.

Magic, which in the hands of the exorcist could protect Mesopotamian man from the attack of demons, in the hands of sorcerers (male or female) could be directed against humans. Such antisocial use of magic is widely attested from the beginning of the second millennium, being legislated against by the Laws of Hammurabi. The typical technique in witchcraft was making an image of the victim which was then destroyed, often by burning, but anything closely connected with the intended victim could be used to gain magical power over him.

Evil persons might also make use of the magical properties of spittle. When one spat, the decent thing to do was to rub it out with the foot, but a worker of black magic might deliberately omit this, in order to gain power over the person walking over it. Sorcerers themselves could be counterattacked by magical means. Thus we find a cylinder-seal employed against a witch. The seal was twirled to the accompaniment of a

The remedy for all these was of the same kind. Incantations were recited by the exorcist and the patient was then handed an onion, a date, a piece of matting, and tufts of wool. Each of these he had to pull apart and throw into the fire. Accompanying the destruction of each was an incantation of the following type: 'Like this onion which he peels and throws into the fire . . . so may oath, curse . . . pain, weariness, guilt, sin, wickedness, transgression, the pain which is in my body, my flesh, my sinews, be peeled off like this onion'.

Another procedure used to dispose of evil influences was to absorb them into some substance or animal. The following simple example describes the method of calming a feverish child by transferring the evil contagion to a dog: 'You shall place a loaf on the child's head; you shall recite a (previously specified) incantation three times; you shall wipe (with the loaf) from the (child's) head to his feet, you shall throw that loaf to a dog. That child will be calm'.

The threat of evil powers, in the form of demons, witchcraft, and other forces released by breach of taboo, came to a climax in relation to the king himself. Many rituals and incantations and a vast corpus of taboo were designed to protect him, and the land whose well-being resided in him, from such perils. He might even resign his throne temporarily to a substitute to escape the dire consequences when particularly grave evils were foretold.

The gods were thought to determine in advance the details of a man's

suitable incantation—'O witch, like the twirling of this seal (of green stone), may your face spin and turn green'—whereupon the witch was herself 'put into a spin'. The principal incantations and rituals against witches and sorcerers were collected in a series known as Maqlu ('Burnings'), so called because the typical rituals involved burning images of the sorcerer or witch or related demonic powers, to the accompaniment of an incantation to the fire god.

Extraction of Curses

Not only the deliberate activities of witches and sorcerers but also the commission, even accidentally and unwittingly, of certain tabooed acts, could bring evil supernatural influences upon a man. Curses (not necessarily spoken words) were regarded as physical things which could enter a man's body and by suitable means could be extracted again.

Troubles of this kind were dealt with by another series of incantations, called Shurpu (a term also meaning 'Burnings', but in a different sense from Maqlu). The victim was diagnosed as suffering from one of an undifferentiated list of offenses, including both deeds which would in terms of modern thought be taken as ethical offenses and those which were simply accidental breaches of a taboo. Thus the sufferer might have:

Eaten what is taboo to his god,
Estranged son from father, father
from son,
Despised his parents, offended the
elder sister,
Said 'There is' when there was not,
Had intercourse with his
neighbour's wife,
Shed his neighbour's blood,
Slept in the bed of a person under
a curse.
Drunk from the cup of a person
under a curse.

life, or events relating to the future of a city or nation. By using proper means, men could obtain a glimpse of these 'destinies'. Many forms of divination developed to this end, some available to the common man, others restricted to the king and matters of statecraft. Amongst the principal techniques were extispicy, observation of animal behaviour, interpretation of dreams, and astrology.

Extispicy involved the slaughtering of a lamb and the examination of its internal organs. A question having been previously put to the sun god, his answer could be read by the experts in the configurations and markings of the organs, particularly the lungs and liver.

Omens could be obtained in simpler manner from random events, in particular the behaviour of animals, and there arose large compilations listing these. If ants were seen fighting, this foretold 'approach of the enemy; there will be the downfall of a great army'. If a white dog cocked its leg against a man, hard times would follow, though if it were a brown dog, the man would receive happiness.

For the interpretation of dreams, to which much importance was attached in later Assyria, a 'Dream Book' existed, giving the interpretation of some hundreds of dream incidents. Astrology, also important in imperial Assyria, used meteorological or celestial phenomena to predict matters relating to the king or the state. For example: 'During the night Saturn came near the moon. Saturn is the 'star' of the sun. This is the solution: it is favourable to the king, (because) the sun is the king's star'. This divination technique was used many centuries before the development of horoscopic astrology, applicable to a particular individual, which, although it also had its origin in Mesopotamian civilization, did not arise until the latest stage, at about 400 BC.

H. W. F. SAGGS

Bust of Roman Mithras, from the Roman colony at Arles (*Colonia Iulia Paterna Arelatensium Sextanorum*, erstwhile province of Gaul)

FURTHER READING: S. N. Kramer. The Sumerians. *(Chicago Univ. Press, 1971); A. L. Oppenheim.* Ancient Mesopotamia, Portrait of a Dead Civilization. *(Chicago Univ. Press, 2nd rev. ed., 1977); R. Thompson, comp.* The Devils and Evil Spirits of Babylonia, *2 vols. (AMS Press, 1976, cl. 903–4); G. Van Driel.* Cult of Assur. *(Humanities, 1969).*

Mithras

During the period between 1400 BC and 400 AD Persians, Indians, Romans, and Greeks worshipped the god Mithras. The god was particularly important in the old polytheistic religion of the Persians between the 8th and 6th centuries BC and again in the Roman Empire in the 2nd and 3rd centuries AD. No direct evidence remains of Persian paganism, and if we wish to get an idea of this polytheistic religion we must fall back on reconstruction from texts of a later period. Plenty of material is available, however, and many points can be discovered which are very probably accurate.

There are four important sources for Mithraism. The first is a cuneiform script tablet from Boghazköi in Turkey which contains a contract between the

Hittites and the Mitanni, an Iranian-speaking tribe in Mesopotamia c. 1400 bc. In this contract, Mithras is invoked as a god before whom an oath may be sworn. Secondly, there are some Indian texts in which the god Mitra appears as a 'friend' and as a 'contract', and has connections with the sun. Unwillingly, he participates in the sacrifice of the god Soma, who frequently appears in the form of a bull or as the moon. Thirdly, great hymns of praise (yashts) were written, probably in the fifth century, in honour of Mithra and the goddess Anahita. The Mithraic yasht extolled the god as the Lord of Contract, who in war grants victory and in peace prosperity. Finally, the Roman monuments reveal some important aspects of Mithraic mysteries that spread to far-flung areas of the Empire.

By comparing these sources we may infer that in Persian paganism Mithras was a god of friendship and of contract and had close connections with the sun. These three points are interrelated, as contracts are the basis of friendship among people; as a witness to contracts the sun has often been called upon, as he is all-seeing. The sacrifice of bulls was also part of the Mithraic cult. It is closely connected with Mithras as god of contracts, as in ancient times contracts were sanctioned through common sacrifice and a common feast. According to Plutarch, Mithras was the 'mediator'. This corresponds to what we know about the old Persian Mithras. The contract as a bond between humans, friendship and feasting after the sacrifice which was a unifying force, and the sacrifice itself linking men with the gods are all examples of Mithras's role as a mediator. Mithras, the sun, was in old Persian times also closely connected with kingship. People swore oaths by the king and

by the sun. Kingship also incorporated above all else the idea of law and order at a time when the abstract concept of the state was still unknown and there were no written laws. Order was visibly present in the person of the king; the king was the law, and when he died chaos erupted, as law and order were gone.

The Persian social system was feudal, in the sense that there were no abstract legal rights and duties but only reciprocal personal obligations between man and woman, parents and children, lord and peasant, and so on. Mithras, who represented law and order, was the divine exponent of the Persian system as god of contracts and of all reciprocal relationships.

Eclipsed by Zoroaster

The Persian religion was completely changed by Zoroaster. The exact period of the prophet's life is uncertain; at the latest it was about 550 bc, perhaps considerably earlier. Zoroaster taught that there was a single god, Ahura Mazdah and he rejected the other

gods of the old Persians. The Persian word *daivas*, which originally meant 'gods', has since Zoroaster signified 'evil demons'. Zoroaster fought passionately against polytheism and against Mithras. He protested against the bull sacrifice, the principal festival of the Mithraic religion. In later generations, the doctrinal teaching of Zoroaster was gradually interspersed with elements of the older polytheism, and the wide gap between the two religions was bridged by compromise. After Darius, who died in 486 bc, the Persian kings were Zoroastrians. But the aristocracy probably continued to be attached to Mithras and the old gods. Despite this difference of opinion, the Persian kings seem to have made allowance for those social groups who did not want to replace the old cults entirely by Zoroastrianism. Indeed, the kings were practical politicians, and considerate of the feelings of their subjects. In the 4th century bc the Kings Artaxerxes II and III mentioned Mithra and the goddess Anahita in their inscriptions. But by this time, Zoroastrianism was

Ardeshir II, the eleventh Sassanid King of Persia from 379 to 383 AD

the dominant factor in the blending of the two religions and we hear no more of the Mithraic bull sacrifice.

After the destruction of the Persian Empire by Alexander the Great, nothing more is heard about the Persian worship of Mithras. Yet over three centuries later Mithras was worshipped in the states between the Parthian Empire and the Graeco-Roman world, for example in Armenia, where Mithras was again god of kings and feudalism. In a Mithraic ceremony, King Tiridates I submitted to the Roman Emperor Nero in the 1st century AD and made his kingdom a fief under Nero's control. Mithras was also the god of the kings of Commagene, to the south of Armenia. It is likely that Mithridates of Pontus (1st century BC), the great enemy of the Romans, worshipped Mithras; his kingdom included the northern coast of modern Turkey, and the Crimea. Finally, we know from Plutarch that the pirates of Cilicia, the south coast of Turkey, also worshipped Mithras during this period. On the other hand, Mithras was of no importance in the Greek-populated areas of Asia Minor. The Persians were the national enemies of the Greeks and consequently their god Mithras had no chance of success with the Greeks.

Powerful Roman Following

It is an open question whether the Roman Mithras mysteries were the same religion as the Persian Mithraic cult. The Persian religion changed to accommodate the different conditions of the Roman Empire. Certainly, many elements of the old religion were retained, but at the same time the Roman theology contained elements unknown to the Persians. For example, the Romans took their doctrine of the fate of the soul from Plato's philosophy. One

could say that the Roman mysteries were a completely new religion. It may be that there were one or more founders of the new cult, dating from perhaps c. 100 AD. The dated Roman Mithras monuments start from c. 140 AD.

It is puzzling how this religion came to Rome. It is unwise to postulate that its spread can be compared to the spread of the Christian mission, for the Mithras mysteries were addressed to entirely different social strata, to the soldiers and officials in the imperial service, and only men were initiated into the cult. It has been suggested that the Mithraic cult spread slowly, by way of Syria and Asia Minor, and then came to Rome by sea. However, this theory is contradicted by the hostility of the Greeks in Asia Minor toward the god. It has also been suggested that the Roman legions became acquainted with the cult of Mithras on the Persian frontier and that when troops were moved from the eastern front to Europe they brought Mithras with them to the west. It should be remembered, however, that a religion would only have been able

to spread in the army of the Roman emperors if it were regarded favourably by those at the top. It is therefore probable that the founder, or founders, of the Roman Mithraic mysteries must have been active in Rome itself, and that he or they must have enjoyed the benevolent encouragement of higher generals, perhaps even of the *praefectus praetorio*, the commander of the Praetorian Guard. The Mithras cult was probably introduced into the legions from above, by officers who were posted from their headquarters in Rome to legions on the frontiers of the empire.

The geographical distribution of archeological finds supports this hypothesis. Many Mithraic remains have been excavated in Rome and in areas of military conflict on the frontiers, such as the Euphrates, Danube, Rhine, and in Britain; but almost none have been found in the pacified provinces such as Gaul or Spain, apart from the Mithraeum or temple in Mérida, Spain, the seat of the Roman governor.

There are numerous Mithras initiation inscriptions that do not originate

Mithras killing a sacred bull (*tauroctony*), side A of a two-faced Roman marble relief, c. 2nd or 3rd centuries AD

Mount Nemrut—West Terrace. On the left, the head of Apollo/Mithra/Helios/Hermes, an indication of the deity becoming interchangeable upon each conquering of the area

from soldiers but from officials in the imperial service, particularly from freedmen who were able to obtain very influential positions in finance and customs administration if they proved their worth. Such men worshipped one god only if it did not prejudice their career. It is characteristic of the Mithraic cult that it was a religion of loyalty, of respect for the social system, unlike Christianity which was a religion of rebellious aloofness from the state, and of revolutionary hope in the Last Judgment.

Initiation Underground

The Mithraic sanctuaries in the Roman world were underground grottoes. The ceiling symbolized the heavens, and the cavern the world. The chambers were never very large, with space for barely 100 men. Around the central chamber there were sometimes labyrinthine systems of artificial passages, as beneath the church of St. Clemente in Rome. There was always a spring in the cavern. The Mithraic monuments were certainly not built secretly below

ground, but a hole was dug in the same way as when a cellar is constructed, perhaps behind a high fence.

There were seven grades of initiation into the Mithraic mysteries, each with a symbolic name: corax (raven), nymphus (bridegroom), miles (soldier), leo (lion), Perses (Persian), heliodromus (courier to the sun), pater (father). The raven wore a raven's mask, the lion a lion's mask, the Persian a Persian cap, and so on. Literary records state that the initiate into the Mithraic mysteries had to submit to corporal punishment, that he was bound and then released. The initiation signified a ritually symbolic regeneration. The person being initiated as a 'soldier' had to undergo a test of courage. He had to force his way, apparently by means of a duel, to a wreath. This done, an officiant came up to him and put the wreath on his head, but the candidate had to reject the wreath and say that Mithras was his wreath. For the rest of his life he was not permitted to wear a wreath, as this honour was due only to the god.

There were various initiation

ceremonies, such as baptism, the common meal, obligation through shaking hands (in this ceremony we can recognize the old Persian god of contract). Those being initiated wandered through the underground passages; at some points passwords were demanded. On one fresco at Ostia, in Italy, the mystic is dressed as a 'bridegroom'. In Rome beneath St. Prisca the fresco depicts a procession of 'lions'. At Capua, Italy, the initiate is being led toward the initiation point with his eyes bound. He then kneels down before the mystagogue (teacher or leader) who wears a Persian cap, and finally lies stretched out, humbly on the ground.

On some occasions lighting effects were used: there were reliefs which could be illuminated from the rear revealing a crescent or the head of Mithras or Sol (the sun) surrounded by a halo. There were also statues of Chronos, the god of time who swallows everything, which were hollow at the back and able to spit fire. At some shrines the relief showing the sacrifice

of the bull, at the end of the grotto, could be turned round, revealing on the other side, for example, the common repast of Mithras and Helios. Either side could be shown, according to the demands of the liturgy.

Some verses from hymns of the Mithraic mysteries have been found as wall inscriptions under the church of St. Prisca in Rome. There are also frescoes testifying to a syncretism of the Persian with old Roman ceremonies. The Mithraic sacrifice of the bull is connected with the old Roman feast of Suovetaurilia (the sacrifice of a boar, a ram, and a bull); this sacrifice was offered up on the day of Palilia, another old Roman festival, when the founding of the city of Rome was celebrated. Suovetaurilia and Palilia were Roman national festivals, which were celebrated under the patronage and with the participation of the emperor. The Mithraeum under St. Prisca, where these representations may be seen, lay in a large complex of buildings which were imperial property. The Persian religion was thus set completely into an 'old Roman' framework, with the approval and even the encouragement of the emperor; in particular the Emperors Commodus, Septimius Severus, and Caracalla probably favoured the Mithraic mysteries, for an exceptionally large number of dated Mithraic inscriptions originate from their period. Also characteristic of the blend of Persian and Roman ideas is a representation found in a Mithraeum at Ostia of the Roman god Silvanus, and instead of *pater* in the inscriptions we sometimes read *Pater patratus*. This is an old Roman title for a priest whose task it was to form alliances. Thus, in the service of the Persian god of contract, there was the renewal of a priest's title which had been in use in ancient Rome for the negotiation of contracts.

From Death to Cosmic Birth

The sacrifice of the bull had been the great holy deed of Mithraism. The sun god, through his messenger, the raven, had commanded Mithras to sacrifice the bull; on some reliefs the raven flies to Mithras on a sunbeam. The god carried out the sacrifice with great reluctance: in many representations he is sadly averting his gaze, he is innocent of the animal's suffering. But when the bull died, a great miracle occurred—the world began: the cloak of Mithras was changed into a celestial globe on which planets, the zodiac and fixed stars were shining; the white bull, now a crescent, was moved into the heavens. (Luna, the moon goddess, is seen in the reliefs frequently averting her eyes from the sacrifice.) From the tail and from the blood of the bull arose ears of corn and the vine. Then came all the trees and plants, the four elements, the winds and the seasons; from the seed which issued from the bull there arose the good animals and all living things. This Mithraic deed was a blessing: 'Thou hast saved us also by pouring out the blood eternal', according to one of the few verses we have obtained from a Mithraic hymn. The power of evil wanted to prevent the creation; the scorpion, snake and lion try to drink the seed of the bull. Evil will not be destroyed until the end of time; as long as he is on earth man must always struggle for good and against evil.

Particularly instructive is a relief in London on which Mithras is sacrificing the bull not in the cavern but in the celestial sphere, which is indicated by the zodiac: the heavens arose following the sacrifice of the bull. Each sunrise signifies a repetition of this cosmogony. The stars began to revolve in the sky, and this was the birth of time. The sun circling around the earth caused the day, the orbit of the moon the months, and the path of the sun through the zodiac (the ecliptic) the years.

There are numerous other Mithraic myths to be seen in the reliefs, often in the small pictures near the main scene: the birth of Mithras from a tree; Mithras shooting at the cloud with an arrow (bringing the rain), or at the rock (causing a spring to gush forth); cutting the corn; taming the bull; his contract with the sun god; the holy meal; the ascent to heaven on the chariot of the sun god. The myth of the birth of Mithras from the rock has the same significance as the sun rising over the mountains on the horizon and the cosmogony in the sacrifice of the bull. The birth of Mithras from an egg depicted on the relief at Newcastle-upon-Tyne shows the egg turning into a celestial globe, represented by the zodiac; here Mithras is equated with the Orphic primeval god Phanes (Eros) who arose out of the egg.

The Mithraic myths have been interpreted into a complete theology, in accordance with the Platonic myths. The cavern of the mysteries was the world, as in the cave allegory of the Platonic state. The mystic had to try to free himself from the shackles of materialism and ascend to the true sun, like Mithras on the chariot of the sun god. The way up led through the spheres of the seven planets, a progress already anticipated on earth in the Mithraic initiations, when the mystics ascended through the seven grades of initiation, each of which was related to a planet. This ascent was symbolized by the seven-runged ladder at Ostia; at each initiation the mystic passed through a new gate. On the reliefs at Capua and Rome there is the Platonic Eros, or the Orphic Phanes (Mithras), guiding the psyche of the mystic. The ascent of Mithras has been compared with the ascent of the soul to the firmament in Plato's *Phaedras*.

The cosmogony of the mysteries was interpreted from the cosmogony in Plato's *Timaeus*. Mithras was named 'father and creator of the universe', in words reminiscent of the *Timaeus* and the attack by the evil animals, shown on the reliefs, corresponds with the attack of the elements on the newborn babe in the *Timaeus*. Above all, however, the dualistic outlook of Persian religion found its philosophical interpretation in the two rotations of the heavens seen on the Mithraic reliefs: the constant rotation of the vault of heaven with the fixed stars to the right and the variable orbit of the planets through the zodiac to the left. From the combination of these revolutions arose inconstant time. But man must strive for the eternal and, by passing the gods of the planets, ascend to the one true eternal.

This Platonizing interpretation of the Mithraic myths is secondary in relation to the old Persian religion; but the Roman mysteries were probably first established on the basis of this allegorical interpretation. The founder or founders of the religion must have been Platonists. They rendered the philosophical teachings into the myths and rites of the Persian god and thus created an entirely new religion.

The Mithraic mysteries were therefore completely Hellenized and Romanized. The Persian god could be accepted as a traditional god of the Romans. There is a characteristic inscription from Carnuntum, near Vienna, from the year 307 AD: the old Emperor Diocletian had consulted with the reigning emperors in order to settle disputes; together they restored a Mithraic sanctuary and dedicated it 'to the patrons of their empire'. The cult was to thrive as long as the emperors supported it.

Under Constantine the Great the Mithraic cult lost imperial favour. He publicly supported Christianity and while there are several dated Mithraic monuments up to 312 AD, after that there is only one from the military frontiers of the empire.

A collection of inscriptions from Rome, in which Mithras is mentioned, are dated from 357 to 387 and originate from the group of pagan Roman senators who had rebelled against the new Christian Empire in Constantinople. They were connected with the Emperor Julian the Apostate, who had wanted to reintroduce paganism into the whole empire. These cults of the Roman opposition are no longer characteristic of the Mithraic mysteries, as at that time in Rome a fierce syncretism was being practiced; the inscriptions mention Mithras only as one of many pagan gods. The genuine Mithraic mysteries ceased under Constantine, and the triumphant Christian Church erected its basilicas above the underground Mithraic caverns in Rome.

R. MERKELBACH

Moloch

This Ammonite god of the sun was also worshipped by Pheonecians and Canaanites, perhaps by Sumerians

Moloch, from Athanasius Kircher, *Oedipus Aegyptiacus*, 1652

as well. Represented with the head of a bull, Moloch is well known for purportedly demanding the burned sacrifice of human children. The Old Testament mentions Moloch a number of times as a false god, and in particular warns Israelites not to allow their children to 'pass through the fire to Moloch', which is understood to warn against allowing children to be sacrificed. Some scholars believe that there is a ritual or nonsacrificial interpretation of 'pass through fire', perhaps a fire ceremony, but not one that involves death. Tales of sacrificing children to gods were spread later by the Greeks in a kind of propaganda campaign against Carthage, their rivals. It may be that Moloch suffered the same fate, being unfairly associated with the killing of children. Whatever the truth of the matter, the name of Moloch has come to be used as a euphemism for a practice or institution that exacts too high a price.

FURTHER READING: Ascalone, Enrico, and Frongia Rosanna M. Giammanco. Mesopotamia. *(Berkeley: University of California, 2007); Suggs, M. Jack., Katharine Doob Sakenfeld, and James R. Mueller.* The Oxford Study Bible: Revised English Bible with the Apocrypha. *(New York: Oxford UP, 1992).*

Mummification

The ancient Egyptians were not unique in their concern to preserve the bodies of their dead. But their practice of embalming dead bodies was not just an exercise of the mortician's craft; it was a religious ritual, inspired by a distinctive conception of human nature and destiny. The custom was already well established when the Pyramid Texts were composed (c. 2400 BC), and it was still being followed in the 4th century AD, when Christian influence led finally to its abandonment. Throughout that immense period, despite great vicissitudes of political fortune, the people of Egypt continued patiently to mummify not only their human dead but sacred animals also. The practice was both costly and gruesome, and its long continuance attests to the strength of the belief that inspired it.

The explanation lies in the Egyptian idea of man. The physical body was regarded as an essential constituent of the human personality, and an afterlife could not be imagined as being possible without it. As the Egyptian funerary texts show, the decomposition of the body consequent on death was profoundly feared. Action was taken to prevent it from a very early period, as passages from the Pyramid Texts show. In the first, Tait, the personification of the linen bandages used for wrapping the corpse (in this case of King Teti) is being invoked: 'Hail Tait . . . protect the head of Teti, so that it becomes not detached. Bind together the bones of Teti so that they do not fall apart'. The purpose of embalming is stated in this assurance given to King Pepi: 'they [the goddesses Isis and Nephthys] prevent thy putrefaction from flowing on the earth . . . they prevent the odor of thy corpse from being evil for thee . . . '

Magical Amulets

These passages in the Pyramid Texts refer to the process of embalming and they show that it was essentially a ritual transaction that was based upon the legend of Osiris. The Egyptians believed that the ritual reenactment, on behalf of a dead person, of the acts that were supposed once to have raised Osiris from death would ensure a similar resurrection.

But this ritual magic was reinforced by practical action, taken in the light of contemporary knowledge and experience, to preserve the corpse from physical disintegration. As the first of the passages above shows, the corpse was wrapped in linen bandages to hold it together; the other passage suggests some action to arrest its putrefaction.

Painting on papyrus of the Opening of the Mouth ritual being performed with attendant priests

This early literary evidence is supported by specimens that have been found of mummies dating from the Thinite Period (3200–2780 BC). Already attempts appear to have been made to preserve the body by the application of salt or natron, a form of soda, while the bandages were impregnated with a resinous substance and moulded to the shape of the body. In these earliest examples the body is contracted, with the arms, legs, and fingers separately bandaged. The contracted position was also used in pre-dynastic burials, when the body was not embalmed but often preserved by direct contact with the dry desert sand. The extended position later became invariable.

The technique of embalming gradually improved, though all its various stages cannot now be discerned from the available archeological material. Obviously experiments were made, with varying success. During the Middle Kingdom (2052–1567 BC), the embalmers had learned how to remove or reduce the flesh, while leaving the skin and bones intact. Mummies of this period are dark-coloured, and the skin is dry and brittle. Amulets of various kinds, giving magical protection, were placed on the body or in the wrappings; the heart scarab was already in use, being set sometimes in the breast cavity.

Artificial Eyes

During the New Kingdom (1567–1085 BC), the art of mummification developed to its highest point of achievement. This was probably due not only to increasing experience but also to Egypt's political power, which enabled the embalmers to obtain costly spices and medicaments from a wide area of Africa and the Middle East. Such notable mummies as those of Thothmes IV and Seti I attest to the ability of the embalmers of this period to preserve the facial features of the dead; artificial eyes were sometimes inserted and the contours of the face filled out by packing mud beneath the skin.

A detailed account of the process of mummification was given by the Greek historian Herodotus, who had

Beautiful Memory Picture

Alas, poor Yorick! How very surprised he would be to see how his counterpart of today is whisked off to a funeral parlour and is in short order sprayed, sliced, pierced, pickled, trussed, trimmed, creamed, waxed, painted, rouged, and neatly dressed—transformed from a common corpse into a Beautiful Memory Picture. This process is known in the trade as embalming and restorative art, and is so universally employed in the United States and Canada that the funeral director does it routinely, without consulting corpse or kin. He regards as eccentric those few who are hardy enough to suggest that it might be dispensed with.

Jessica Mitford,
The American Way of Death

The mummified head of pharaoh Seti I

The mummified head of Egyptian pharaoh King Ahmose I

Canopic jars of Neskhons, wife of Pinedjem II. Made of calcite, with painted wooden heads. Originally from the Deir el-Bahri royal cache, c. 990–969 BC

visited Egypt in the 5th century BC. Although he wrote long after the zenith of Egyptian civilization and was quite often fanciful, or misinformed, in his descriptions, his account of mummification is generally confirmed by examination of mummies. After describing the lamentation that follows a death and the taking of the body to the embalmers, he writes: 'There are a set of men in Egypt who practice the art of embalming . . . These persons, when a body is brought to them, show the bearers various models of corpses, made in wood, and painted so as to resemble Nature. The most perfect is said to be after the manner of him whom I do not think it religious to

name (Herodotus means Osiris) in connection with such a matter; the second sort is inferior to the first, and less costly; the third is the cheapest of all. All this the embalmers explain, and then ask in which way it is wished that the corpse should be prepared'.

Herodotus then describes the process: 'They take first a crooked piece of iron, and with it draw the brain through the nostrils, thus getting rid of a portion while the skull is cleared of the rest by rinsing with drugs; next they make a cut along the flank with a sharp Ethiopian stone, and take out the whole contents of the abdomen, which they then cleanse, washing it thoroughly with palm wine, and again

frequently with an infusion of pounded aromatics. After this they fill the cavity with the purest bruised myrrh, with cassia, and every sort of spicery except frankincense and sew up the opening. Then the body is placed in natron for seventy days, and covered over. After the expiration of that space of time, which must not be exceeded, the body is washed, and wrapped round, from head to foot, with bandages of fine linen cloth, smeared over with the gum which is used generally by the Egyptians in the place of glue, and in this state it is given back to the relations who enclose it in a wooden case which they have made for the purpose, shaped into the figure of a man'.

Herodotus then describes the other two methods, the first of which consisted of injecting cedar oil by syringes, which, according to the historian, dissolved the stomach and intestines and was drained out through the anus. The body was also steeped in natron, which dissolved the flesh, leaving only the skin and bones. In the third method, used by the poorer classes, the intestines were removed by clyster, a process involving the injection of a liquid, and the body soaked in natron for seventy days.

This account by Herodotus omits to mention the frequent use of bitumen for packing the cavities from which the organs had been removed. This substance had the effect of making the body black and heavy, but rendered it almost indestructible except by burning. The word 'mummy' derived, incidentally, through Byzantine Greek and Latin, from an Arabic word meaning bitumen.

The organs that were removed from the body, namely, the heart and lungs and the viscera, were separately embalmed in bitumen and wrapped in bandages. They were then placed in what are traditionally known as 'Canopic' jars, of which four were used for each person. The covers of the jars were shaped, respectively, as the heads of the four sons of the god Horus, under whose protection their contents were placed. These jars were put into a special chest and interred with the mummified body.

For burial the mummy was enclosed in a coffin. From the Middle Kingdom period onward this coffin was usually anthropoid, in the shape of a human body with the facial features carefully moulded and depicted. It was also brightly painted both inside and outside with images of protective deities,

Egyptian canopic jar

particularly of Nut, the sky goddess, and magical symbols and hieroglyphic texts taken from the Book of the Dead. The bodies of royal persons and nobles were often placed in a number of anthropoid coffins; Tutankhamen (c. 1354–1345 BC) was enclosed in three, the inner one being of pure gold. These coffins were usually placed in a massive stone sarcophagus, as if to ensure the utmost security to the dead.

The tomb in which the embalmed and coffined body was finally laid was furnished with a variety of goods, according to the status of the deceased, and it became his 'eternal house', at which food offerings were regularly made. Among this funerary equipment were 'ushabtis', little mummiform figures on which a magical text was inscribed commanding the ushabti to answer in the next world for its owner, if he were called upon to labour there.

S. G. F. BRANDON

Mut

Ancient Egyptian mother goddess, associated with the waters from which all creation sprang. Mut is depicted as a royal woman, wearing the crowns of Egypt and carrying the ankh. She is also connected to the vulture, which Egyptians believed was a species entirely composed of females and produced offspring without sexual reproduction. Female pharaohs promoted Mut in particular, with Hatshepsut establishing the largest point of worship in a temple at Karnak. Ultimately the Mut mythology blended together with Isis, after a period of time when she was said to be the wife of Ra, the sun god, and mother of Khonsu, the mood god. These three—Ra, Mut, and Khonsu—formed a triad, a typical arrangment of sacred characters in Egyptian religion. 'Mut' is the ancient Egyptian word for 'mother'.

FURTHER READING: Hornung, Erik. Conceptions of God in Ancient Egypt: The One and the Many. *(Ithaca, NY: Cornell UP, 1996); Brewer, Douglas J., and Emily Teeter.* Egypt and the Egyptians. *(Cambridge, UK: Cambridge UP, 2007); Teeter, Emily.* Religion and Ritual in Ancient Egypt. *(Cambridge: Cambridge UP, 2011).*

Ohrmazd

Ohrmazd is the Middle Persian (c. 200–700 AD) form for the Zoroastrian God who first appears in the Avesta (the sacred book of the Zoroastrians) as Ahura Mazdah, the 'Wise Lord' or the 'Lord Wisdom'. It is not known whether such a god existed before the appearance of the Iranian prophet Zoroaster, who probably flourished in the 6th century BC. It seems, however, most probable that he assumed overriding importance only with Zoroast-

Ahura Mazda (right, with high crown) presents Ardashir I (left) with the ring of kingship. (Naqsh-e Rustam, 3rd century AD)

er himself, who regarded himself as Ahura Mazdah's prophet and believed himself to be in direct communication with the god.

The oldest part of the Avesta, the Gathas, is usually considered to be, if not Zoroaster's own words, then at least directly inspired by him; and the centre of this 'revelation' is the god Ahura Mazdah, creator and sustainer of the universe. There are other divine beings beside Ahura Mazdah himself, but these are always subordinated to him and he is sometimes called their 'father'. These divine beings were later formed into a group of seven, who constituted God's 'court'. Originally, however, they seem to have been aspects of God: they are the Holy Spirit, Truth, the Good Mind, the Kingdom, Right-Mindedness, Wholeness, and Immortality. Collectively they would later be known as the Bounteous Immortals.

Ahura Mazdah, however, stands above and beyond them in the Gathas: he is their 'father' and their creator. By 'father' Zoroaster did not understand anything physical (since his God was pure spirit) but simply the origin of all things. Ahura Mazdah creates Truth, for instance, by his will or wisdom and he maintains it by the Good Mind. So too at the beginning of existence Ahura Mazdah thinks: 'Let the wide space be filled with lights', and it is so. And it is 'by his mind' that he 'fashioned forth corporeal things, consciences and wills', that 'he created bodily life, and deeds and doctrines among which men could freely make their choices'.

Ahura Mazdah is holy: and by 'holiness' the Zoroastrians understood creativity and fruitfulness. He is the creator of all good things, both spiritual and material. He thinks creation into existence and there does not seem to be any preexistent matter from

which he creates: he creates out of nothing. He is omnipotent and 'rules at will'; he is judge and in the last days will judge all men according to their good and evil deeds.

There is one thing, however, that Ahura Mazdah did not create, and that is death. His Holy Spirit is the spirit of life, and death was the work of another spirit, Angra Mainyu or the 'Destructive Spirit', who was later to be called Ahriman. In the Gathas this Destructive Spirit is the eternal adversary of God's Holy Spirit but not of God—of Ahura Mazdah—himself. The Holy Spirit is the author of life and holiness, while the Destructive Spirit is

> *Ohrmazd was on high in omniscience and goodness, for infinite time he was ever in the light. That light is the space and place of Ohrmazd.*

the author of death and diminution. And so we read: 'Of these two Spirits he who was of the Lie chose to do the worst things: but the Most Holy Spirit, clothed in rugged heaven, (chose) Truth . . .'

There is, then, an evil spirit beside the life-giving Holy Spirit of God, who brings death and destruction into the world. The evil spirit is not particularly prominent in the Gathas but was later to become an independent principle and the antagonist of God himself.

In the later Avesta the ancient 'pagan' gods reappear as helpers of Ahura Mazdah and his role is seriously impoverished. This process can also be discerned in the inscriptions of the Achaemenid kings, in the latter of which the old god Mithra and the goddess Anahita appear alongside Ahura Mazdah. Yet Ahura Mazdah remains essentially the creator of heaven and earth and of 'what is excellent on

earth'. He is the source of increase and fertility, of good order in general and of the particular 'good order' among men established and assured by the Achaemenids, the royal house of the first Persian Empire (546–330 BC).

Adversary of Evil

With the sack of Persepolis by Alexander the Great in 330 BC, Zoroastrianism, of which Ahura Mazdah was the Supreme God, ceased to have any privileged position; and it was only with the foundation of the second Persian Empire by the Sassanians in 226 AD that Zoroastrianism not only rose out of obscurity, but became the official religion of the Empire. Ahura Mazdah reemerged as Ohrmazd but, though still the same God, he was yet not quite the same.

In the course of the centuries Ohrmazd (as he was now called) had been identified with the Holy Spirit of the Gathas; and this identification caused a quite new picture to appear. The Holy Spirit had been the eternal adversary of the Destructive Spirit (Angra Mainyu, now called Ahriman), but this role now fell to Ohrmazd himself. This meant that God and the Devil were independent powers—the first wholly good and the second wholly evil, the first dwelling in eternal light, the second in eternal darkness.

'Ohrmazd was on high in omniscience and goodness; for infinite time he was ever in the light. That light is the space and place of Ohrmazd . . . omniscience and goodness are his totality . . . Ahriman, slow in knowledge, whose will is to smite, was deep down in the darkness: (he was) and is, yet will not be. The will to smite is his all, and darkness is his place'.

Such was the state of affairs in the beginning, and so it would have remained if Ahriman had left well done, but seeing 'valour and supremacy superior to his own', he was jealous of it and longed to possess it. He was not strong enough, and so he created other devils to assist him. Ohrmazd in self-defense first created the Bounteous Immortals and other kindly spirits and then the material creation—the sky, water, the earth, plants, cattle, and finally man. Strictly speaking Ahriman cannot create material things, he can only destroy or corrupt them. His first attack on Ohrmazd's spiritual creation failed, for Ohrmazd repulsed him by the power of the holy Word. His second attack on the material creation was only too successful, however. 'Like a serpent he darted forward, trampled on as much of the sky as was beneath the earth, and rended it . . . Then he fell upon the waters . . . which are below the earth; and he bored a hole in the middle of the earth and entered it thereby. He fell upon the plants . . . and upon the (primal) Bull and Gayomart (primal man); and he slew them both'. Thus the second battle ended in a complete defeat for Ohrmazd, or so it seemed.

Even so, Ohrmazd's spiritual creation remained untouched; and once Ahriman had entered the sky he found himself imprisoned within it. Moreover, the seed of Gayomart, the primal man, and of the Bull had fallen into the ground; and from there human life and the life of man's friends in the animal creation were to grow up and to carry on the good fight against Ahriman and his demonic hordes. For 3,000 years the two spiritual armies are locked in indecisive battle but in the last 3,000 years allotted to this world Ohrmazd's victory becomes every day more apparent, until in the last days Ahriman is defeated by a war of attrition; and the whole demonic creation, seeing Ohrmazd's creation elude it, falls upon itself in a suicidal civil war. Finally Ohrmazd smites Ahriman and he is expelled

into the eternal darkness in which he will remain forever unconscious, never to rise again: and all Ohrmazd's creation will be reunited with him in the eternal light and in unceasing joy forever and ever.

R. C. ZAEHNER

FURTHER READING: The Hymns of Zarathustra *tr. by M. Henning. (Hyperion, 1980); R. C. Zaehner.* The Teachings of the Magi. *(Oxford UP, 1976); and* The Dawn and Twilight of Zoroastrianism. *(McClelland, 1961).*

Osiris

The ancient Egyptian god Osiris is one of the most interesting and significant deities known to historians of religions. He is also one of the oldest gods of whom records survive; and he may rightly claim to have been worshipped longer than any other god—his cult was already well established by 2400 BC, and it continued until the forcible suppression of paganism, in favour of Christianity, in the 4th century AD.

Because Osiris was so important to them and they were so familiar with his myth or legend, the Egyptians never seem to have written a formal account of their beliefs about him. Their literature, both sacred and secular, is replete with references and allusions to him, and he is one of the figures most abundantly portrayed in their art. Yet it was left to the Greek writers Diodorus Siculus, in the 1st century BC, and Plutarch, in the following century, to provide posterity with descriptive accounts of this ancient Egyptian god, who was still a potent figure in their day. Their accounts must, inevitably, be treated with much caution; for it is unlikely that they had any direct access to Egyptian records, and they were concerned to rationalize and philosophize what they had learned from their Egyptian guides and interpreters.

However, there is reason to think that they did preserve some authentic traditions, and their accounts are significant as evidence of what Osiris had come to mean to Graeco-Roman society more than 2,000 years after he first appears in Egyptian records.

In the Pyramid Texts, which are concerned with the afterlife of the pharaohs of the 5th and 6th Dynasties, Osiris plays a strange but vital role in the mortuary ritual. Among its rubrics and spells, reference is made to his murder and the finding of his body: 'Isis comes and Nephthys . . . They find Osiris, as his brother Set laid him low in Nedjet'. Nedjet in historical times was located near Abydos, in Upper Egypt, which was the chief sanctuary of Osiris. In another text of about the same period (2400 BC) there is reference to the drowning of Osiris in the River Nile at Memphis, the ancient capital of Egypt. There are references also in other texts to the casting of Osiris's body into the Nile or to finding it upon its banks. The two traditions are not mutually exclusive; but what is consistently attested throughout all Egyptian records is that Seth murdered Osiris.

Raised by Magical Chants

The Egyptian evidence is also agreed that the corpse of Osiris was found by Isis and Nephthys, who either prevented its decomposition or restored it when decomposed by various acts of embalmment. After effecting the preservation of his body, the dead Osiris was then raised to life again. Various deities are associated in the texts and iconography with this resurrection, namely, Isis and Nephthys, Atum-Re, Anubis, and Horus. The means by which it was effected varies. Generally it would seem that magical incantation

was envisaged to resurrect the god. Sometimes a more practical way was imagined, as in depictions showing Isis and Nephthys fanning air into the inanimate Osiris with the falcon wings attached to their arms.

Although he was thus raised to life again, Osiris did not resume his earthly life in Egypt where, as the texts indicate, he had been a king. Instead, his cause against his murderer Seth was tried before a tribunal of the gods of Heliopolis. The verdict was concise: 'Guilty is Set; Osiris is just'. Osiris then became 'the lord of the West', the underworld or realm of the dead.

The legend of Osiris also involves a number of other divine figures. Isis is both the wife and sister of Osiris. Nephthys, her sister, is the consort of Seth, who is represented as both the brother and murderer of Osiris. Horus was regarded as the posthumously begotten son of Osiris. Grown to man's estate, he is represented as fighting with Seth to avenge his father and secure his patrimony. He is also described, inconsistently with his posthumous birth, as performing various mortuary offices for his father, including the ceremony of 'Opening the Mouth'.

Such, then, is the story of Osiris as it can be reconstructed from Egyptian texts. The versions of Diodorus Siculus and Plutarch are fuller narrative accounts, composed according to contemporary Graeco-Roman taste; but they preserve some outline of the basic pattern of the Egyptian original. Diodorus presents Osiris as an ancient king who taught the Egyptians the arts of civilized living, including agriculture—Isis had discovered the use of wheat and barley, which had hitherto grown wild. He is murdered by his brother Typhon (Seth is here identified with an evil monster of Greek mythology), who divided his body into twenty-six pieces, which he gave to his followers in order to implicate them in his crime. The death of Osiris is avenged by Isis and Horus, who slay Typhon. Isis recovers the parts of her husband's body, except the phallus, and buries them secretly. In order to promote the worship of Osiris, she then made exact replicas of his body and entrusted them severally to colleges of priests to bury in their local centres—this is obviously an attempt to explain the fact that several places in Egypt claimed to have the tomb or some relic of Osiris. After reigning for many years, Isis died and was deified. Memphis claimed to have her tomb; but many believed that both Osiris and Isis were buried in the island of Philae in Upper Egypt. This account by Diodorus shows no insight into the real nature of the deity or his place in Egyptian religion.

Treachery at a Banquet

According to Plutarch, Osiris was also a king who civilized both the Egyptians and the rest of mankind; he was identified by the Greeks with their god Dionysus. After the return of Osiris from his world travel, Seth planned his death with the help of seventy-two fellow conspirators. Having secretly measured the body of Osiris, Seth made a beautiful chest, richly decorated, exactly to its dimensions. Then, at a banquet to which Osiris was invited, he offered to give the chest to any guest whom it fitted. When Osiris laid himself within it, Seth slammed the lid and secured it fast. The chest was thrown into the River Nile, carried to the sea, and drifted to Byblos, on the Phoenician coast. It came to rest on the shore,

and a lovely tree grew up and enclosed it. The tree's size and beauty caused the King of Byblos to cut it down and use it as a pillar of his palace.

The sorrowing Isis, who had long been seeking her husband's body, eventually located it, and by a display of magical power, obtained it from the King of Byblos and brought it back to Egypt. There it was discovered by Seth, who cut it into fourteen pieces and scattered the parts throughout the land. Isis patiently searched for the parts, burying each where it was found—another explanation of the many burial places of Osiris in Egypt. The phallus was not found; it had been devoured by a fish that became tabu to the Egyptians. Osiris then emerged from the underworld, to train and equip his son Horus to punish Seth. Horus conquered Seth after a hard struggle, and his legitimacy, questioned by Seth, was vindicated by the gods. Isis conceived a son called Harpocrates by her dead husband—Plutarch here mistakes one of the Greek names ('Harpocrates', derived from the Egyptian 'Horus the child') of Horus for another deity. Plutarch also regarded Osiris and Isis as demigods who,

because of their virtue, were translated into gods.

These Greek versions are evidence of the fascination that Osiris had for Graeco-Roman society. But although Egyptologists today are better placed to evaluate the ancient god than the Greek men of learning, many problems still remain unsolved.

The Mighty One

The Pyramid Texts show that the kings of Egypt were associated with Osiris in death. This association was clearly not a novel one, and it must have extended far back into the past, possibly into the predynastic period. The name 'Osiris' has been the subject of much study in the hope that it might provide a clue to the deity's origin, but none of the many interpretations that have been offered has yet been generally accepted. The most recent suggestion, which has much to commend it, is that the name meant originally 'the Mighty One'. Equally obscure is the problem of the original location of the cult of Osiris. Busiris (from an Egyptian word meaning 'House of Osiris') in the eastern Delta of the Nile was an ancient cult centre of Osiris, but the local

Osiris as he appears on the wall of an inner room in the temple of Deir el-Medina

deity there was Anzeti. However, since Osiris is invariably depicted wearing the tall white crown of Upper Egypt, it would seem that he had originated from that province.

The royal aspect or character of the god is presented in his traditional iconography: besides the white crown, he holds the symbols of Egyptian royalty—the crook and flail. The image, however, is a curious compromise between a living and a dead king. For the body of Osiris is represented in the form of a mummy, yet the face and head are free of mummy wrappings and the hands protrude from the wrappings and firmly grasp the royal insignia.

The association of the pharaoh with Osiris in death, which constitutes one of the most notable themes of the Pyramid Texts, was designed to effect the resurrection of the dead king. It was based on the principle of imitative magic, the dead king being ritually assimilated to Osiris. The whole drama of the mortuary ritual was, in fact, modeled on that of the legend of the death and resurrection of Osiris. In the Pyramid Texts the subject was the dead king; but gradually the royal mortuary ritual was democratized, so that by the New Kingdom all persons who could afford the expense could hope for re-vivification through ritual assimilation to Osiris.

Because of his connection with the fundamental mysteries of death and the afterlife, Osiris became the most significant of the gods for the Egyptians. At Abydos, the chief centre of his cult, a dramatic presentation of his death and resurrection was periodically performed. Osiris was also connected with the cult of the Apis bull, from which was derived his transformation into Serapis, the great deity of Hellenized Egypt, whose worship was promoted by King Ptolemy I (304–282 bc) as part of his policy to unite his Greek and Egyptian subjects. In the form of a Mystery religion, the cult of Isis

and Osiris spread far into the Roman Empire; and the famous Golden Ass of Apuleius (2nd century AD) attests to the power of its appeal—although Isis, as the great compassionate goddess of the universe, tended to dominate the attention of the devotees, leaving Osiris a somewhat background figure invested in deep mystery.

The ever-increasing importance of Osiris to the Egyptians resulted in his association with natural phenomena, especially with the growth of corn and the fructifying waters of the Nile. This has led to his identification as a vegetation deity of the dying-rising type by many scholars, preeminently by Sir James G. Frazer. The identification appears to be strikingly confirmed by the custom of placing in tombs moist earth shaped in the form of Osiris: the seed sown in it quickly sprouted in the dark warmth, thus symbolizing new life rising from the dead Osiris, and perhaps facilitating the resurrection of the dead person buried in the tomb. However, although a fertility role was certainly assigned to him, Osiris's character of a vegetation god was later and subordinate to his mortuary significance.

Judge and Redeemer

Another role which Osiris acquired was that of judge of the dead; but it was not until the New Kingdom that he appears in this guise, and it is not clear how he came to acquire it. In the Book of the Dead Osiris is presented as exercising his fateful office in two different ways: the dead are directed to make their first 'Declaration of Innocence' to him; and he presides at the weighing of the soul. The role of judge of the dead logically contradicted that of saviour of the dead which Osiris had in the mortuary ritual. This discrepancy is extremely interesting because a similar one occurs in Christianity where Christ is both saviour and judge. The cause, however, is not the same in each case: Osiris probably

came to be regarded as the judge of the dead because he ruled the land of the dead; the diverse roles of Christ derived from the Pauline and Jerusalem traditions that were eventually fused together in orthodox Christology.

It is difficult for us today to appreciate what the ancient Egyptians felt when they looked on the image of Osiris. But some insight is perhaps given, if we bear in mind that the image was that of a divine hero who had suffered and died, and then rose from the dead. Thus Osiris was not some remote transcendent deity such as Re, the sun god, but one who had endured the grim ordeal that awaited all men. In his image, moreover, the Egyptian devotees saw also the promise of their own resurrection from death and eternal life in the realm of Osiris. Phenomenologically, if not historically, Osiris was thus a prototype of Christ.

S. G. F. BRANDON
FURTHER READING: E. A. W. Budge, Osiris and the Egyptian Resurrection, *2 vols. (Dover, 1973); S. G. F. Brandon ed.* The Saviour God. *(Greenwood Press, 1980); J. G. Griffiths.* The Origins of Osiris. *(Argonaut); E. Otto.* Egyptian Art and the Cults of Osiris and Amon. *(Abrams, 1967).*

Phoenicians & Carthaginians

A degree of mystery invests both the name and origin of the Phoenicians. Phoenix was a Greek word meaning 'purple-red' and 'palm tree'. The Greeks seem originally to have applied the name 'Phoenician' to the inhabitants of the coastal lands of the eastern Mediterranean, between the Nahr-el-Kabir and Mount Carmel. It is not certain whether the name referred to the darker complexion of these people in contrast to the lighter colouring of the Greeks, or to the fact that palm

trees were a distinctive feature of their land. Phoenicia was also the home of the celebrated purple dye, made from the *murex mollusc*, which was highly prized in the ancient world. The Roman form of the name was Poeni, which was also used to designate the Carthaginians who had originated from Phoenicia. The Phoenicians, however, called themselves 'Canaanites' and their land was 'Canaan', so well-known from the Hebrew Bible.

According to Greek writers, the Phoenicians had originally lived in the Persian Gulf area, but had migrated westward at a remote period and settled on the Mediterranean coast. This account of their origins has not been confirmed by modern archeology. There is, indeed, much evidence of migrations of Semitic peoples from Arabia and the Persian Gulf into Syria and Palestine during the third and second millennia BC. But it would appear also that Semites were living in this area from at least the third millennium, and they cannot be distinguished from any 'Canaanite invaders'. We have, therefore, to consider the Phoenicians as Canaanites, that is, as Semitic inhabitants of the coastal area of the eastern Mediterranean. The term may also be used in a special sense after about 1200 BC, for as a result of the settlement of the Israelites and Philistines about this time in the district later known as Palestine, the area of Canaanite political independence became limited approximately to the territory occupied by the four chief Phoenician cities of Tyre, Sidon, Byblos, and Aradus.

The Father of Men

Since the Phoenicians were Canaanites, the earlier form of their religion can now be studied from the ritual and mythological texts discovered since

Statue of a woman, from the Phoenician port city Ibiza

Adorned statue of the goddess Tanit

1928 by excavation of the Canaanite city of Ugarit, close to the modern Ras Shamra. The Ugaritic texts reveal that the Canaanites of the 15th and 14th centuries BC worshipped a number of gods. The presiding deity was El, described as 'the Father of Men', who was regarded as benevolent and merciful. He was 'the Creator of Created Things', and 'the Bull'; the latter title doubtless indicated strength and virility. He is depicted on a stele as a bearded man, seated on a throne, and shown with a tall crown adorned by a pair of bull's horns. A worshipper, probably a king, stands before him, making an offering.

Although El was the supreme deity, the most active god of the Canaanite pantheon was Baal. He was represented as young and vigorous, armed with an axe and a spear, symbolizing lightning. These weapons indicate his original name and nature—he was Hadad, the weather god. 'Baal' was a title meaning 'lord', and signified ownership or sover-eignty of the land. The use of this title denoted the deity's connection with the fertility cult of Canaan; as the weather god he brought the winter rains that fertilized the land. In the mythological texts Baal is described as 'the son of Dagon', the corn god, and at Ugarit their temples were adjacent.

Closely associated with Baal was the fertility goddess Anat, who in later forms of Canaanite-Phoenician religion was called Astarte. On a stele found at Bethshan, Anat is described in Egyptian

Inside the tophet of Salambo, in the Phoencian port of Carthage

hieroglyphs as 'Antit, Queen of Heaven and Mistress of all the gods'. She seems also to have been known as Qodshu, which could be interpreted as 'sacred prostitute' and refer to the licentious fertility rites which were practiced in her sanctuaries. Anat or Astarte was generally depicted in art as nude, with the sexual attributes emphasized.

Among the texts recorded on the tablets found at Ugarit is a long mythological poem which tells of the conflict between Baal and Mot, the personi-

fication of drought and sterility. The theme was probably inspired by the annual struggle between vegetation and drought. Baal was apparently conceived of as the spirit of vegetation as well as a fertility god. In the poem, Baal is slain by Mot and descends into the underworld. His death is mourned by El; and Anat seeks for his corpse, which she finds and buries with lamentation and the appropriate funerary rites. There is doubtless some connection here between the actions of Anat and those of

the Egyptian goddess Isis in her quest for Osiris. Anat takes revenge on Mot by killing him and treating his body as grain, winnowing, parching, and grinding it. Baal eventually returns from the underworld, and Anat announces that rain will come again and the parched earth will revive. This mythological text was doubtless related to an annual ritual commemorating the death and resurrection of vegetation.

Evidence found at Ugarit and other sites shows that the Canaanites were attracted to other religions. Ugarit itself was a cosmopolitan port, where many languages were spoken and where Egyptian, Mesopotamian, Hittite, Hurrian, and Aegean-Mycenean influences were current. A notable memorial of Aegean-Mycenean religion is an ivory carving of the fertility goddess known as the Potnia Theron or 'Mistress of the Animals', which was found in a tomb. The stele unearthed at Bethshan, depicting Anat-Astarte, also shows on either side of the goddess the ithyphallic Egyptian god Min and the Canaanite god Reshef, who holds an ankh, the Egyptian symbol of life. In this connection, too, there are the Egyptian mummiform sarcophagi found at Sidon, one of which bears the funerary inscription in Phoenician of Eshmunazar, a king of Sidon probably in the 6th century BC. This readiness to accept foreign deities was also a feature of Carthaginian life. The acceptance, however, often took the form of identifying the foreign deity with a Canaanite, Phoenician or Carthaginian deity, which led to confusion of conception: thus the Baalat ('lady') of Byblos was identified with the Egyptian Isis or Hathor; and Melkart, the patron god of Tyre was assimilated with the Greek Hercules.

As the titles Baal ('lord') and Baalat ('lady') were used in conjunction with some other designations to denote the patron deity of some particular place, so other titles were used. A notable instance is the name Melkart, for the chief god of Tyre: it was composed of two words meaning 'ruler' or 'king', and 'city'. As Baal Melkart, this god became one of the leading deities of Carthage, the daughter city of Tyre. More difficult to explain is the name of Sidon's patron-god, Eshmun. It has been suggested that the name derives from *shem*, 'name', meaning 'the

Name' above all others. Eshmun was assimilated to the Greek healing god Asclepios. He appears to have had chthonic (underworld) attributes, which would account for his close association with the fertility goddess Astarte.

Exporting Religion

Carthage, which was destined to become Rome's great rival in the Mediterranean world, was traditionally founded in 814 BC by colonists from Tyre; it was one of many Phoenician settlements on the western Mediterranean coasts. Its position, in command of the straits between North Africa and Sicily, was one of great strategic opportunity, which it exploited to build up a commercial empire. Carthage

A demiurge, Ptah is creation incarnate who willed the world into being.

steadily outgrew its mother city in size and importance, and even after its final destruction by Rome in 146 BC, Punic culture lived on and the old Punic gods continued to be worshipped under Roman names.

The Phoenician colonists took their native religion with them to North Africa, and it formed the fundamental pattern of Carthaginian religion. Some differences, however, did develop at Carthage, particularly with regard to the status or character of certain gods. Thus, although Melkart, the patron god of Tyre, was accorded a special position in the daughter city and an annual offering was sent to his temple at Tyre, two other deities had greater prominence at Carthage. They were Baal Hammon and Tanit Pene Baal. The origin of the former is obscure, though it has been suggested that 'Hammon' means 'altars

of incense' or more plausibly, that it derives from 'Ammon', the name of the Libyan god of the Siwa oasis, whose oracle Alexander the Great once consulted. This Ammon was identified with the ancient Egyptian god Amun and the Greek Zeus.

The goddess Tanit, although her full title 'Pene Baal' meant '(Tanit) Face of Baal', seems to have had precedence over Baal Hammon, with whom she was often associated. Tanit was undoubtedly the Carthaginian counterpart of the Phoenician fertility goddess Astarte, for the latter does not appear independently of Tanit in the Carthaginian area. In Roman Carthage, Tanit was identified with Juno Caelestis, which indicates that she was also associated with the heavens. The crescent and the disc naturally suggest her connection with the moon. The emblem of the hand, with palm turned outward, probably symbolizes protection and benediction, and anticipates the famous Islamic amulet of the 'Hand of Fatima'. But essentially mysterious is the 'sign of Tanit', which could be interpreted as a schematic figure of the goddess with arms raised in blessing, or as a Carthaginian transformation of the ankh, the Egyptian sign of life.

Centuries of Child Sacrifice

One of the most significant but sinister discoveries made on the site of Punic Carthage was that of the 'topheth' within the precinct of Tanit. The Hebrew word topheth occurs in an account of the reforms carried out by King Josiah at Jerusalem (2 Kings 23:10): 'And he defiled Topheth . . . that no one might burn his son or his daughter as an offering to Molech'. It used to be thought that 'Molech' was a Phoenician god, but recent research suggests that it was a term for child sacrifice practiced in Canaanite-Phoenician religion. The topheth of Tanit has provided grim evidence of the longevity of the rite at Carthage, in fact from the 8th century BC to the Roman destruction of the city in 146 BC. Thousands of urns were found there containing the calcined bones of small children and birds and small animals—these latter were possibly substitute sacrifices. Small stelae, marking the burial places of the urns, mostly had dedications to Tanit Pene Baal and Baal Hammon. The purpose of these child sacrifices was probably either propitiatory or to promote fertility.

Among other Phoenician gods worshipped at Carthage were Eshmun of Sidon and Reshef. The cult of the Greek goddesses Demeter and Persephone was introduced in the 4th century BC, and after the Roman conquest the Punic deities were generally identified with the Roman deities deemed to be equivalent in character and status. The grim fanaticism that characterized both Phoenician and Carthaginian religion has been thought by some scholars to have left its impress upon ancient African Christianity.

S. G. F. BRANDON

FURTHER READING: M. Edey. The Sea Traders. (Time-Life, 1974); J.C. Gibson. Canaanite Myths and Legends. (Attic Press, 1978); J. Gray. The Canaanites. (Praeger, 1964); D. Harden. The Phoenicians. (Praeger, 1962); S. Moscati. The World of the Phoenicians. (Praeger, 1968).

Ptah

Egyptian god of builders, shipbuilders, metalworkers, designers, sculptors, and architects; sacred creator of the city of Memphis. Analog of Hephaestus in the Greek tradition and Vulcan in Roman mythology. A demiurge, Ptah is creation incarnate who willed the world into being. The staff he carries in many representations is a combination of the three royal and divine symbols, the ankh, the djed, and the was. Ptah also presided over royal ceremonies that were meant to preserve the power of the pharaohs.

FURTHER READING: Teeter, Emily. Religion and Ritual in Ancient Egypt. (Cambridge: Cambridge UP, 2011); Wilkinson, Richard H. The Complete Gods and Goddesses of Ancient Egypt. (New York: Thames & Hudson, 2003).

Pyramidology

The theory first proposed by John Taylor in 1859, and developed by the Astronomer Royal, Charles Piazzi Smyth, in 1864, maintained, firstly, that the Pyramid of Cheops (the 'Great Pyramid') was built to express a knowledge of the mathematical irrational pi; secondly, that its measurements embodied a totality of geodesic and astronomic knowledge; and thirdly, that these measurements also embodied in cipher form prophesies relating to the events that would later form the body of the Old Testament, as well as the

The only ancient wonder still standing, the great pyramid of Khufu (Cheops) is a structure of profound importance.

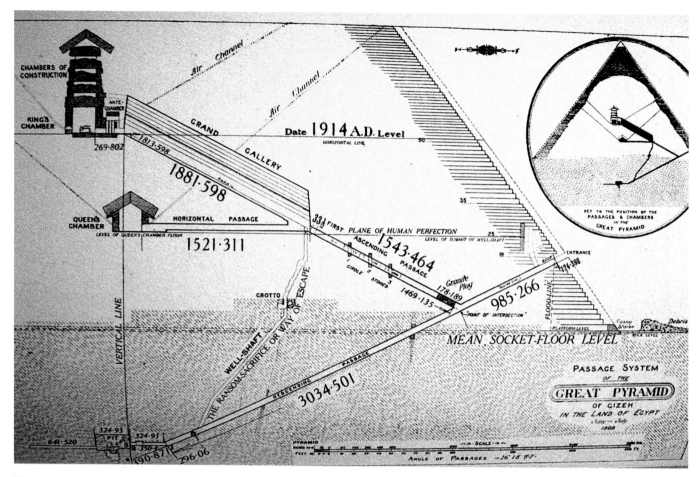

Pyramid chart from the 1911 Bible Students Convention Souvenir Report. At this time, the Bible Students in association with Pastor Charles Taze Russell believed that the Great Pyramid of Gizeh in Egypt confirmed biblical chronology. They believed the Great Pyramid confirmed their predictions for the year 1914. Pyramidology was rejected by the Bible Students in 1928 by J. F. Rutherford, Russell's successor, who later renamed the movement Jehovah's Witnesses.

complete future history of Christendom up to and including the Second Coming of Christ.

Though the pyramids of Egypt had been a subject for speculation since the time of Herodotus in the 5th century BC, pyramidology proper was an essentially Victorian phenomenon and can only be understood in reference to its time. Napoleon's expedition to Egypt had opened the eyes of the West to the magnitude of the civilization of ancient Egypt. The French archeologist Jean Champollion (1790–1832) succeeded in deciphering the Rosetta stone, giving access to the meanings of the hieroglyphs, and the new field of Egyptology was born.

The intellectual world at this time was split into two rough but distinct camps. On the one side the scientists and academicians—the inheritors of

the beliefs of the previous century's 'Enlightenment', violently antireligious and atheistic, convinced that the secrets of the universe would shortly yield to a mechanistic Newtonian explanation, and firm in the belief that man had progressed gradually but inexorably from savage or animal beginnings to a state of civilization.

The religious camp formed the opposition; equally violent in its belief, perhaps more numerous, but disorganized, and adhering to a form of fundamentalism, the belief in the literal truth of the Bible. A strong, specifically English and American, subgroup of this movement were the British Israelites (or Anglo-Israelites), who believed that the Anglo-Saxon race descended from the ten lost tribes of Israel.

The fundamentalists, in their way, were as materialistic as their opponents,

and required some material 'scientific' proof in order to support their views. The Great Pyramid of Giza provided an admirable cornerstone upon which to build. The magnitude of this structure, its rigorous geometry, the fact that it was oriented precisely to the cardinal points of the compass, and sited to within minutes of the 30th degree of latitude; that double its height divided into the length of its perimeter gave a close approximation to the value of pi; that amazing technical expertise had gone into the leveling of the plateau upon which it stood, and into the joining of its huge blocks of stone; all this seemed to the fundamentalists to be evidence that a mighty civilization had existed, possessed of advanced science and divine knowledge.

However, since they were reviled in the scriptures as representing all that was unholy, and shown by the new translations to have been worshippers of dog-headed gods and crocodiles, the builders of the Great Pyramid could not have been Egyptian. Charles Piazzi Smyth wrote, in *Our Inheritance in the Great Pyramid*: 'In speaking of anything in this book as simply sacred, I mean, to the best of my poor and limited ability, to distinguish such things as sacred to the God of Israel, i.e., to the one and only true God who lived forever and ever, and I have no respect of the same kind nor similar comprehensive word, for anything attributed to the gods of Egypt, Assyria, or Babylon . . .'

The Pyramid Inch

It was in this climate that pyramidology was born. It was virtually complete at its inception in John Taylor's book *The Great Pyramid; Why Was It Built? And Who Built It?* Among the many intrigued by this work was Charles Piazzi Smyth who, on Taylor's insistence, travelled to Egypt to take rigorously scientific measurements, no mean task at that time; and it was Smyth's book, *Life and Work at the Great Pyramid*, which, with the apparent authority of science upon it, struck the public imagination.

Smyth's great contribution to pyramidology was the 'pyramid inch', corresponding to 1.001 standard inches (the other 0.001 having been lost over the course of history), upon which all subsequent pyramidological prophecy was based.

The subject of Egyptian weights and measures was in any event a complex one. The ancient Egyptians employed a variety of different cubits, spans, palms, and digits, which obeyed no discernible single standard. Thus it was in no way disturbing that no known Egyptian measure corresponded to Smyth's 'pyramid inch'; it was even used as necessary evidence to support the contention that the Great Pyramid, alone among the many ruins of Egypt, had been constructed by a divinely inspired non-Egyptian race. Then, in 1865, another early pyramidologist Robert Menzies put forward the idea that prophecies and biblical history were inscribed into the Pyramid in the ratio of one pyramid inch per solar year—and pyramidology was complete.

By taking detailed measurements of the perimeter, sides, outer courses of masonry, inner chambers, galleries and corridors, by dividing the result by certain numbers held to be significant

in the construction of the pyramid, and by relating the results to biblical chronology and to the history of Christianity, exact correspondences were discovered. By the same token, an understanding of the cipher was supposed to permit the making of prophecies up to the Second Coming which, following the pyramid-inch-per-year theory up the Grand Gallery, was clearly close at hand.

Argument arose, however, over the method of dating; one faction maintained that the birth of Christ should stand at the starting point, so placing the Second Coming in 1911, while others decided that the starting point should correspond to the Resurrection, pushing the Second Coming back to 1936. Pyramidologists claimed that such events as the accession of the first Labour Government to power, and the Papal Bull inviting all Catholics to Rome to attend Holy Year (1924), were foretold and duly inscribed into the measurements of the Grand Gallery. Though a society of pyramidologists still exists, the movement appears to have lost most of its popular appeal.

There was a flurry of interest in 'pyramid power' during the 1970s, following the report of the filing of a

Divine Plan of the Ages

Much and rapid traveling and unprecedented increase of knowledge are outstanding characteristics of our present day. We are therefore in 'the time of the end', and since 1914 the Old Order is being broken up. Accordingly, the due time has come when God said He would reveal the future 'times and seasons' of His plan, hitherto concealed throughout all ages. Consequently, the major matters in the Book of Daniel and other prophetic Books of the Bible have been revealed right on time, and in addition, like any wise architect, God has disclosed where His drawings are. Moreover, these plans are portrayed on better material than paper, namely, in stone, within the largest and most substantial building in the World, the Great Pyramid of Giza—in what seems to be a most unlikely place, camouflaged and concealed, ostensibly in a pharaoh's pyramid so as to keep them a profound secret and unsuspected all down the ages till the present due time, divinely appointed . . .

It is not yet generally known that the Almighty arranged for His great and wonderful plan to be portrayed in symbols of stone long before the Bible was written. Modern discovery and research

have revealed the fact that this, the World's most massive edifice, symbolically and by measurement, declares the great Divine Plan of the Ages from the beginning to the consummation.

As we can now demonstrate that the Great Pyramid was built under Divine inspiration, this fact in itself proves that God thought that it was necessary for us, therefore it does not matter what we think. It is not for puny man to begin debating with the Almighty as to whether the Pyramid is necessary or not if God Himself in His infinite wisdom sees that it is necessary. Had it not been necessary God would not have had it built. Therefore if we ignore or neglect the Pyramid in these perilous days at the close of this Age we will miss something valuable which God has specially provided for us in this day and generation. The Great Pyramid displays the Christian religion upon a scientific basis in response to the scientific appeal of our age.

Adam Rutherford,
Pyramidology

patent in 1959 by a Czech engineer named Karel Drbal. He maintained that used razor blades kept beneath a cardboard model of a pyramid would remain mysteriously sharp, and for a time sold his patented cardboard and styrofoam pyramids in Czechoslovakia.

Drbal said he had been told that the dead bodies of animals which had strayed into the Great Pyramid and died there did not decay in the normal way but became mummified. It seemed as if the pyramid shape somehow affected the physical, chemical and biological processes going on inside it.

The concept was publicized in Sheila Ostrander and Lynn Schroeder's *Psychic Discoveries Behind the Iron Curtain* (1970), and taken up by Lyall Watson in his bestseller *Supernature* (1972). For a time pyramids of all sizes were sold as meditation aids, healing, and longevity devices and general spirituality boosters.

Although orthodox authorities insist that there is nothing mysterious whatever about the pyramids, it remains possible to suggest that there is a mystery, and that it has not yet been solved. According to I. E. S. Edwards, Keeper of Egyptian Antiquities in the British Museum, 'The true pyramid was merely a representation in stone of the sun's rays shining to earth through a gap in the clouds, and by its possession the king could transport himself at will to the celestial kingdom of the sun god'. But set against the statement that 'Egypt lies in an almost rainless area, where the temperature is high by day and sinks quickly at night in consequence of rapid radiation under the cloudless sky' (Encyclopedia Britannica), this conclusion seems open to question. Since the celestial

kingdom of the sun god was visible most of the time, it may seem odd to the nonspecialist that the Egyptians should expend such effort emulating a phenomenon they seldom, if ever, saw.

J. A. WEST

FURTHER READING: William R. Fix. Pyramid Odyssey. *(Mercury Media, 1978); John Michell.* View Over Atlantis. *(London: Garnstone Press, 1969); C. Piazzi Smyth.* Our Inheritance in the Great Pyramid. *(Steiner Books, 1978); Peter Tompkins.* Secrets of the Great Pyramid. *(New York: Harper & Row, 1978); Max Toth and Greg Neilsen.* Pyramid Power. *(Warner, 1976).*

Re

Or Ra, sun god and 'great god' of ancient Egypt, closely connected with the kingship of the pharaohs; as the sun at dawn, represented as a beetle or beetle-headed man; as the declining sun, he was Re-Atum, an old and wise man; linked with the god Amun at Thebes; frequently linked with the falcon-headed sky god Horus.

Scarab

The ancient Egyptians made numerous amulets, of which the most familiar is the scarab. Fashioned out of various materials, scarabs have been found in Egypt on habitation sites, in tombs and on mummies. These amulets are usually oval in shape, one side being convex and the other flat. The convex side is carved or moulded to represent the back of a beetle; the flat side generally bears a hieroglyphic inscription.

The name 'scarab' has been given to amulets of this kind by Egyptologists, because they represent the *scarabaeus*, a beetle of the genus Lamellicorn. The reason why the Egyptians chose the image of this particular beetle for an amulet is twofold; its explanation affords a significant insight into their thought and imagery.

The Egyptian name for the scarab beetle was *kheprer(i)*. The verb *kheper* meant 'to believe', or 'to come into existence'; while *kheperu* signified 'forms', or 'stages of growth and development'. The Egyptians also called the sun god Khepri, because to them

A pectoral, in this case a brooch, made of gold, lapis lazuli, and semiprecious stones depicting scarab, solar disk, and crescent, from Treasure of Tutankhamen

he was 'He who exists himself', that is, was self-existent. In turn, they believed that he was the creator of the world and the source or author of life. The similarity of the scarab beetle's name to that of the sun god therefore held a deep significance, which was reinforced by another curious fact.

It is the habit of the scarab beetle, which feeds on dung, to make a ball of dung and roll it into a hole which it has already prepared. The beetle enters the hole, closing the entrance, and lives there until it has consumed the ball. Certain ancient writers have recorded the significant analogy which the Egyptians drew from this remarkable habit. The Roman author Pliny explains: 'The people of a great part of Egypt worship these insects as divinities; an usage for which Apion gives a curious reason, asserting as he does, by way of justifying the rites of his nation, that the insect in its operations pictures the revolutions of the sun'. According to Horapollo, a late Egyptian writer, the scarab beetle 'rolls the ball from east to west, looking himself toward the east. Having dug a hole, he buries it for twenty-eight days; on the twenty-ninth day he opens the ball, and throws it into the water, and from it the scarabaei come forth'.

The curious idea which Horapollo expresses here, that the male scarab beetle thus produced the young, is more clearly stated by the Greek writer Plutarch: 'The Egyptians also honoured . . . the beetle, since they observed in them certain dim likenesses of the power of the gods, like images of the sun in drops of water . . . The race of beetles has no female, but all the males eject their

Scarab motif for a necklace piece

Statue of a scarab dedicated to Khepri by Amenhotep III in the Karnak temple complex

sperm into a round pellet of material which they roll up by pushing it from the opposite side, just as the sun seems to turn the heavens in the direction opposite to its own course, which is from west to east'.

This quaint error that scarab beetles were of male sex only, together with their habit of rolling balls of dung and the suggestion contained in their name, all conspired to produce a strange piece of religious imagery. Since Re, the sun god, is called Khepri, the 'Self-Existent One', who of himself generated all forms of existence, and since he rolls the ball of the sun daily across the sky, he must be the original divine Scarab. Thus, in religious iconography Re is frequently represented as a large black scarab beetle, sitting in the solar boat and rolling the sun disc, or as a man whose human head is replaced by a scarab beetle. This strange imagery was already current by the middle of the third millennium BC, as the following passage from the Pyramid Texts shows. It concerns the union, or reunion, of the deceased pharaoh Unas with the

sun god. 'This Unas flieth like a bird and alighteth like a beetle upon the throne which is empty in thy boat, O Re'. There are even more ancient indications of the currency of this evaluation of the scarab beetle; for jars of them have been found in graves dating from before 3500 BC.

The significance that the Egyptians saw in the scarab beetle rendered its image an amulet of supreme potency. For it represented Re, the sun god, as the source of all existence and thus was itself, in terms of sympathetic magic, endowed with vitalizing virtue. Hence its use as a life-giving amulet for the dead was obvious. But it was used also by the living as a talisman, conferring daily well-being and protection against evil. The inscriptions cut upon the flat side were very varied. Some give the names and titles of the owner, often with a pious or 'good luck' phrase; many have the names of pharaohs, since these were names of great magical power. The authentic 'royal scarabs' are of considerable historical value, especially those of the New Kingdom (1567–1085 BC), when the custom

grew up of recording historical events on them.

The most notable scarab amulet was the 'heart scarab'. This was placed upon the breast of the mummy and inscribed with Chapter 30 of the Book of the Dead. The text contained a petition addressed by the dead person to his heart, asking it not to witness against him when it was weighed against the symbol of truth at the awful judgment after death.

Serapis

The god of Alexandria and the chief deity of Ptolemaic Egypt was Serapis or Sarapis, about whose origin there was much speculation in the ancient world. According to the Roman historian Tacitus, writing in the 2nd century AD, Ptolemy I, the first Greek monarch of Egypt (305–283 BC), was instructed in a dream to send to Sinope, a city on the shores of the Black Sea, for the statue of the god of that place. Ptolemy consulted the Egyptian priests about his dream, but they could not interpret it. It was eventually interpreted by an Athenian named Timotheus who, significantly, was connected with the Eleusinian Mysteries. He identified the god of Ptolemy's dream as Pluto, who was associated with the underworld goddess Persephone at Sinope. After some difficult negotiations, the statue was obtained and brought to Alexandria. Tacitus adds some further explanatory details about Serapis: 'The god, himself, on account of his healing art, is called by many Aesculapius; by others, Osiris, the most ancient deity of the country (Egypt); and many give him the name of Jupiter, as lord of the universe. But the most maintain that he is Pluto—either from tokens which are discernible in the deity himself, or by a circuitous process of 'probable reasoning'.

This account of the origin of Serapis is not accepted by scholars today. But it is recognized as probable that Ptolemy I did promote the cult of Serapis as a means of uniting his Greek and Egyptian subjects in the worship of a god whom both could appreciate. This god was a hybrid conception of Egyptian origin, venerated already by some Greeks resident in Egypt. The origin and development of the conception provide a curious example of religious syncretism. At Memphis, the ancient capital of Egypt, there had existed from a remote period the cult of the Apis bull as a symbol of divine procreativity. When one of these sacred animals died, it was identified with Osiris, the god of the dead, and named Oserapis, that is Osiris-Apis. The body of each Apis was mummified and buried, amid public lamentation, with the bodies of its predecessors in the Serapeum, a vast subterranean labyrinth at Sakkara.

Head of Serapis, found in Carthage, Tunisia

Seth

One of the major gods of ancient Egypt, Seth was said to be the son of Geb and Nut and he is conspicuous on the monuments and in texts. In particular he is assigned a prominent role in representations of symbolic rites relating to the paranoiac state. The best known of these is the ceremony of 'Uniting the Two Lands', which is impressively portrayed on the limestone reliefs from List near Memphis, now in the Cairo Museum.

Seth is figured here facing the god Horus. Both are animal gods, but here their bodies have human shape; only their heads retain their original form—the falcon head of Horus and the canine head of Seth. The two deities are shown tying the symbolic plants of Upper and Lower Egypt to the sign which connotes unity. In these reliefs Seth is clearly the representative of Upper Egypt.

There is little doubt that the scene mirrors an enacted ritual in which priests impersonated the gods. Seth is depicted too in other related ceremo-

nies, such as those connected with the purification and the coronation of the pharaoh. In an oft-recorded rite which has been called 'the Baptism of Pharaoh' he is shown, together with Horus, pouring water over the king's head.

Unidentified Animal

Seth's original cult centre was probably Ombos, the modern Naqada, where a figure of the Seth animal has been found amid vestiges of Naqada's earliest predynastic culture, which derives from the middle of the fourth millennium BC. But what the Seth animal really was still constitutes a problem. Suggestions made include the ass, oryx, antelope, the fennec (a small fox with huge pointed ears), jerboa (a rodent), camel, okapi, long-snouted mouse, giraffe, and various types of hogs or boars. Another view is that the animal is fabulous, like the griffin or dragon. The narrow snout and upraised ears and tail suggest a canine type; perhaps the species was already extinct in Egypt in early times. In later phases of his development Seth was associated with the ass, the pig and the hippopotamus, and in these cases the interpretation of his character was usually unfavourable.

Indeed a striking fact in the history of the cult of Seth is that after the New Kingdom, from about 1000 BC, the god is involved for the most part

The gods Seth (left) and Horus (right) adoring Ramesses II in the small temple at Abu Simbel, in far southern Egypt

er, Thoth replaces Seth in some of the symbolic rites, such as the 'Baptism of Pharaoh'. Seth is identified with the victim offered in sacrificial rites, and the slain offering is equated with the defeated enemy. The Book of Victory over Seth and the texts of the Temple of Edfu are virulently antiSethian, but they derive from sanctuaries of Osiris and Horus. It is true that even in the first millennium BC Seth was specially honoured by the Libyan Dynasty; and if the escalating popularity of Osiris told heavily against him, there were centres of Seth worship even in the Roman era.

In the legend which describes his conflict with Horus there are some clear pointers to a historical and political substratum. Cosmological explanations become prominent later, and one modern view would interpret the myth as being inherently of this type. Seth, however, is not easy to fit into such a scheme. As a god of heaven, Horus represents light, it may be argued; he is eventually equated with the sun god Re, and his eyes are the sun and moon. If so, what does Seth represent? He is not simply a god of darkness; sometimes he is a storm god, a thunderer, while at other times his name is linked with the desert. One recent writer H. te Velde, sees the polarity as that between light and sexuality. Seth is certainly endowed by the Egyptian texts with strong, if somewhat perverse, sexual powers. It is very doubtful, however, whether they are felt to be opposed to the cosmic concept of light. Nephthys, sister and partner of Isis, is usually named as his wife, but the union is not credited with offspring.

in a position of increasing degradation. One reason is that the roles he occupies in mythology are inauspicious. In the legend about his fierce fight with the falcon god Horus, Seth is said to have been deprived of his testicles, and although he in turn ripped out one of the eyes of Horus, the final victory, including justification in the divine tribunal, went to his opponent. In the myth of Osiris the role of Seth becomes still more sinister: he is the murderer who felled Osiris in Nedjet. The opposing gods in each case were incorporated in the concept of kingship, Horus being identified with the living pharaoh,

Osiris with the deceased one, so that Seth was fated from the start to follow a difficult course.

In relation to the living pharaoh, Seth's place in the official theology was at first protected, as we have seen, by the concept of reconciliation. If Seth represents Upper Egypt in a rite celebrating the unity of Egypt, this means that an early stage of disunity is reflected, when Seth was the patron god of a part of the country, espousing its strife against another part. But the retrospect is now a happy one, and the dominance of Horus in the royal theology does not deny Seth an honoured second place. Later, howev-

'A Kind of Satan'

Seth is himself sometimes equated astrally with the Great Bear, and in the texts and representations which portray the fight of Re against Apophis, the serpent demon of darkness, Seth is the champion-in-chief of the sun god. What contributed especially to his decline in status was the tendency to identify him with foreign invaders such as the Assyrians and Persians. In the magical papyri his position remains tremendously influential, even if he is often regarded now as a kind of Satan. By this time he has been identified with the Greek monster Typhon, likewise a challenger of the established divine order. Seth-Typhon is sometimes referred to as 'the head-less demon', but this term is applied in the papyri to other gods too, including Osiris. Since the magician is anxious to deploy the powers of Seth-Typhon, his attitude to the god may be ambivalent. On the one hand he may address him with great respect and declare himself to be his partisan in the struggle against Osiris or Horus; on the other hand, he may call him 'the slayer of his own brother', just to remind him that the magician is acquainted with his crimes and will use his knowledge unfavourably unless the god is prepared to show sympathy in the matter which is the subject of his appeal.

One of the Gnostic sects went by the name of Sethians, paying special honour to Seth, the biblical son of Adam and Eve. Suggestions concerning a second relationship involving the Egyptian god seem to be rather speculative.

J. GWYN GRIFFITHS

Shamash

Sun god in the Akkadian pantheon, also the god of justice in Assyrian and Babylonian mythology. Part of a triad of gods with his father Sin, the moon god, and his sister/wife Ishtar, feminine mother goddess. Shamash sometimes carries a saw, a tool that symbolizes the ability to make clear legal decisions. The lawgiver, Shamash is depicted on the famous stele known as the Code of Hammurabi handing the king a series

Relief image on the Tablet of Shamash, British Library room 55. Found in Sippar (Tell Abu Habbah), in Ancient Babylonia; it dates from the 9th century BC and shows the sun god Shamash on the throne, in front of the Babylonian king Nabu-apla-iddina (888–855 BC) between two interceding deities. The text tells how the king made a new cultic statue for the god and gave privileges to his temple.

The Great Sphinx of Giza

of tablets. Hammurabi was inspired to write the code by Shamash's divine justice and laws. Shamash plays a key role in the Epic of Gilgamesh by giving Gilgamesh powerful weapons to fight the forest demon Humbaba as well as intervening in the battle to enable Gilgamesh and Enkidu to defeat the monster.

FURTHER READING: Wilkinson, Richard H. The Complete Gods and Goddesses of Ancient Egypt. *(New York: Thames & Hudson, 2003); Wilson, John Albert.* The Culture of Ancient Egypt. *(Chicago: University of Chicago, 1956); Pinch, Geraldine.* Egyptian Mythology: A Guide to the Gods, Goddesses, and Traditions of Ancient Egypt. *(Oxford: Oxford UP, 2004).*

Sphinx

Hybrid creature combining human and animal parts, typically a lion's body and the head of a man (or sometimes of a hawk or ram): pairs or avenues of sphinxes guarded the en-

trances to palaces, temples, and tombs in Egypt; the Great Sphinx is a colossal image near the pyramids of Giza; in Greek mythology, the woman-headed Sphinx of Thebes strangled passersby when they failed to solve the riddle she put to them.

Sumerians

One of the earliest human civilizations, the Sumerians inhabited an area of land surrounding the Tigris and Euphrates Rivers in modern day Kuwait, Iraq, and Saudi Arabia. Sumerian civilization can be traced from approximately 4000 BC to its occupation by Akkadian peoples in around 2000 BC. The Sumerians invented some of the earliest known features of human civilization, including writing, cities, fast wheels, advanced agriculture, specialized divisions of labour, taxation, literature, monarchy, and empire. Even after the Sumerian dynasties were destroyed by conquest their achievements had lasting effects.

Urban Centres, Agriculture, and Centralized Power

The Sumerians invented the city or urban centre. As wheat farmers, livestock herders and fisher-hunters gathered together, they began to form even more organized and cohesive communities of specialists. Eventually larger, more complex societies could be supported. Eridu, established in around 5300 BC, was probably the first such settled city; its centre of power was a temple complex dedicated to the god Enki (or Ea). As populations grew and climate shifted, newer larger cities emerged further north in the Tigris-Euphrates River plains. By the early 4th millennium BC Uruk had become the dominant power in the region, symbolized in the myths of Inanna (goddess of Uruk) receiving the secrets of civilization from Enki. Within 1,000 years of the rise of Uruk there were dozens of independent city-states in the Fertile Crescent. During that period Uruk grew to be the largest urban population in the world, with 45,000 to 50,000 citizens.

The Uruk Period, which scholars place between approximately 4000 and 2900 BC, was a time of incredible invention, innovation and progress. Sometime around 3100 BC, from pictographic markings on small clay pieces—for the purposes of record keeping—emerged a complex logosyl-labic writing system called cuneiform that used abstract symbols to represent sounds and grammatical meaning. This marked the advent of recorded human history and literature. Archaelogical evidence shows that the Sumerians used their writing technology to support a large network of traders, religious leaders and urban centres. The Uruk Period Sumerian trade network stretched as far west as Turkey and east as Iran. The Sumerians of this period developed sophisticated irrigation techniques in order to feed their growing populations. Archaeological evidence also points to improved

Sumerian Religion

Sumerian myth and religion is rich and varied, and has much in common with later Semitic myths as well as Egyptian, Greek, and Roman polytheism. The cosmos of the Sumerian mythos consisted of heaven, earth, and the underworld. Anthropomorphic gods were organized hierarchically, with four main deities at the top, a committee of seven deities that determined the fates, and then a large population of lesser deities that accepted individual prayers and sacrifices. The most prominent gods were An, the great creator; Enlil, An's successor and the ruler of the gods, Enki, another designer/creator god, and Ninhursag, the mother of all.

The religious hierarchy extended to the system of priests involved in worshipping the gods as well as civic adminstration. High priests, poets, singers, libation bearers, and a number of other roles were fulfilled by specific priestly figures. Temples, which began as small single rooms but grew, by the end of the Sumerian civilization, to ziggurats, were at the heart of Sumerian politics, religion, and city life. Ziggurats are large step-pyramidal structures that formed the core of a larger religious complex.

Epic of Gilgamesh

The Epic of Gilgamesh is one of the earliest recorded works of literature, dating from the Uruk period of Sumerian civilization. Several poems about the mythical king Gilgamesh of Uruk from this era were later combined by the Akkadians, with the oldest complete version of the epic surviving from the 18th century BC. The epic concerns

wheel-based technologies, such as pottery and modes of transportation.

Sumerian Language

The Sumerian spoken language is, as far as linguists can discern, a language isolate, which means that it is unrelated to any other language before

or after. Sumerian was the dominant language of the region for 2,000 years until the rise of the Akkadian Empire in 2300 BC, when Semitic Akkadians conquered the former Sumerian kingdom. Even then, Sumerian survived as a religious and scholarly language until the 1st century AD.

Gilgamesh, King of Uruk, and his friendship with Enkidu, a powerful man from the wilderness sent by the gods to temper Gilgamesh's iron rule. Enkidu is killed after a sensational battle with the forest demon Humbaba, and Gilgamesh, devastated by the death of his best friend, goes on a quest to find the source of immortality. At first his quest is to find a way to bring his friend back to life, but eventually he is merely seeking the antidote to death itself. Gilgamesh meets Utnapishtim, a Sumerian precursor of Noah from the Hebrew Old Testament, who, along with his wife, is the sole survivor of the Great Flood. Utnapishtim gives Gilgamesh the secret to immortality, but Gilgamesh loses it on his way home to Uruk. The epic ends with Gilgamesh understanding that all men die, but that his immortality is with the grand city that he has built. The triumph of the Sumerian invention—the city—in the Epic is a testament to the pride the Sumerians felt at their great achievement. The Epic of Gilgamesh has become a model for hero's journeys and epic quests.

FURTHER READING: Kramer, Samuel Noah. The Sumerians: Their History, Culture and Character. *(Chicago: University of Chicago, 1979); Van, De Mieroop, Marc.* A History of the Ancient Near East, Ca. 3000–323 BC. *(Malden, MA: Blackwell Pub., 2007).*

Syria and Palestine

The fullest contemporary record of religion in Syria is the texts in alphabetic cuneiform from ancient Ugarit Ras

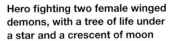
The Fertility Cult

In this myth Baal is the god of thunder, lightning and winter rains, 'He who Mounts the Clouds', and is, like the Mesopotamian Tammuz, a dying and rising god, whose fortunes fluctuate with the vegetation he promotes. In his eclipse in the summer season his sister and consort Anat (the north Syrian counterpart of Astarte) is particularly active. Baal, as the vegetation he promotes, succumbs to Mot. His dead body is sought over hill and dale by Anat, called in the Ras Shamra texts 'the Virgin Anat', a rite which had its counterpart in the fertility cult throughout the Near East. There is definite reflection of the mourning of Anat on the recovery and burial of the body of Baal in the Old Testament (Zechariah 12.11) in 'the mourning for Hadad-Rimmon in the plain of Megiddo'. Anat proceeds to avenge Baal. She cuts down Mot, winnows him, parches him with fire, grinds him with a millstone and scatters his remains in the fields for the birds to eat. This obviously relates to the desacralization of the new crop, setting it free for common use, as in the offering of the first sheaf of 'new grain from fresh ears, parched with fire', in Leviticus 2:14.

In myth related to ritual, strict logical consistency is not expected, and Baal revives. His revival is anticipated in a dream by El, who is the final authority in these texts and intervenes at significant junctures to confirm a decision or to foreshadow the future. El's vision is of the skies raining olive oil and the wadis running with honey, which recurs in the liturgies of Israel reflected in Amos 9:13 and Joel 3:18. With similar lack of consistency Mot is introduced in a final 'showdown' with Baal, out of which Baal emerges victor

Shamra, about twelve miles north of Latakkia and two miles from the coast. Theophoric names (personal name including in its form a divine name) as in the Egyptian Execration texts, lists of offerings to various gods, ritual texts, incidental references in legends, and, above all, myths of the fertility cult illustrate the religion of Syria in the 14th century BC. The many gods, both Semitic and non-Semitic, reflect the mixed population of this city in north Syria, but only the cult of the fertility god Baal and the goddess Anat and their associates is documented sufficiently to permit a reconstruction of the cult.

From these texts we learn that the senior god was El ('god'), the King Paramount, Father of the Exalted Ones, and Father of Men and Creator, depicted as enthroned at the remote 'source of the streams'. His strength and procreative influence is expressed in his title

'the Bull', but he was the principal god in social relationships, and this aspect of his character is expressed by his title, 'the Kindly, the Compassionate'.

El's executive king is Baal, whose proper name was Hadad ('the Thunderer') or Baal Ramman ('the Thunderer'), which Jewish scribes parodied as Rimmon ('pomegranate'). He establishes his kingly power and order in Nature in a primeval conflict with Sea-and-Ocean Currents and associated monsters like Letan (Leviathan of the Old Testament) and Tannin, also known in this connection in the Old Testament, and has his 'house' built as a visible token that he is the reigning king. He is obliged, however, to reassert his kingship in a seasonal conflict against Sterility, or Death (Mot), in a myth which is believed to be related to the chief seasonal crisis in Syria, at the autumn equinox.

and again vindicates his kingship. This conflict is set 'in the seventh year' and may be related to the seven-year cycle marked in Israel by an artificial famine, when the land lay fallow on the principle that drought must be given full play in order that its force might be exhausted. Thus in the seasonal tension after the long dry summer, pending the coming of the 'early rains', the Syrian peasant relieved his anxiety and predisposed providence by homoeopathic magic, which was the genesis of drama in Greece in the cult of the wine god Dionysus at Athens. In Syria no such dramas are attested, but all the elements of drama are in the Baal myth.

It will be seen that Israel inherited this liturgic theme of the great autumn festival, which she developed in the light of her own historical tradition of the great deliverance from Egypt and the Covenant, but the essential features of the seasonal festival survive, conflict with the forces of destruction and disorder, the demonstration of the effective kingship of God and the establishment of his government, often by judgment. This is expressed notably in the Enthronement psalms in the Old Testament, in passages in the Prophets which reflect this liturgical theme and in passages on the Day of the Lord in Jewish and Christian apocalyptic, for example, Revelation. There the sea and certain sea monsters are archenemies of God's ordered government, as in the Baal myth of Ras Shamra in the New Year festival in Canaan.

The role of the king in his sacral function as executive of Baal as the Divine King in his 'passion' and triumph in the great autumn festival cannot be established on the evidence of the Ras Shamra texts, but on the analogy of the corresponding occasion in Mesopotamian religion it is likely. With the necessary changes, it may certainly be

demonstrated that in Jerusalem the Davidic king was the temporal guarantee of the effective Kingship of God, which was expressed in the liturgy of the great autumn festival. For Canaan Ezekiel's denunciation of the King of Tyre (chapter 28) expresses the conception of the king as the representative of God, the channel of divine blessings, and, as representative of the community, the royal man in the garden of God. The Legend of King Krt at Ras Shamra speaks of the king as 'the son of El', and the crown prince is 'suckled by the fertility goddesses

Reshef was the god who slew men by war and plague.

Anat and Athirat'. The conception of the king as the upholder of the social justice which is the concern of God is expressed in the royal texts from Ras Shamra and, as in Psalm 72 and Isaiah 11:1–9, he is the medium of blessings in Nature. It is not difficult to see here an ideology from which the conception of the Messiah in Israel developed.

The protagonists of this cult are well known through texts, sculpture, and figurines. Baal is the active young warrior god, El is an elderly god on his throne and footstool, both being associated with the bull in virtue of procreative interests. Anat, like Astarte in the Old Testament, is the goddess of love, and appears naked in moulded reliefs and pendants, either devoted to shrines or given in return for the payment of a vow and used as amulets to promote childbirth. Sexual rites of imitative magic associated with the Canaanite fertility cult survived in Israel and are constantly denounced by the Prophets. Anat was also the goddess of war, like

Ishtar in Mesopotamia, and is involved in what is evidently a bloody massacre in her temple in an episode in the Baal myth at Ras Shamra, which may really describe a bloodletting rite, like the self-laceration of the devotees of Baal at Carmel (1 Kings 18:28), or perhaps circumcision. The mother goddess Athirat (Ashera of the Old Testament) appears as the consort of El, and is probably the goddess represented as the nourisher of life who offers ears of corn to two rampant caprids (goats) on an ivory relief from the seaward quarter of Ugarit. The motif is a development of the rampant caprids reaching up to the fruit of the Tree of Life, which is familiar throughout the Near East. In the references in the Old Testament to the ash era as a feature of sanctuaries this is a tree, either natural or stylized, representing the mother goddess Ashera as the receptive element in Nature and as the universal nourisher. The Tree of Life is closely associated in the ancient Near East with the king in his sacral function as mediator of the divine blessing, as in Assyrian sculpture and on the royal couch from the palace of Ras Shamra.

The Will of the Gods

Significant as the fertility cult of Canaan undoubtedly was, it is possible that the dramatic nature of the Baal myth gives an incomplete picture of the actual situation. In royal legends for instance, in dynastic succession and other historical and social situations the predominant deity is not Baal but El, to whom chiefly sacrifice is made in a fast liturgy on the occasion of a national emergency. This and a certain text from Ras Shamra containing oaths by certain attributes of El indicate a more spiritual conception of El, which is nearer to the Hebrew conception of God.

Among many other deities in Canaanite religion Dagan, the god of corn (dagon), is known at Ras Shamra from offering lists, from Baal's stock epithet 'the Son of Dagan', and from dedication inscriptions on stelae from a temple adjoining that of Baal at Ras Shamra, which dates from c. 2000 BC. Reshef was the god who slew men by war and plague. He is known from Egyptian sculpture and may be recognized in bronze figurines of a striding warrior with offensive weapon and shield, well known from archeological sites in Syria and Palestine. In one of the Ras Shamra texts he is called Reshef of the Arrow, and in the Graeco-Roman period he was assimilated to Apollo with his pestilential arrows. From later inscriptions from Sidon, Eshmun is known as the god of healing, assimilated to Asclepius in the Graeco-Roman period, as Baal was to Hercules, by whose labours also order was sustained against the constant menace of chaos. The sun, regarded as a goddess, is a minor figure in the Baal myth of Ras Shamra, and the moon god and his consort Nikkal were also worshipped, particularly at Harran in northwest Mesopotamia, and in north Syria. Ritual texts from Ras Shamra indicate that special rites and sacrifices, in which the king was involved, were observed at certain days of the month, probably at lunar phases.

The will of the various gods was consulted and communicated in various ways. In the 2nd century AD, Lucian of Samosata mentions oracles according to the movement of statues of the gods, doubtless at the manipulation of

Ram perched on the tree of life, covered with gold leaf. The horns, eyes, and back of the animal are of lapis lazuli. Found at a pit of the Royal Cemetery of Ur. c. 2600–2400 BC. British Museum, London

Syrian deities, shown in relief

priests in response to specific questions, conveying a simple 'Yes' or 'No', like the sacred lots Urim and Thummim in early Israel. Divination by the entrails of sacrificed animals was also practiced, the liver being especially significant, as is indicated by clay models from archeological sites, charted and annotated for consultation or instruction. The medieval Arab writer Ibn an-Nadim mentions divination at Harran by the direction of the gaze or the expression in the eyes of the dying victim. Texts from the Amorite city of Mari on the mid-Euphrates mention diviners who consulted the auspices in this way and communicated their findings to the king in matters of ritual or state. There were also communications by ecstatic devotees, who suggest 'the sons of the prophets' in the Old Testament and dervishes of later Islam.

At Byblos c. 1100 BC there is an instance of the will of the god communicated to the king in an affair of state by an ecstatic of his household and considered authentic by the king. The account of the distress of King Saul before his last battle (1 Samuel 28) mentions prophets and dreams as the media of the communication of the will of God in a crisis, and the patriarchal narratives in the Old Testament and the passage in the Baal myth where El sees the revival of Baal in a dream indicate the significance attached to dreams as communications of the will of God in future events or on the significance of the present situation. People would often resort to shrines in ritual incubation when dreams were taken as sure communications of the purpose of the god.

The temple in Syria varied in form, but the general conception was a large area within the sacred precinct in which the temple proper was the focal feature. This conception is best illustrated in the sanctuary of Bel, or Baal, in the early Roman period at Palmyra in the Syrian desert and the Moslem sacred precinct at Jerusalem. At Ras Shamra and Hazor in the 14th and 13th centuries BC, the tripartite temple is known, comprising an outer court with a great altar, shallow vestibule, main nave, and inmost shrine, or 'Holy of Holies'. This is the plan of Solomon's Temple at Jerusalem, which was constructed by Phoenician craftsmen. Administrative texts from Ras Shamra attest hereditary office in a large number of professions among temple personnel, priests, votaries both male and female, temple prostitutes, singers, makers of sacred vestments, sculptors, potters, launderers, slaughterers, augurers, or possibly Temple herdsmen, and merchants who traded on account of the Temple. The king of course was the supreme priest, though except on special occasions he would delegate his duties.

Sacrifice of the Infants

The myths and legends of Ras Shamra in their fuller context amplify the simple listing of various types of sacrifice in the offering lists. Thus from the description of the duties of the son and heir of the king in the royal legend of Prince Aqhat at Ras Shamra it is known that communion meals were eaten in the sanctuary. The blood and vitals were offered to the god, and the rest was cooked and eaten by the community, thus effecting solidarity of the participants with the god and with one another. The shrine might also house memorials of the ancestors of the community, represented by standing stones, as in the Canaanite sanctuary of Hazor, and probably also at Gezer. By offerings at this tangible token of a favoured ancestor the community hoped to continue to share in the blessing which had been his.

Besides communion sacrifices there were those that were offered wholly to the gods either as food or as an act of total renunciation on the part of the worshipper, being wholly burned on the altar; and other such offerings were made for purification, as doves were sacrificed in Israel after childbirth, and as firstlings of crop and flock and of game in hunting. In Israel and among the Carthaginians in North Africa animals were sacrificed in redemption of first-born sons, and this was almost certainly done also in Syria.

Archeological evidence has been claimed from Gezer and Tell al-Fara by Nablus for foundation sacrifice of children, but this is disputed. Multiple infant sacrifice, however, is attested by jars full of calcined bones of infants and

young animals from the sanctuary of the fertility goddess Tanit at the Tyrian colony of Carthage (see Phonecians), in Punic inscriptions and in the writings of the African Church father, Tertullian (3rd century AD). Those may have been first-born children dedicated thus as firstlings, but in King Mesha's sacrifice of his eldest son (2 Kings 3), like those in Judah in the latter period of the kingdom, they may have been sacrifices in extremity, to which Philo of Byblos (64–161 AD) alludes. Other cases, such as that which Diodorus Siculus attributes to the Carthaginians in Sicily after a victory over the Greeks in 307 BC, may be a case of 'death-devotion' (herem), a great act of renunciation of the spoils of war, to which King Mesha also refers in his inscription recording his war of liberation from Israel (c. 835 BC). The sacrifices would thus correspond to Samuel's 'hewing Agag in pieces before the Lord' (1 Samuel 15:33).

The Dead and the Afterlife

Besides the commemoration of the dead as recipients of the divine favour ritual texts from Ras Shamra refer to the family god ('il' ib), certain of these alluding to 'offerings at the aperture of the divine ancestor'. This is amplified by the discovery of grave-installations of such apertures as pipes of bottomless jars to communicate offerings, especially libations, to the defunct, probably to promote fertility of the earth, over which the dead were believed to have some influence. Such offerings to the dead may be the substance of the ban on offerings of a portion of the harvest to the dead in Deuteronomy 26:14. The dead were termed repa'im by the Phoenicians as in Israel, the name for the 'weak' shades in the Old Testament, and were possibly referred to in funerary inscriptions of King Tabnith of Sidon (5th century BC) as 'divine', or at least supernatural, as in the passage on

King Saul and the Witch of Endor (1 Samuel 28:13), where the shade of Samuel is described as 'a god'. In this case, the king sought revelation of the future.

As recipients of offerings, givers of fertility and revealers of the future, the departed in ancient Syria were regarded as not quite defunct. The Aramaean king Panammu in his inscription (c. 750 BC) expects his descendants to invoke him when they make an offering to Baal, so that 'his soul may eat and drink with Baal'. The existence of the shade in the gloomy underworld is familiar in the Old Testament, particularly in Job (chapter 3). Though quite undesirable this was apparently still an existence, however insubstantial, and this attenuated life was sustained by offerings, particularly libations, though one of the more recently discovered texts from Ras Shamra refers to animal sacrifice 'for the life of the family god', or the divine ancestor. The belief in this insubstantial life of the dead who require to be revived by libation survives among Arab peasants in Syria and Palestine, who believe that the dead come at dusk to wells, springs and rivers to drink; however, this was but a tenuous existence. In the Legend of Prince Aqhat in the Ras Shamra texts occurs the passage:

> As for mortal man, what does he get
>   as his latter end?
> What does mortal man get as his
>   inheritance?
> Glaze will be poured out on my
>   head,
> Even plaster on my pate,
> And the death of all men will I die,
> Yea I shall surely die.

These lines express the typical view of the afterlife in ancient Canaan.

Incantations and Amulets

Apart from the regular cults, men in Syria, as elsewhere and at all times,

sought to enlist the powers of the supernatural or to ward off their evil influences by charms and amulets. Prophylactic charms in Aramaic are known, and at least one excerpt from the Baal myth of Ras Shamra was probably used as an aphrodisiac charm. The figurines of the nude fertility goddess were probably also used to promote procreation and childbirth. Besides, a great number of amulets have been found in excavations. Those are chiefly Egyptian, the cat and the intelligent ape, the hippopotamus, which was both a sinister force to be placated as the representative of chaos or, in the form of an upright female, a beneficent patroness of mothers.

The grotesque dwarf Bes, the protector of children and pregnant women was also popular. From the Egyptian cult of the fertility god Osiris, the goddess Isis and their son Horus, who survived a hazardous infancy to avenge Osiris' death (see Horus), small images of the infant Horus were favourite amulets, and also the 'Eye of Horus' with its fertilizing teardrops. Small gold flies and other insects resembling lice, which were found by Sir Flinders Petrie at a site at the mouth of the Wadi Ghazzeh in Palestine, may have had a prophylactic purpose to ward off disease, such as the gold mice referred to in 1 Samuel 6:4, which were sent back with the ark by the Philistines.

In describing the religion of Syria the documents of Ras Shamra have been taken as the basis of this account, firstly because they are a contemporary statement, the fullest and most reliable that is available, and secondly because they document the fertility cult, which was the most conspicuous aspect of local religion that impressed Israel as she settled in Palestine. Ugarit, however, was but one city-state in Syria, and in the history of the land it is notable

View of the ruins of Palmyra, Syria

that, despite a general community of religion in any given period, there were local variations and different emphases. So, too, over the long period of paganism, until Christianity was established as the faith of the majority (c. 500 AD), different variations of the old religion developed through time and in different localities.

The Blood of Adonis

In the settled land the old gods were assimilated to the gods of Greece and Rome, as Baal to Zeus the sky god with his thunderbolt, the fertility goddesses Astarte, Anat, and Ashera to Aphrodite and Juno. Baal in his role as a dying and rising vegetation god was assimilated to Adonis, the lover of Aphrodite, or Venus, but retained his Syrian title Adonis ('lord'); their cult was practiced at the source of the River Adonis just south of Beirut. When it ran red, as it did at a certain time in summer, it was considered to be discoloured by the blood of Adonis, who was lamented at that time by the Syrian women. Baal, the divine king who must always struggle to vindicate his kinship and order against the forces of chaos, was assimilated to the labouring Hercules, particularly at Tyre and her colonies in the coastal plain of Palestine south of Jaffa. The god Reshef, with his power of life and death, was assimilated to Apollo with his bow and arrows as plague-shafts, and Anat, the goddess of love and war was assimilated to Athene and Minerva. The sea was assimilated to Poseidon, who appears as the city god of Beirut on coins from the Graeco-Roman period, and the healing god Eshmun to Asclepius with his serpents. The latter was particularly venerated at Sidon, judging from the name Eshmunazzar, which was borne by two kings of Sidon.

In the caravan city of Palmyra, between Damascus and the Euphrates, the needs of the caravan merchants in the first three centuries of the Christian era are indicated by the cult of the moon, which was also venerated at Harran, another great caravan city in north Mesopotamia. The moon had evidently a peculiar significance for those merchants and their distant and protracted enterprises. The Venus star Athtar, the brightest star in those latitudes, the first to rise at evening and the last to disappear in the morning, was also greatly venerated at Palmyra, whereas two gods Arsu and Azizu ('the Gracious and the Fierce') they are represented as mounted respectively on a camel and a horse.

Christianity did not easily oust the Nature religion of Syria, even after it became the official religion of the Roman Empire. Indeed when Porphyry the Bishop Elect of Gaza went to his see at the end of the 4th century AD the

To the god Dumuzi, the lover of thy youth, thou hast ordained lamentation year by year.

lusty heathen impeded his journey; and according to his deacon and biographer, there were eight pagan temples and many private shrines in Gaza and only 280 Christians out of between 50,000 and 60,000 inhabitants, and that after an Imperial edict against paganism.

JOHN GRAY
FURTHER READING: John Gray. The Canaanites. (Thames & Hudson, 1965); Near Eastern Mythology. (Hamlyn, 1970).

Tammuz

The Hebrew prophet Ezekiel tells how, in the year 592 BC, in a mystic vision he saw the iniquity of the Jewish inhabitants of Jerusalem. In particular, he relates how he was brought to 'the north gate of the house of the Lord; and behold, there sat women weeping for Tammuz' (8:14). The prophet thus, unintentionally, witnesses to the widespread influence of the cult of the Mesopotamian god Tammuz and to a notable feature of that cult. The Jewish women were performing a ritual lamentation for the death of Tammuz, which was annually mourned at the summer solstice when the year begins to wane and vegetation has withered under the sun's heat. The mourners chanted in their lament:

How long will the springing up of
verdure be withheld?
How long will vegetation
be withheld?

The Hebrew name 'Tammuz' derived from the Sumerian 'Dumuzi', which was both the name of an ancient Sumerian deity and of the month in which he was specially commemorated. In the Jewish calendar there is also a month 'Tammuz', as there is with the Arabs under the name 'Tamuz'. The god was known, too, by the title Adoni, 'my Lord', which passed into Greek and Latin as Adonis. Although this ancient deity was so widely known and abundant reference is made to him in Mesopotamian texts, our modern knowledge of him is pieced together from a variety of material, most of it fragmentary.

The Sumerians, who originally conceived of this deity, called him 'Dumu-zi-abzu', meaning 'True son of Apsu'. The Apsu was the personification of the sweet waters, as opposed to Tiamat, the personification of the salt waters or sea. Since it was the sweet waters (as rivers or rain) which fertilized the earth, Dumuzi's filial relationship to the Apsu doubtless indicates some original connection with fertility.

Detail of ancient Mesopotamian so-called 'Ishtar Vase'. Terracotta with cut, moulded, and painted decoration, from Larsa, early 2nd millennium BC

There is indeed evidence of this aspect of his nature; however, in Sumerian mythology the god appears in various guises. Thus, in one myth concerned to exalt agriculture over a pastoral economy, Dumuzi is a shepherd god, who competes unsuccessfully with Enkimdu, the farmer god, for Inanna, the fertility goddess.

Dumuzi's connection with Inanna ('Ishtar' in Akkadian) constitutes the most celebrated feature of his mythology, but the evidence about it is curiously ambivalent. Although represented in the previous myth as the rejected suitor of the goddess, in another myth he appears as her husband, but the relation had direful consequences for him. For Inanna became desirous of ruling in the underworld as she did in the world above. Consequently she descended to the realm of Ereshkigal, the Sumerian goddess of the dead, to challenge her sovereignty. But Ereshkigal was too strong for her, and Inanna was held prisoner in the 'Land of No Return'. Eventually the god Enki secured her release and return to the upper world, but on condition that she found a substitute to take her place. To save herself, Inanna delivered Dumuzi to the demons who accompanied her, as the required substitute, and Dumuzi was carried off to the grim domain of Ereshkigal.

Sacred Prostitutes

In the famous Epic of Gilgamesh, curious reference is made to Ishtar's responsibility for the fate of Dumuzi. In repelling the amorous advances of the goddess, the hero Gilgamesh includes Dumuzi among the list of her victims; but he adds 'To the god Dumuzi, the lover of thy youth, thou hast odained lamentation year by year'. This cryptic statement doubtless refers to some aspect of the myth which found expression in an annual ritual lamentation for Dumuzi, in which Ishtar was involved. Further information, though still of a cryptic nature, is provided in the later Akkadian version of the myth of Ishtar's descent into the underworld. In this version there is no mention of Dumuzi's being a substitute for Ishtar. However, at the end of the narrative, after the account of Ishtar's return from the 'Land of No Return', reference is suddenly made to Tammuz (Dumuzi): 'Tammuz, her young husband, wash with pure water; anoint him with goodly oil; clothe him with a resplendent robe; let him play on the flute of lapis lazuli; let the courtesans appease his wrath! . . . On the day when Tammuz comes up to me, and the lapis lazuli flute with him, and the carnelian ring, come up to me. When those who lament, men and women, come up with him to me. May the dead arise and smell the incense'.

These invocations or injunctions clearly relate to an elaborate ritual drama in which the death and resurrection of Tammuz were portrayed. The 'courtesans' were undoubtedly the sacred prostitutes who served in the temples of Ishtar. However, it is difficult, in turn, to relate the myth of Ishtar's descent into the underworld to these rubrics concerning Tammuz. The obvious explanation that Ishtar descended there to rescue the dead Tammuz is not actually supported by the Akkadian text; and it is certainly contradicted by the Sumerian version. However, the Akkadian text does imply a ritual connection of some kind.

The general bearing of the extant evidence indicates that, whatever may have been his original Sumerian form, in Mesopotamia later, and in other adjacent lands, Tammuz was the central figure of a death and resurrection ritual which was related to the annual cycle of vegetation, and in which the fertility goddess Ishtar was intimately implicated.

As a 'dying-rising god', Tammuz naturally suggests comparison with similar types of deity, and above all with Osiris of Egypt. Such phenomenological similarity makes it reasonable to ask whether Tammuz also played the role of the saviour god in Mesopotamian religion which Osiris so notably did

in the religion of Egypt. The answer is that Tammuz did so, but in a different way, and the reason for the difference is interesting and important.

The religion of the ancient Mesopotamian peoples was based upon an evaluation of human nature that precluded any hope of a happy afterlife. Death irreparably shattered the constitution of the individual person, and what survived (the etimmu) descended to the grim Land of No Return. Hence, Tammuz could never assume that role in a mortuary ritual which Osiris had in Egypt, whereby the dead participated in the resurrection of the divine hero. However, ritual texts do exist in which salvation was sought through Tammuz; but the salvation was from sickness, not from death.

An attempt has been made to show that there existed in Sumer a myth and

ritual pattern in which a divine king represented Tammuz. This pattern involved the sacred marriage of the king and the chief priestess of Inanna, and the death and resurrection of the king. The purpose of the rites was to ensure the fertility of men, flocks and land. The theory has not, however, found general acceptance among scholars.

S. G. F. BRANDON

FURTHER READING: S. N. Kramer. Sumerian Mythology. *(New York: Harper, 1961); H. W. F. Saggs.* The Greatness That Was Babylon. *(Sidgwick & Jackson, 1962).*

Tiamat

Monstrous personification of the sea in Babylonian mythology: from her mingling with the fresh waters the first

Marduk and the Dragon Marduk, chief god of Babylon, with his thunderbolts destroys Tiamat the dragon of primeval chaos

generation of the gods was born; she threatened to destroy the gods but was killed by Marduk, the god of Babylon, who fashioned the universe from her body and created mankind from the blood of the leader of her army.

Was

A scepter with a stylized animal head on the top, it is often seen being carried by the Egyptian gods and symbolizing divine power. In particular, the was is connected to the god Set (or Seth), at one time the god of storms and foreigners, and later the god of chaos. The was thus came to represent power over Set's chaos. The was scepter also served to keep and protect the dead; to that end it is often included in scenes of gods giving various symbols and amulets to dead kings, and an actual was scepter might be included in the objects accompanying a royal mummy. Was scepters are associated with the ankh, or key of life, and the djed pillar, which symbolized stability and strength. All three objects are typical in Egyptian steles involving gods and pharaohs.

FURTHER READING: Teeter, Emily. Religion and Ritual in Ancient Egypt. *(Cambridge: Cambridge UP, 2011); Shafer, Byron E., John Baines, Leonard H. Lesko, and David P. Silverman.* Religion in Ancient Egypt: Gods, Myths, and Personal Practice. *(Ithaca: Cornell UP, 1991); Pinch, Geraldine.* Egyptian Mythology: A Guide to the Gods, Goddesses, and Traditions of Ancient Egypt. *(Oxford: Oxford UP, 2004).*

Zoroastrianism

Zoroastrianism is the name given to the religion founded by the Iranian prophet Zoroaster, probably in the 6th–7th centuries BC. Modern scholarship tends

Was scepter

to accept the traditional date of the prophet, '258 years before Alexander'. For the Iranians, 'before Alexander' could only mean the final extinction of the First Persian Empire at the sack of Persepolis by Alexander the Great in 330 BC. Hence Zoroaster's 'date' would be 588 BC. But what period in his life would this refer to? It might refer to his

birth, to his first revelation at the age of thirty, to his conversion of the local king Vishtaspa at the age of forty, or to his death at the age of seventy-seven.

Whichever date we accept, Zoroaster's life will have spanned the 7th and 6th centuries BC. This, however, like so much in Zoroastrian studies, cannot be regarded as at all certain. So too

School of Athens (detail), Raphael (1483–1520)

with the place in which he operated. The later tradition placed him in western Iran, in what is today Azerbaijan; but this is almost certainly not true, for the internal evidence the dialect and the place names mentioned in the early Zoroastrian texts—points to the east, the country near the Oxus River, now in Soviet Central Asia. Modern scholarship would have it that Zoroaster's field of activity was in ancient Chorasmia, corresponding roughly to what is today the Turkmen Republic of the Soviet Union. This again is highly probable but far from certain.

Gods and Demons

It must be emphasized at the outset that in practically every aspect of Zoroastrian studies uncertainty prevails, and this for a variety of reasons. The principal reason is that our main sources do not agree. The sacred text, the Avesta, itself only a fraction of the original scripture and handed down orally for at least 1,000 years, is (as is the way of sacred scriptures) not consistent with itself, nor is it consistent with the contemporary sources—the inscriptions of the Achaemenian kings and the various Greek accounts of the Iranian religion from Herodotus onward.

The same is true of the second period of Zoroastrian supremacy during the Second Persian Empire, the so-called Sassanian Empire, which lasted from 226–651 AD. It cannot be claimed, then, that all that will be said in this brief article is authoritative; for Zoroastrian scholars have disagreed with a vehemence of acerbity rare even among academics.

Zoroaster, or Zarathushtra, as he is called in the Avesta, was born sometime in the 7th century BC, fled from his native land because he preached a doctrine which his fellow countrymen refused to accept, and found asylum with a certain King Vishtaspa in eastern Iran, who finally accepted his teaching. That his teaching was at variance with the traditional religion is clear. Just what that earlier religion was is less clear. One thing is certain, however: that the Aryans, the common ancestors of the 'Aryan' invaders of India (who were responsible for the earliest sacred book of the Hindus, the Veda), and the Iranians who inhabited the Iranian plateau had a common religion which was polytheistic.

The ahuras (the Iranian form of the Indian asuras) were able to retain their divine status, whereas the daivas were reduced to the status of demons. This probably happened before the appearance of Zoroaster, as the terms ahuro-tkaesha ('the religion of the ahuras') and daevo-data ('the law of the daivas')

Priests procession at Persepolis. This relief decorates the Tachara, Darius the Great's private palace at Persepolis, Iran.

would seem to show. Already, it would appear, the ahuras were considered to be beneficent powers, and the daivas were maleficent.

New Message from God

Zoroastrianism has been described both as an ethical monotheism and as a classical form of dualism. How can one religion be described in two such contradictory ways? The answer is that Zoroastrianism, like any other religion, developed and changed, now emphasizing one aspect of the prophet's message, now another. In any case, the Zoroastrianism of the prophet himself was very different from the form of Zoroastrianism which became prevalent in the later stages of the First (Achaemenian) Persian Empire (550–330 BC), and this again differed considerably from the official Zoroastrianism of the Second (Sassanian) Empire (226–651 AD). The

first could be designated monotheism, the second modified monotheism, and the third dualism.

Zoroaster was born into a priestly family, but he saw himself as a prophet, the bringer of a new message from a god called Ahura Mazdah, the 'Wise

Two Groups of Deities

The original Aryan pantheon was, it seems, divided into two distinct groups of deities, the asuras (or ahuras) on the one hand and the daivas on the other. The asuras seem to have been remote gods who dwelt in the sky, while the daivas were nearer to men and more intimately associated with them. From the beginning there seems to have been tension between the two groups. In India the asuras, because they were held to possess magic powers which they were likely to use against mankind, finished up by becoming demons. But in Iran precisely the opposite happened.

Lord', who revealed himself as the true God. This message is preserved in the oldest part of the Avesta, the Gathas or 'Songs' of Zoroaster himself.

Zoroaster was a prophet every bit as much as were the Hebrew prophets—who prophesied at much the same time. He was convinced that he was inspired by God and that he was charged with a message from him to man. He claimed to 'see' him and also to hear his voice. Indeed, his relationship is so close that he can speak of it as one of 'friend to friend'.

The essence of Zoroaster's message is that God is One, holy and righteous, the Creator of all things, both material and spiritual, through his Holy Spirit, the living and the giver of life. He is good because he is productive and gives increase. His 'oneness', however, is a unity in diversity, for he manifests himself under many various aspects: the Holy Spirit, as and through whom God creates; the Good Mind, as and through which he inspires the prophet and sanctifies mankind; Truth, Righteousness, or Cosmic Order (Asha), as and through which he shows mankind how to conform to the cosmos in accordance with true righteousness; Sovereignty, as and through which he rules over the entirety of creation; Wholeness, which is the plenitude of his being; and Immortality, as and through which he will annihilate death.

The Bounteous Immortals

These aspects of the Wise Lord were later to be called the 'Bounteous Immortals', and in the later periods of Zoroastrianism they were to be associated with various material elements: they appear as God's creatures and are thus assimilated to the archangels of other traditions. Two of them demand particular notice: Truth and the Holy Spirit. Like the other Bounteous Immortals, they have acknowledged opposites or 'adversaries' which thwart and restrict them. Ahura Mazdah, as Supreme Deity, has no opposite but, insofar as he is associated with Truth and the Holy Spirit, he is (indirectly) at variance with the 'Lie' and the 'Destructive Spirit'—the later Ahriman—just as the Hebrew God is opposed to Satan in the later Judaeo-Christian scriptures.

Hence it is not wholly illogical to describe the Zoroastrianism of the prophet himself as both a 'monotheism' and a 'dualism'; and in so far as Ahura Mazdah reveals himself under different aspects, it is not wholly absurd to describe it as a modified 'polytheism'.

The towers of silence at Yazd, in Iran

Truth and the Lie

In the Gathas the basic dualism is between Truth and the Lie—Asha and Druj—which can also mean the established cosmic order and whatever disrupts it. This dualism remains throughout all the phases of Zoroastrianism. The Lie also means the disruption of the established political order (Darius described the rebels against his authority as 'liars'), and the disruption of the truthfully spoken word, or what we normally understand by a lie. As God, Ahura Mazdah is beyond both Truth and the Lie, but as and through Truth he is inexorably opposed to its opposite, which is also the spirit of disruption.

Similarly is the case of the Holy Spirit. The Holy Spirit is irreconcilably opposed to the Destructive Spirit and this opposition was later to be regarded as characteristic of Zoroastrian dualism. Of these two Spirits it is written: 'In the beginning those two Spirits who . . . were twins known as the one good and the other evil in thought, word and deed . . . And when these Spirits met they established in the beginning life and death that in the end the followers of the Lie should meet with the worst existence, but the followers of Truth with the Best Mind. Of these two Spirits he who was of the Lie chose to do the worst things; but the most Holy Spirit, clothed in rugged heaven, (chose) Truth as did (all) who sought with zeal to do the pleasure of the Wise Lord by (doing) good works'.

Although the two Spirits choose to do good and evil, the Holy Spirit can nevertheless say to 'him who is Evil: "Neither our thoughts, nor our teachings, nor our wills, nor our choices, nor our words, nor our deeds, nor our consciences, nor yet our souls agree"'.

Ahura Mazdah, the Wise Lord, is himself described as being the 'father' of the Holy Spirit (as he is of several other Bounteous Immortals), but he is also in a sense identical with him. As and through the Holy Spirit, then, he is as irreconcilably opposed to the Evil or Destructive Spirit, the author of death, as he is to the Lie, for he is both Life and Truth. But if he is the father

Zoroastrian temple in present-day Iran

of the Holy Spirit, and the Holy Spirit is the Destructive Spirit's twin, does it not follow that he is the father of the Destructive Spirit too? In the later literature, the Wise Lord is roundly identified with the Holy Spirit, and once this has happened Zoroastrianism becomes a classically dualist religion.

A minority, however, remembering that the two Spirits had been spoken of as twins, insisted that they must have had a common father. This could no longer be Ahura Mazdah (the later Ohrmazd), so some other entity had to be found. They finally settled on 'Infinite Time', who thus became the supreme principle beyond good and evil.

The Two Houses

In all its phases Zoroastrianism is the religion of free will. Man is judged in accordance with the nature of the thoughts, words, and deeds he has thought, spoken, and done in his lifetime. The reward of the good is heaven, the 'Best Existence'; that of the wicked is hell, an 'evil existence'. At death the soul must cross the 'Bridge of the Requiter' which, in the later literature, is broad and free from danger for the righteous but becomes as narrow as a razor's edge for the wicked, who thereby fall helplessly into hell. In the Gathas it is Zoroaster himself who guides the righteous across the awesome bridge, but when the wicked reach it 'their souls and consciences trouble them when they come to the Bridge of the Requiter, guests for all eternity in the House of the Lie'.

Heaven and hell are states rather than places—the best existence and the worst existence or, more graphically, the House of the Good Mind and the House of the Worst Mind, the House of Song and the House of the Lie. In the one there is 'ease and benefit', in the other discomfort and torment, 'a long age of darkness, foul food, and cries of woe'.

In addition there is a final reckoning 'at the last turning point of existence', when there will be a Last Judgment in the form of an ordeal by fire and molten metal which will allot to the righteous and the unrighteous their final destiny of weal or woe. The Last Judgment then, merely confirms the individual judgment at death: salvation and damnation are fixed for all eternity. This 'black-and-white' doctrine was to enter Judaism and, through Judaism, Christianity, and Islam. The Zoroastrians, however, were later to modify it themselves, for in the later texts the Last Judgment (which seems unnecessary anyhow) becomes not a judgment at all but a purgation by molten metal in which the wicked are finally purged of their sins and the just suffer nothing since the molten metal has no terrors for them: they experience it as if it were warm milk.

These, then, are the basic doctrines preached by the prophet Zoroaster himself: there is one supreme God, Creator of all things, spiritual and material; aside from him there are two irreconcilable principles—Truth and the Lie, the Holy Spirit, and the Destructive Spirit. Alongside these there are 'aspects' of God and also, though less markedly, 'aspects' of the Lie and the Destructive Spirit. Man must choose between the two, and in accordance with his choice he will either be blessed with eternal bliss or chastised with everlasting torment. By 'good' is meant Truth, the proper ordering of things, life, and prosperity; by evil, the Lie, disorder, death, and misery. The dualism is not one of spirit and matter but one of spirit and spirit, matter being in itself good because it was created by God, though later corrupted by the Devil.

The Later Avesta

Only the Gathas purport to be the work of the prophet Zoroaster himself. The rest of the Avesta (or rather what survives of it) is later and contains much material that seems to be totally at variance with the prophet's teaching.

According to the later tradition the 'original' Avesta consisted of 21 Nasks or 'books', a summary of which survives in the Denkart, a work, like all the works written in Pahlavi (Zoroastrian 'middle' Persian), that dates from after the Mohammedan conquest but which draws on much earlier material. Of these 21 Nasks only one remains in its entirety—the Videvdat or 'Law against the Demons', a tiresome book largely concerned with the punishments of sins, ritual purification, and mythology. Apart from this there is the Yasna, the 'sacrifice', or ritual texts accompanying the main Zoroastrian liturgy together with minor liturgical texts, and the Yashts or 'hymns of praise' celebrating a whole gamut of pre-Zoroastrian deities which the prophet had certainly ignored and may even have proscribed.

The Yasna, or sacrificial liturgy, centres round the immolation of the sacred plant haoma (the Iranian equivalent of the Indian soma), the juice of which is considered to be the elixir of immortality. The Yasna is both sacrifice and sacrament: the plant god is slain by being pounded in a mortar and its juice is consumed in order to win eternal life. There seem to be references to this cult in the Gathas themselves, and it seems certain from these references that the

> *Man . . . will be blessed with eternal bliss or chastised with everlasting torment.*

prophet disapproved of it strongly, at least as practiced by the 'worshippers of the daivas'. Be that as it may, the haoma cult appears very soon to have become central to Zoroastrian worship and it has remained so to this day, both among the 10,000 Zoroastrians who still survive in Iran and among the 100,000 Parsees ('Persians'), as the Zoroastrians who emigrated from Iran to India some centuries after the Mohammedan conquest are called (see Parsees). The haoma sacrifice is the central act of the liturgy, but from beginning to end the material object around which the rite is celebrated is the sacred fire which, like haoma itself, is called the 'son' of Ahura Mazdah.

The Sacrificial Haoma

The sacrifice opens with a confession of faith in the following terms: 'I confess myself a worshipper of Mazdah, a Zoroastrian, a renouncer of the daivas, an upholder of the ahuras'. The formula helps us to see how the Zoroastrians of a later date regarded their religion. They are worshippers of (Ahura) Mazdah, the only God, proclaimed by Zoroaster as supreme Creator and Lord: hence they are 'Zoroastrians'. But when they add that they are 'renouncers of the daivas' and 'upholders of the ahuras', they seem to be upholding a religion that probably preceded the coming of the prophet and in which there were many ahuras or gods just as there were many daivas or demons who, like Satan and his angels in the Judaeo-Christian tradition, had once themselves been gods. In any case the ahuras, now

called yazatas or 'worshipful ones', are constantly invoked throughout the Yasna. They may either be material manifestations of divinity, preeminently fire and water, but also the winds, mountains, and so on, or they may be spiritual, invisible beings who are in fact the ancient Aryan gods, once common to Iran and India; slightly refurbished, it is true, in that they are subjected to the ultimate authority of Ahura Mazdah, the Wise Lord.

But these divinities though they are constantly invoked throughout the

He is the great god 'who created this earth, who created yonder sky, who created man, who created happiness for man, who made Darius king'.

Yasna, are not essential to it. The central figure, as we have seen, is the sacrificial haoma, but next to him and the sacred fire is a 'god' who figures quite prominently in the Gathas, Sraosha. In the Gathas he is, like the Bounteous Immortals, an abstract idea. He is the faculty of 'hearing' God's word and therefore of obeying it. In the Yasna he is fully personified and is, in a sense, the mediator between man and God. As the spirit of obedience, he also enforces obedience among men and chastises the wicked, as he chastises the demons. His continued importance, his relevance, and his popularity are attested by the fact that he alone among all the Zoroastrian pantheon was later identified with a Mohammedan angel (with the angel Gabriel, so familiar to Christians too).

The second main division of the later Avesta is the Yashts and it is in some ways remarkable that they have survived; for they are hymns of praise to deities, some of whom are quite certainly pre-Zoroastrian and others

almost certainly so. In the Yasna these deities are always clearly subordinate to Ahura Mazdah but this is not always so in the Yashts, for in two cases at least Ahura Mazdah himself is represented as doing obeisance to them—to Vayu, the wind god, and to Anahita, the goddess of the waters.

The Faith of the Achaemenids

From the Achaemenian inscriptions, from proper names like Mithradates, from rock reliefs of much later date, and from the extraordinary diffusion of the cult of Mithras throughout the Roman Empire shortly after the rise of Christianity, it is clear that the most important of these ancient deities was Mithra—like Ahura Mazdah himself originally a god of the sky and later identified with the sun.

As with everything connected with Zoroastrianism, there has been furious debate as to whether or not the Achaemenid kings were Zoroastrians. About the religion of the earliest of them, Cyrus and Cambyses, there is no evidence, but about that of Darius the Great (521-485 BC) there is plenty, for there are many inscriptions dictated by him. Ahura Mazdah is the only god the Great King invokes. He is the great god 'who created this earth, who created yonder sky, who created man, who created happiness for man, who made Darius king'. This is recognizably the same god as that of Zoroaster. Similarly, when speaking of the rebels against his authority, Darius says they 'lied' in that they claimed to be kings, 'lying' thus being equivalent to the disruption of the established order—again a Zoroastrian conception. Thus, in his conception of the nature and supremacy of Ahura Mazdah and in his identification of evil with the 'Lie', Darius is at one with Zoroaster. Though it can be argued that he was not formally a 'Zoroastrian', he was certainly a 'worshipper of Mazdah'.

The case of Darius's successor Xerxes (485–466 BC) is even clearer, for he claims to have suppressed the cult of the daivas and to have established some sort of 'Mazdean' orthodoxy: 'Where the daivas had previously been worshipped, there did I worship Ahura Mazdah in accordance with Truth and using the proper rite'. Further he refers to an afterlife in which the good will be 'blessed': 'The man who has respect for the law which Ahura Mazdah has established and who worships Ahura Mazdah in accordance with Truth and using the proper rite, may he be both happy when alive and blessed when dead'. Xerxes, then, was both a 'worshipper of Mazdah' and a 'renouncer of the daivas', and since he refers to 'the law which Ahura Mazdah established', presumably through his prophet Zoroaster, he was almost certainly a 'Zoroastrian'.

During the reign of Artaxerxes I (465–425 BC) the Zoroastrian calendar was introduced, but in this calendar the days and months are named not only after Ahura Mazdah and the Bounteous Immortals but also after the ancient gods who now appear beside them. The Zoroastrianism of the later Achaemenian kings was that of the Yasna rather than that of the Gathas. And so we find in the rare inscriptions of Artaxerxes II and III the god Mithra and the goddess Anahita invoked together with the supreme god, Ahura Mazdah.

The Last Contest
With the collapse of the Achaemenian Empire, Zoroastrianism disappears as an organized religion until it becomes once more the state religion of the Second (Sassanian) Empire from 226 to 651 AD. To judge from rock reliefs during this period, it would appear that Mithra and Anahita still enjoyed considerable favour both with the royal house and among the people. It was, however, the policy of the new dynasty to seek to establish religious conformity throughout the empire. Now for the first time one can speak of religious orthodoxy; and this, to judge from the Pahlavi books which draw their material from this period, was a rigid dualism in which the Bounteous Immortals and the ancient gods resuscitated in the late Achaemenian period were reduced to the status of angels. The scene was now dominated by two eternal principles, Ohrmazd (Ahura Mazdah) and Ahriman, Ohrmazd being identified with all goodness and light and dwelling in the Endless Light above, Ahriman being equated with all evil and darkness and dwelling in the Endless Darkness below. The two kingdoms are totally separate and independent, but the time comes when Ahriman becomes conscious of the light of Ohrmazd, envies it, attacks it, and invades the material world which Ohrmazd had created as a bulwark against him. For 3,000 years the issue of the battle is in doubt, but in the last 3,000 years of the existence of this world the power of evil is slowly but relentlessly ground down until the Saviour, the Saoshyans, appears to make all things new. The souls of men, whether they be in heaven or in hell, are reunited with their bodies and are purged in a sea of molten metal. When this is done, Ahriman is expelled back into his native darkness and rendered unconscious for ever. Then the whole creation enjoys eternal bliss in the presence of Ohrmazd, the Lord.

This dualist orthodoxy, however, was questioned by a theological deviation called 'Zurvanism' which subordinated both Ohrmazd and Ahriman to a higher principle, Infinite Time or Zurvan. However, no matter what the main theological trend may have been at the time, Sassanian Zoroastrianism was so wedded to the Sassanian state that, when the latter was overthrown by the forces of the new religion, Islam, which had arisen in the Arabian desert in the 7th century AD, the Zoroastrian Church, no longer being the 'established' church, rapidly and irreversibly declined. Iran, once the centre of two great empires of which Zoroastrianism had been the official religion, now became a Moslem country; and the Zoroastrian community, having steadily lost ground throughout the centuries, has now been reduced to a mere 10,000 souls living mainly in Yazd and Kerman in the southeast, while another 100,000 or so, descendants of refugees from persecution, survive as the rich and enlightened community of the Parsees in Bombay and other Indian cities. Such has been the fate of a religion that once ruled proudly throughout the Iranian lands.

R. C. ZAEHNER

FURTHER READING: tr. by M. Henning. The Hymns of Zarathustra. (Hyperion, 1980); M. Boyce ed. Zoroastrianism. (Barnes & Noble Imports, 1984); R. C. Zaehner. The Dawn and Twilight of Zoroastrianism. (Putnam, 1961); The Teachings of the Magi. (Oxford University Press, 1976).

Zurvan

Zoroastrianism and Manicheanism are commonly regarded as being the two classical dualist religions, and this is true. But there is all the difference in the world between them, for Manicheanism is a dualism of spirit and matter, spirit being identified with good, matter with evil. Zoroastrianism, on the other hand, is a spiritual dualism of two spirits, the one good and the other evil, and they are irreconcilably opposed. Matter,

Opposite page:
Zeus/Serapis/Ohrmazd with worshipper. Bactria, 3rd century BC

however, is created by Ohrmazd, the good God, though it comes to be corrupted by Ahriman, the 'pure' spirit of evil. The basic text for this dualism is to be found in the Gathas or 'Songs' of Zoroaster himself where the prophet is represented as saying: 'I will speak out concerning the two Spirits of whom, at the beginning of existence, the Holier thus spoke to him who is Evil: "Neither our thoughts, nor our teachings, nor our wills, nor our choices, nor our words, nor our deeds, nor our consciences, nor yet our souls agree."'

The irreducible antagonism between the two Spirits seems clear enough here. But there is another text (quoted in the article on Zoroastrianism) in which it is unambiguously stated that the two Spirits were twins; and that would imply that they had a common father.

God of Infinite Time

Now in the later Avesta, as the sacred book of the Zoroastrians is called, an entity with the name of Zrvan akarena ('Infinite Time') is sometimes mentioned. Nothing much is said about him, but at least he is infinite, whereas Ohrmazd and Ahriman, God, and the Devil, had by now become independent principles, each limiting the other. A different view is quoted by Eudemus of Rhodes, a pupil of Aristotle, who lived in the 4th century BC. He is reported as having said that 'the Magi and the whole Aryan race call the whole intelligible and unitary universe either Space or Time from which a good god and an evil demon were separated out, or, according to others, light and darkness before these . . . One of these (higher principles) is ruled by Ohrmazd, the other by Ahriman'.

This is the philosophical account of the 'Zurvanite' position. Light and darkness are ruled respectively by Ohrmazd and Ahriman, God and the Devil; but the highest principle is beyond all these, and this principle is Space-Time, Zrvan akarena, who in the later language becomes Zurvan I akanarak, 'Infinite Zurvan-Time'.

By the time of the Sassanian Empire (226–651 AD), however, Zurvan had become a proper name and a personal god, the word for 'time' in Persian now being zaman, as it is to this day. During the Sassanian period, to judge from the Zoroastrian books which,

In the beginning, all is One in Zurvan who, philosophically, is Time-Space. Basically he is good and light . . .

though actually written as late as the 9th century AD, are generally held to represent the views of Zoroastrian orthodoxy during the last century or so of the Sassanian Empire, one would not realize that the god Zurvan was of any importance at all, let alone that he was regarded by some as being the father of both Ohrmazd and Ahriman. Indeed, in these so-called 'Pahlavi' books, Zoroastrianism (or the 'Good Religion' as the Zoroastrians themselves now called it) was defined as the religion of the two principles as distinct from the monotheism of the Jews and Christians. 'I must have no doubt', a Zoroastrian catechism reads, 'but that there are two first principles, one the Creator, and the other the Destroyer. The Creator is Ohrmazd who is all goodness and all light; and the Destroyer is the accursed Ahriman who is all wickedness and full of death, a liar, and a deceiver'. Nothing could be clearer than that.

There is no question that there is a principle beyond these two. In the whole corpus of the Pahlavi books there is only one mention of the theory (explicitly stated in the Gathas though it is) that Ohrmazd and Ahriman are twins, and in this one passage it is denounced as a doctrine thought up by a demon.

The Pahlavi books, as they now stand, reflect a doctrine that was current at the end of the Sassanian period, and we can be fairly certain that this complete dualism was official doctrine then. So too was it after the death of Shapur (Sapor) I in 271 AD as we now know from a long inscription of the high priest of that time, one Kartir. Unfortunately this agreement between the ninth century books and the third century inscription is not conclusive; for if neither had survived and we had to rely exclusively on Christian, Manichean, and Moslem sources, we would be inclined to think that Zurvanism was the predominant trend in the Zoroastrianism of the Sassanian period, not the neat dualism of the Pahlavi texts, and this for two principal reasons. First, when the Christians attack Zoroastrianism, they attack not the dualism we know from the Pahlavi books but the theory that Ohrmazd and Ahriman are twins. Secondly, when the Manichees started to translate their own scriptures into Persian they called their own supreme Spirit, the 'Father of Greatness' and king of the kingdom of light—not Ohrmazd but Zurvan. And this is very odd indeed since the Zoroastrian Ohrmazd who is 'all goodness and all light' corresponds as exactly as you could wish to the Manichean 'Father of Greatness'. The Zoroastrian Zurvan, on the other hand, as we know him from the Christian sources, is rather 'the whole intelligible and unitary universe, either Space or Time', of Eudemus, but now transferred onto a purely mythological plane.

The Zurvanite myth is preserved in several sources which substantially agree and must go back to a common original. In this myth (quoted in the article on Ahriman) Zurvan is the father of Ohrmazd and Ahriman.

The message of the myth is clear. In the beginning, all is One in Zurvan who, philosophically, is Time-Space. Basically he is good and light, but there is a fundamental flaw in his nature represented by his 'doubt', and this is materialized in the shape of Ahriman who is 'dark and stinking', 'a liar and a deceiver'. Unless Zurvan is to be false to his vow, he must make Ahriman king of this world for 9,000 years, though Ohrmazd may be high priest in heaven above. In any case, Ahriman's power will be broken in the end, and then Ohrmazd will be 'all in all' in 'infinite time' of which Zurvan is the mythological representation.

In the Selections of Zadspram, the only one of the Pahlavi books where Zurvan plays a prominent part, we learn a little more about his 'testament' to Ohrmazd and Ahriman and about Ahriman's 9,000-year rule:

When first creation began to move and Zurvan, for the sake of movement, brought that form, the black and ashen garment to Ahriman, he made a treaty in this wise: 'This is that implement like unto fire, blazing, harassing all creatures, that hath the very substance of Az (Greed, Lust, Concupiscence). When the period of 9,000 years comes to an end, if thou hast not perfectly fulfilled that which thou didst threaten at the beginning, that thou wouldst bring all material existence to hate Ohrmazd and to love thee, . . . then, by means of this weapon, Az will devour . . . thy creation; and she herself will starve'.

From other texts we can deduce that Zurvan gave a corresponding 'implement' or 'form' to Ohrmazd—'a form of fire—bright, white, round, and manifest afar', which is associated with priesthood and wisdom as it is in the 'classic' Zurvanite myth.

How are we to interpret all this? The birth of Ahriman from Zurvan's doubt is a 'Fall' in the divine nature itself, the manifestation of an essential imperfection in the godhead.

To compensate for this Fall Zurvan endows Ohrmazd with wisdom, the priestly virtue par excellence, but to Ahriman he gives Az who is Greed, Lust, Concupiscence, Acquisitiveness, and who is insatiable. Ultimately, then, Az is self-destructive and so in the end Ahriman's kingdom is destroyed by the very 'implement' he had accepted from Zurvan and made into his own 'selfhood'. Having supplied Ohrmazd and Ahriman with the 'implements' appropriate to each, Zurvan plays no further part in the cosmic struggle. Only at the very end does he appear to help Ohrmazd administer the coup de grace to Ahriman, Az, and their evil creation. Even so, Zurvan must be seen as a god that failed.

S. R. C. ZAEHNER
FURTHER READING: R. C. Zaehner. The Dawn and Twilight of Zoroastrianism. (New York: Putnam, 1961); Zurvan, A Zoroastrian Dilemma. (Biblo and Tanner, 1973).

Glossary

Amulet An ornament or piece of jewelry worn to protect the wearer and ward off evil spirits or harmful supernatural forces.

Assimilation The merging of traits, language, and beliefs from previously distinct cultural groups into another existing, dominant one.

Augur A seer or priest, usually in ancient times, who observes natural signs, especially the behaviour of birds, and reads into them divine approval or disapproval of some course of action.

Brandishing Carrying or waving about an implement, especially a weapon.

Capricious Moods or judgments that are unpredictable, given to change course without reason.

Collusion Participation in secretive or illicit plans.

Cuneiform Among the earliest forms of writing, slim triangular or wedge-shaped elements used as characters and forming words by the ancient Sumerians, Assyrians, Babylonians, and others.

Deified Acknowledged as, or being made into, a god or goddess.

Deluge A great flooding by water, in the literal sense; figuratively, a heavy or numerous amount of something.

Divination The mystical or prophetic act of discovering previously unknown information, the power for which comes from the supernatural or occult.

Dualism A theory that reduces its view on any given subject or matter into two opposing principles, such as good/evil, mental/physical, natural/supernatural, etc.

Emanate When a subject gives off a particular effect, which then spreads outward from the place of origin.

Enigmatic Inherently vague or difficult to understand; puzzling.

Euphemism A milder, more acceptable term for something shocking, unpleasant, or blunt.

Functionaries A person who performs a role in an important, often religious, event.

Funerary Relating to ritual burial of the dead.

Hegemony Dominance in governing or influencing a culture, place, or group of people.

Heretical Opposing or contradicting established beliefs and practices, especially those surrounding a well-established religion.

Iconography The study and interpretation of symbols, themes, and subject matter in the visual arts.

Incantations The saying of prayers, chants, or words believed to be holy or magical.

Inveighed Strongly opposed verbally.

Licentious Promiscuous and unprincipled in sexual matters.

Malevolent Intentions and actions that are evil or purposefully harmful.

Monotheism A belief system that recognizes one deity.

Obeisance Behaviour that shows respect and reverence to another person.

Omniscient All-knowing, particularly in a deity.

Perpetual Everlasting and ongoing.

Plinth A heavy block, base, or solid platform for displaying statues, vases, and, in architecture, columns.

Polytheism Religious belief in the existence of many gods and goddesses.

Primordial Something that has been around since the beginning of the world.

Ruse A clever attempt to mislead or deceive.

Slough To shed or shrug off.

Stele A large stone or hewn rock slab that is chiseled with words or images, placed upright on display.

Summarily To treat something decisively, directly, and totally.

Tabu (taboo) Forbidden, especially something contrary to accepted religious practices.

Truncated Shortened, especially by having some part broken off or removed.

Ubiquity Seeming to appear everywhere.

Vicissitudes Changes and fluctuations in circumstances or fortune, usually in a negative context.

Index

scarabs, 106
pyramidology, 101–104
    Great Pyramid of Giza, 102
pyramids, Step-Pyramid, 53

Q
Qedeshat, 14
Qodshu, 14

R
Ra, 104
    Amun-Ra, 10
Ras Shamra Baal myth, 16, 117
Re, 30, 104
    Amun-Re, 30, 104
    as scarab beetle, 106
rebirth. *See also* reincarnation
    Tibetan Book of the Dead, 24
religious dualism, 7
resurrection of Osiris, 92, 94
Rimmon, 40
Roman Empire, Mithras, 82
Rosetta stone, 102

S
sacred prostitute, 14
sacrifice
    children, 100–101, 119
    communion sacrifices, 119
    divination from animal entrails,
       118
    haoma sacrifice (Zoroastrianism),
       133
    Harranian religion, 41–42
Saklas, 68–69
Sassanian Empire, Zurvan and, 136
Saudi Arabia, 111
scarabs (dung beetles), 28, 104–106
Serapis, 106
Seth, 32, 107
    cult center, 108
    Great Bear, 110
    Horus and, 46–48, 107, 109

Osiris and, 57–58, 94–95
    Thoth and, 109
Shamash, 110–111
Sin cult, 41
Song of Ullikummi, 43–44
soul, ba, 34
sphinx, 111
    avenue of ram-headed sphinxes, 10
spirits, Mesopotamia, 78–79
spiritual twin, 67
Step-Pyramid, 53
Sumeria, 111–112
    Dumu-zi-abzu, 122–123
    early deities, 74–76
    The Epic of Gilgamesh, 113–114
    language, 111–113
    religion, 113
    Uruk period, 111–113
Sun (Egyptian religion), 30
Syria, 114–115
    Adonis, 122
    afterlife, 119
    amulet, 119–122
    Baal, 115–116
    communion sacrifices, 119
    divination, 118
    El, 115–116
    fertility cult, 115
    great autumn festival, 116
    incantations, 119–120
    Mot, 115
    Ras Shamra Baal myth, 117

T
Tammuz/Dumuzi, 122–124
Tanit, 100
Taylor, John, 103
temples
    Astarte, 14
    Egypt, 36
Teshub, 40
The Epic of Gilgamesh, 113–114
    Babylonia and, 39, 43

Dumuzi, 123
the Great God, 33
theophoric names, 115
Thoth, 33
    Seth and, 109
Tiamat, 124–125
Tibetan Book of the Dead, 23–24

U
Uruk period, 111–113

V

W
was scepters, 125
Wise Lord, 127–128
Wrathful Dieties, 24
Wurusemu, 42

Z
Zarathrustra/Zoroaster, 126
Zeus
    Baal and, 18
    Hadad and, 40
Zoroastrianism
    Achaemenids and, 133–134
    Ahriman, 7–10
       Ohrmazd and, 8–9
    Ahura Mazdah, 7, 10, 133–134
    Avesta, 126, 131, 133
    Az, 9–10
    Bounteous Immortals, 128
    Christianity and, 131–134
    disappearance, 134
    dualism, 7–10, 127–128, 130–131,
       134
    ethical monotheism, 127
    Evil Spirit, 8–9
    free will, 8, 131
    Gathas, 38, 127
    haoma sacrifice, 133
    Holy Spirit, 8–9
    Infinite Space, 8

Author List

Contributors to *Man, Myth, and Magic: Beliefs, Rituals, and Symbols of Ancient Egypt, Mesopotamia, and the Fertile Crescent*

Rev. S. G. F. Brandon was professor of comparative religion and dean of the faculty of theology at Manchester University. The author of numerous books, he also edited the *Dictionary of Comparative Religion.*

John Gray was a professor of Hebrew and Semitic literature, Aberdeen; and the author of books including *The Canaanites;* and *The Legacy of Canaan.*

J. Gwyn Griffiths was a Reader in Classics, University College, Swansea, as well as author of *The Conflict of Horus and Seth* and other books.

O. R. Gurney was a professor of Assyriology, Oxford, and the author of *The Hittites; The Geography of the Hittite Empire* (with John Garstang) and other books.

Jacquetta Hawkes is the author of *Prehistoric Britain* (with Christopher Hawkes); *Early Britain; A Land; Man on Earth; Journey Down a Rainbow* (with J. B. Priestley); *Man and the Sun; The Dawn of the Gods,* and other books.

Sir Max Mallowan was a Fellow of All Souls, Oxford; formerly professor of Western Asiatic Archaeology, London. Mallowan has written numerous books, including *Prehistoric Assyria; Excavations at Brak; Early Mesopotamia and Iran;* and *Nimrud and Its Remains.*

R. Merkelbach was a professor of classics, Cologne; author of *Untersuchungen zur Odyssee; Die Quellen des Griechischen Alexander-romans; Roman und Mysterium; Fragmenta Hesiodea* (with M. L. West), and other books.

G. Quispel was a professor of the history of the early church, Rijksuniversteit of Utrecht; author of *Gnosis als Weltreligion; The Gospel of Thomas* (with H. C. Puech), and other books.

B. R. Rees was a professor of Greek at University College, Cardiff; Rees has published editions of Greek papyri; author of *The Use of Greek* and other books.

H. W. F. Saggs was a professor of Semitic languages, University College, Cardiff, and the author of *The Greatness that was Babylon.*

J. A. West is a novelist and playwright, as well as the co-author of *The Case for Astrology* .

R. C. Zaehner was Spalding professor of Eastern religions at Oxford, and a distinguished scholar. A Roman Catholic, he was an authority on Oriental religions and mysticism. He was a Fellow of All Souls, Oxford. His books include *Mysticism, Sacred and Profane; The Dawn and Twilight of Zoroastrianism; Hinduism; The Catholic Church and World Religions;* and, as editor, *The Concise Encyclopedia of Living Faiths.*